Routledge Revivals

Prison from Within

First published in 1937, *Prison from Within* is a first-person account of a prisoner sentenced to imprisonment for eighteen months for fraud. It is a linear narrative honestly recording the various facets of prison culture, along with candid character analysis. The book touches upon philosophical notions of sin and remorse; the social groups of prisoners and the camaraderie shared among them; the poor living condition of prisons and the exploitation of prison labour; and the general politics of the time. The book successfully humanizes criminals and is an excellent reminder of the fact that the prison industry has only worsened with time. Prisons were designed for the purpose of 'cleansing' bourgeoise society; therefore, it is important to revisit the institution and question its utility in modern times. This book will be of interest to students and teachers of history, sociology, criminology, criminal justice, literature, and penology.

Prison from Within

Richmond Harvey

Routledge
Taylor & Francis Group

First published in 1937
by George Allen and Unwin

This edition first published in 2022 by Routledge
4 Park Square, Milton Park, Abingdon, Oxon, OX14 4RN
and by Routledge
605 Third Avenue, New York, NY 10017

Routledge is an imprint of the Taylor & Francis Group, an informa business

© 1937 George Allen and Unwin

Publisher's Note
The publisher has gone to great lengths to ensure the quality of this reprint but points
out that some imperfections in the original copies may be apparent.

Disclaimer
The publisher has made every effort to trace copyright holders and welcomes
correspondence from those they have been unable to contact.

A Library of Congress record exists under ISBN: 37022343

ISBN: 978-1-032-34693-9 (hbk)
ISBN: 978-1-003-32338-9 (ebk)
ISBN: 978-1-032-34696-0 (pbk)

Book DOI 10.4324/9781003323389

PRISON FROM WITHIN

by

RICHMOND HARVEY

LONDON
GEORGE ALLEN & UNWIN LTD
MUSEUM STREET

FIRST PUBLISHED IN 1937

PRINTED IN GREAT BRITAIN BY
UNWIN BROTHERS LTD., WOKING

PRISON FROM WITHIN

CHAPTER I

THE curtain was about to fall on the judicial drama in which for two days I had been the central figure. For months the threat of imprisonment had hung over my head, but now the fateful moment was at hand, and the Jury were filing out to make a decision which meant freedom, and an opportunity to restore my fallen fortunes, or incarceration for a term which only one man in that assembly knew.

Curious eyes were bent on me from all parts of the crowded Court. The legal fraternity employed in the case seemed to be debating my chances of acquittal, as every now and then Counsel would look up and engage in an eager conversation with his neighbour. But I had become inured to the vulgar gaze, and was long past taking any interest in the speculations of professional advocates. All I wanted, and wanted urgently, was to get the business over, and if possible to get away with it.

I had not long to wait. Within half an hour the Jury returned. The shortness of their deliberations was ominous, and I read disaster in their faces. As soon as they had resumed their seats the Clerk of the Court rose and enquired their verdict. The Foreman of the Jury, a gentleman with a bald head, a sense of his own consequence, and an even greater sense of his importance as an instrument for the execution of British justice, rose to his feet, and replied calmly, deliberately, and with an air of complete finality: "We find the prisoner guilty on all counts."

At these fateful words I reeled, but I pulled myself together, although the subsequent proceedings passed as in a dream. I could hear, while I grasped the rail of the dock, the far-off voice of the Judge, saying that I had been found guilty by a jury of my fellow-men on what appeared to him to be clear and unimpeachable evidence; that I had betrayed a great trust, and that he would be doing less than his duty if he did not sentence me to a term of imprisonment. "But," and his voice trailed on, "there are certain extenuating circumstances in your case, and you have received a heavy punishment already in the loss of an honoured position, and an assured pension. You will undergo imprisonment for eighteen months in the Second Division."

Although I had been prepared for the worst, the realization that my world had collapsed under me, and that I had lost for ever the badge of decent citizenship, came upon me with sudden and overwhelming force. Eighteen months in prison! What a calamity, and what a disgrace! But I had no time to think. A touch on the arm, and I stumbled down the dock steps, not daring to look at the back of the Court, where sat my wife, supported by a few friends. Along a lengthy corridor the gaoler led me, and then down a dozen stone steps. Unlocking an iron grille at the bottom, we entered a long, low-roofed, narrow room lined with cells on either side.

The gaoler halted and said briskly: "This will do for you. Seem to have seen your face before, sir!"

"Possibly you have," I answered, mustering a feeble

smile. "I pass this Court almost every day, but I have never been in it before."

"Oh, well," he added, "I'm sorry you've got this packet, but don't take it too badly. I've never been in one, but they tell me there are worse places than prison."

With this piece of rough philosophy he turned the key in the door, and I was alone in the cell. But the gaoler was not yet gone. Pushing back a sliding board in the door he thrust his face against the grating and said: "I'll see you again in less than an hour's time, when you can have something to eat." And then I heard his retreating footsteps, and the clang of the outside door as it was shut.

The cell was about twelve feet in length, and six or eight feet wide. A low bunk composed of very hard boards ran down the side. At the foot of the bunk was a tiny lavatory. The cell had evidently served as a temporary resting-place for gentlemen who had faced their troubles lightly, as well as for law-breakers like myself. Many of them had taken the trouble to express on the walls, in poetry and prose, their heartfelt opinions of their captors, and their contempt for the British judiciary.

At any other time I might have found these opinions amusing, but I was in no mood to appreciate the literary efforts of those who had come into conflict with the guardians of society. My head throbbed like a steam-engine, and my hands were trembling violently. I would have given the world for a double whisky, but the law does not provide stimulants for malefactors suffering from nervous exhaustion. Fortunately I had a *Daily Express* in my pocket, and sitting on the bunk I began to read. I had no idea of what the paper contained, but the exercise served to distract attention from my wretchedly nervous state, and kept at bay the mental and torturing images of a ruined career.

After what seemed at least an hour the grille rattled again, and footsteps approached the cell. The gaoler appeared at the grating with the brief announcement: "Your wife," and retired to a respectful distance until the interview was over. I suppose he was the silent witness of many such scenes. My wife had applied for and obtained permission to bid me good-bye. She was accompanied by a woman friend, and at the gaoler's request the interview was to be as short as possible.

We did not keep him waiting. A few broken words and hysterical promises to write as soon as it was possible, and they were gone. But the outside door did not clang. Back came the gaoler with his face to the bars. He looked me over critically—the tears were running down my cheeks—and said, gruffly but not unkindly: "Here, stop this nonsense. Perhaps a cigarette would help to pull you together. I can see by your fingers that you smoke a lot."

Here was manna from heaven. I hurriedly explained that I had brought in nothing, owing to the fear of search —not even matches—but he was already groping in his pockets, and in a few seconds I had three cigarettes in my possession, and a box of matches. "When you've finished," went on the gaoler, deaf to my grateful thanks, "put the matches under the bed at the near end, so that they won't be seen, and I'll know where to find them. Now buck up, forget the worst, and remember your wife's a well plucked 'un." The grating closed. Good-hearted gaoler. I shall never forget your bluff, robust kindness! Nor shall I forget the aroma and the comfort of those three cigarettes, the last I was to smoke for fifteen long and often weary months.

So I lit up, and started again on the *Daily Express*, but a few minutes later footsteps passed the door. There was the sound of voices, one of them raised in shrill protest, and a door banged to. Another prisoner had come in, and he proved to be a singularly noisy one. Hardly had the gaoler withdrawn than the newcomer started to shout aloud. It was impossible to understand a single word he said, but there was no doubt that he was either drunk or in a very dreadful state of mental distress.

Sometimes he shrieked what appeared to be violent imprecations; at other times his voice sank to a groan, and then he abandoned himself to hopeless sobbing. This infernal din continued without intermission for at least half an hour, and the man's agony was no soporific for my jangled nerves. Would his damned clamour never cease? I rose and paced the cell like a caged animal, but the arrival of the gaoler put a stop to any further apprehension.

On this occasion he opened up the cell, and handed in a mug of tea, with two large slices of bread and a slab of cheese. "Here are your rations, sir," he said cheerfully, "and take my advice, get 'em down your throat, whether you feel like it or not."

"What on earth," I inquired irritably, "is the matter with that fellow next door?"—"Oh, him!" said the gaoler. "He's a Polish Jew; sentenced in another Court from yours for a long firm fraud. He expected to get off, but landed the mustard. When the Judge said three years, he made a scene in the dock, and fell into a sort of swoon. We aren't certain yet whether he's shamming, or whether it's a case of genuine mental breakdown. But he's making a hell of a row, isn't he?" he added somewhat anxiously, as a more penetrating shriek than ever reached our ears. "Anyhow, the quack will be along in a few minutes, and he'll find out whether he's gone bats or not."

Sure enough the doctor did arrive shortly afterwards. One could hear the murmur of voices amidst the animal noises produced by the convict, noises which presently subsided into a low moaning like that of a dog in pain, and then silence.

The food was unpalatable enough, and anxiety is no spur to appetite, but I took the gaoler's advice, and forced it down, not knowing what further demands would be made that day on my physical and mental resources. The cries of newspaper boys could be plainly heard above the dull roar of London's ceaseless traffic. I visualized the office over which I had presided for so many years. There wouldn't be much work done there to-day. One and all would be discussing my fate, and somewhere my wife was weeping. What a crash! Youth was no longer on my side, and on top of losing position and reputation there was the vile stigma of imprisonment, with all its degrading associations. Wolsey's speech occurred to me:

> And when he falls, he falls like Lucifer
> Never to hope again.

For two hours I wrestled with painful thoughts, and almost wished that I had had the courage to take another way out. But about four o'clock in the afternoon there was a great bustle and commotion outside. Doors were being opened, and men were moving. It was not long before a key turned in my lock and the door was pushed inwards to reveal the face of my friend the gaoler.

"The carriage is ready, sir," he said with a grin. "You'll be all right," he continued, more earnestly, "if you keep your pecker up." He held out his hand and I grasped it as firmly as I could. "Thank you," I said. "I can't say much now, but perhaps we shall meet later on."

The prisoners, about eight in number, were taken out to the back of the building, where stood a motor vehicle with the engine purring. It was a Black Maria, familiar to most Londoners by sight. Few people stop to realize the load of anguish and despair which it carries daily.

The prisoners filed in, and were locked up in narrow compartments hardly big enough to hold a fully grown man. I am about 5 feet 10 inches in height, but my head touched the roof, and there was not sufficient room to enable me to stretch my legs. The cell had no light of its own, and the window consisted of wooden shutters the slats of which sloped abruptly to the ground, so that only the roadway immediately below was visible. To anyone subject to claustrophobia this experience must be terrifying, and the close confinement following the mental torture of the trial nearly drove me crazy.

We followed the Embankment, and then turned into Bow Street, where another batch of prisoners was taken on board. Some of them were young men who sang noisily and defiantly, and shouted pleasantries at one another.

The journey was resumed, and after a run of ten or fifteen minutes the Black Maria pulled into a yard. I believe it was Rochester Row, Westminster. Here the doors were unlocked; the prisoners were surrounded by police, and herded into a large cell at the back of the station. Most of them were young men, excited, talkative, and irresponsible. They spoke loudly and boastfully of the exploits that had brought them within the clutches of the law. One of them, a lad of nineteen, related how he had gone out "to do a job" and had been betrayed by a girl of whose intimacies he had tired. His language was not pretty.

The older men were silent and gloomy. Some were obviously labouring under great nervous tension; others were marked with the consciousness of final and irretrievable defeat. One of them, a tall man, spoke to me. "How long are you staying?" he inquired briefly. "Eighteen months." I replied. "God!" he ejaculated, as if appalled at the prospect; "I'm lucky, I've only got six weeks."

It appeared that he was a bookmaker's runner, and had been caught for the third time. Previous offences had produced only a fine, but on the third occasion the magistrate said that fines having proved ineffective he would be sentenced to six weeks in gaol.

The Police, he said, usually let them know when it was intended to make an arrest, thus giving the bookmaker the opportunity to put up a runner with a blameless record, who would escape with a small fine; but on this occasion a sudden change of officers had upset the routine.

The new serjeant was not familiar with, or preferred to ignore, the working arrangements of his predecessor, and our friend had fallen into the net. He was quite philosophical about his misfortune. His employer had paid his expenses, and would not only take him back on release but would look after his wife and children during his enforced absence.

Rochester Row seemed to be a receiving depôt for prisoners from a number of London Courts. Groups of men were continually coming in, and our room grew uncomfortably full. The younger element talked and laughed, and even indulged in vigorous horseplay, but the older men, without exception, seemed to feel their position keenly.

About six o'clock in the evening we were ordered out and sorted into two groups, one for Wandsworth and the other for Wormwood Scrubs. As soon as this business was completed the prisoners re-embarked, and began the final stage of the journey to prison.

And an interminable journey it seemed to be, sitting in a cramped position in that dark and narrow cell. Rain was falling heavily, and the vehicle moved slowly. After about twenty minutes it occurred to me that we must be passing very close to my old home, where I had lived for so long, and had so many years of real happiness. The thought was not cheering.

At last the Black Maria pulled up with a jerk. The opening of iron gates could be heard. We moved on again, and came to a full stop. Doors were unlocked, and in obedience to a gruff word of command I passed out to the back of the vehicle, and descended the steps. We had arrived at journey's end. The grim and frowning walls by which we were surrounded bespoke Wormwood Scrubs.

Under the direction of prison warders we marched in twos for some distance, and were finally herded into the reception-room. A lightly built, bespectacled officer with a sandy, wispy moustache sat at a high desk. He was assisted by a dozen prisoners, who constituted the reception staff. The newcomers were ordered to sit on low forms facing the warder. He called the roll, and inquired from each man if he had ever been convicted before. Wormwood Scrubs is a prison for first offenders, and any person admitting a previous conviction is liable to be transferred to Wandsworth, where the discipline is said to be much more severe.

We were then ordered to empty our pockets. The articles were collected by the reception staff and handed to the warder. From the urgently whispered inquiries as to whether we had any tobacco or cigarettes, one could judge that the reception staff had no intention of allowing contraband to reach the prison authorities. After all valuables and trifles had been taken, entered in a prison register, and signed for, boots were removed, and the business of fitting on prison shoes began. Each man was also issued with a pair of cell slippers.

By eight o'clock we had received practically the whole of our prison kit, including trousers, underpants, coat and waistcoat, two coarse shirts, two vests, mug and tin plate, a Bible, a religious manual, a hymn book, brush and comb, a towel, soap, and a hold-all, and we were then allowed a cup of cocoa, with bread and margarine.

As soon as the food was dispatched the prisoners were handed over to another warder, who had just arrived on the scene, and whose business it was to take our fingerprints, an operation which was soon completed. Then every man was weighed by a prisoner wearing a band round his arm.

Next we were ordered to remove collars and ties, and to be prepared to strip naked at any moment, and before long we were filing into the prison doctor's room to submit to a cursory medical inspection. A rapid examination of the heart, a search of the body for distinguishing marks, and it was all over. On leaving the M.O.'s room our civilian clothes were taken from us, never to be seen again until our release, and we passed on to the baths.

There was plenty of hot water, and after the trials and tribulations of the previous forty-eight hours I think that hot bath was one of the most comforting and soothing experiences that have ever come my way. The attendant, a prisoner, eyed me gravely, and then, after a moment's pause, inquired how I liked it. I replied that it was splendid, and that I felt a different man already. "I don't mean the bath," he said, "they're always good here, but this bloody outfit generally." I told him that I had scarcely had time to form an opinion, but that it was almost impossible to conceive of an agreeable prison.

"Oh, it's not so bad as you might think," he went on. "If you behave yourself, and are not fool enough to worry, a year passes in no time. I'm going out to-morrow."

"Then," I ventured, "you are probably the happiest fellow in this building to-night."

"Well, I ought to be," he reflected, "but I'm not. You know," he continued, lowering his voice and becoming more confidential, "I'm in here for bigamy, and I've just received word that they'll both be at the gate to-morrow morning to meet me. I'd sooner stay here another week than start the old nonsense all over again, but they won't keep you a day over your time."

B

I suggested that his was probably a case of

> I've got a wife and a woman too,
> The wife don't love me, but the woman do.

He grinned, and said that it was something like that, the only difference being that his wife always protested that she loved him to distraction, but behaved as if she had found in him an object on which to wreak the pent-up vengeance of dozens of previous lives. "How is it," he inquired, with the air of a dispassionate seeker after information, "that when you sign up with a woman she seems to acquire an exclusive right to rob, defame, and otherwise molest you?"

I replied that his experience was shared in some degree by all Benedicts, and that the only ideal unions were those between deaf men and blind women.

In any case, what was the other woman like?

"Ah, now you're talking," he said, with sudden energy in his voice.

It was easy to see where the man's inclinations lay, but there seemed to be no alternative but to face the music, and after suggesting that it must be a novel and exciting experience to have two strong women fighting for one's body, an idea with which he vehemently disagreed, we shook hands and wished each other good-bye and good luck.

I was now, like the others, dressed in prison garb, and at the word of command all the newcomers fell in, carrying their small belongings, and passed out of the reception-room into the open air. We marched for some distance under gloomy porticoes, with only an occasional gleam of light from windows where officers were on duty. The prison itself was wrapped in total darkness, and towered above us like a giant's castle.

At last we reached our destination, and passed through iron gates, and a great door, into C Hall, where we were to spend the probationary and disciplinary stage of prison existence. It was a vast and rather dreadful-looking building, like a great steel safe, four stories high, cells running the whole length on either side, with wire netting of a narrow mesh on the level of each floor, to prevent prisoners from hurling themselves to death.

An officer sat at a high desk, but our business with him was brief. He handed me a small cloth badge with the lettering C2 33, and a buttonhole at either end. This meant that I was to be lodged in Cell No. 33 on the second floor of C Hall, and the badge had to be attached to two buttons on the tunic pocket, so that any officer meeting me knew my address without inquiry. "Come on," said the officer, "this way!"—and up the steel gangway we padded. In another minute we stood at the door of Cell 33. "Get your bed down at once," he ordered. "In fifteen minutes I'll turn the light out, whether you're ready or not," and with that he shut the door, and I was alone.

There was no time for the moment to think of my situation. I had no wish to be caught in the dark, and without more ado I turned my attention to bed-making. Three planks attached to two pieces of scantling stood against the wall, together with a hard coir mattress, on which reposed a pillow of the same material, two sheets, and two blankets. The whole formed a bed raised about two inches from the floor. An electric light burned dimly above the door, but its feebleness only emphasized the general depression of the place and the weariness of my own mind.

The warder was as good as his word. Within fifteen minutes his footsteps could be heard approaching, there was a loud click outside the door, and the cell was plunged in Egyptian darkness. But sleep was out of the question. The day had been too eventful, and my nerves and brain were strung to a pitch which precluded rest. Moreover, the bed was abominably hard and uncomfortable, and I tossed and turned about, vainly endeavouring to banish the thoughts that kept clamouring for admission. Long after midnight, however, being utterly exhausted, mentally and physically, I dropped into a troubled sleep, racked with dreams—but a sleep that was preferable to consciousness.

CHAPTER II

IN the morning I woke early, long before daylight. Sleep could not be wooed again, but my nerves were more settled, although I felt absolutely done up. And so I lay, until a bell like an auctioneer's clanged noisily some distance away. It was answered by another, obviously from our own Hall. Footsteps could be heard in the distance, and the click, click, of electric switches as they were turned on by the night watchman on his last round of duty.

Presently my own cell was lighted up, and I struggled out of bed, and dressed painfully. It was then half-past five. After arranging the bed and the clothes in the same position as I had found them, I washed, and emptied the contents of the basin into the bedroom utensil.

There was time to take stock of the furniture and equipment of the cell. It was scanty enough. A stout piece of timber wedged into the wall near the door served as a table, near which stood a wooden chair. In one corner was a washstand with an enamel basin and jug, a receptacle for soap, and a towel. In another corner there were two bookshelves. A printed menu of the regulation prison diet hung on the wall, and a small plain mirror beneath the window completed the inventory.

The window was high up, with iron bars outside, and the only way to get a glimpse of the outer world was by standing on the chair, a practice which was strictly forbidden. The window could be opened by pushing sideways a sliding pane of glass.

As six o'clock struck I could hear the shouting of

warders and the opening of cell doors. Presently the key
turned in my lock, and an officer, a man with long fiddle-
shaped features, whom I soon discovered was popularly
known as "Horse-Face," poked his head into the cell,
crying, "Open your windows, and throw out your
slops!" He then passed on to the next cell, where the
same formula was repeated.

The order, of course, was not to be taken literally, but
I saw through the open door a file of men passing with
bedroom utensils in their hands, and promptly joined
the party. They were making for the lavatories and
washing-places, where the "jerries" were emptied and
washed. The accommodation here was hopelessly inade-
quate, and the odour was overpowering. It was obvious
that a good number of prisoners regarded the night as
the proper time for evacuation.

Half an hour was allowed for this performance, during
which the air was rent with injunctions against talking.
Even when the men had retired to their cells, the shouting
still continued, but now it was directed against any
prisoners who put their heads out of the doors to ascertain
what was going to happen next, or stood on the threshold,
Every man was supposed to stand well back in his cell,
so that communication with other prisoners, either by
signal or speech, was made as difficult as possible.

A few minutes later prison orderlies carrying steaming
buckets came clambering up the stairs, and were taken
charge of by an officer on each landing. And then began
a round of the cells, prisoners holding out their china
mugs for half a pint of cocoa, which was poured from
the bucket, and receiving as well a small piece of dry
bread at the hands of the warder. When the little pro-

cession arrived at my door, the officer said gruffly to the orderly, "Go on, he don't like it," and they went on. I learnt later that cocoa was served only to men who engaged in morning drill.

As soon as the cocoa was dispatched, the bell rang a warning note. A loud cry of "Men for Drill" arose from the bottom floor, and prisoners dashed for the staircases in a wild rush to get there first. The building shook with the tread of hundreds of feet.

One could hear the officers lining the men up, commanding silence, and issuing threats, and then the gaol doors were opened, and the squads filed out into the courtyard. The men who took drill were divided into two squads, A and B. The A squad were all fit men, and were compelled to carry out every movement ordered. B men were fit too, but if through some slight physical disability they had any difficulty in performing the more strenuous type of exercise, they were not obliged to do so, and could stand idle while their more active comrades carried on.

All other men, who through disability or age were unable to engage in drill, were posted to the exercise squad. Every prisoner from the age of forty-six onwards joined this squad automatically, although any man who was certified as sound in wind and limb by the doctor could at his own request join B drill.

As soon as the Drill men had been seen off the premises there was a shout for Exercise men, and the middle-aged, the decrepit, and the disabled moved to the ground-floor, where a count took place; then the doors were again opened, and the prisoners marched into the exercise ring.

The exercise consisted in walking round a circular path in a yard between C Hall and the Part Worn Store. There were inside walks for men who were slow on their feet. A fast pace was maintained, and officers stood at either end of the court to see that a proper interval was kept between prisoners, and that no talking took place. But talking went on despite their precautions, and the only interludes in the monotonous business of marching without an objective were shouts for silence, and an occasional "About turn."

At the southern end of the court there was a row of lavatories, one of them marked with a red cross for the use of V.D. prisoners, and the northern end opened on a path which ran along the wall. The A and B squads passed along this path frequently, sometimes in quick step, and sometimes at the double, the marching being in the nature of a warming up before the physical drill began.

Any man wishing to use the lavatory had to apply for permission, and woe betide the prisoner who made a break without first holding up his hand, and obtaining the warder's consent. There was no such thing as privacy as the doors extended only from two feet above the ground to two feet from the roof.

Half an hour of this business fairly tired me out, and I was more than grateful when the order came to march in C Hall gate. A count was made as we entered, and as soon as we were inside the Hall the shouting and clamour arose with redoubled fury. "Keep to the right!"— and there were officers stationed at intervals to see that we did keep to the right, and close to the wall. "Stop that bloody talking!"—"Get inside your cells and close the doors"—these and other orders assailed our ears, and the din was simply deafening. One young warder of immense physical proportions was the noisiest of the whole crew. He suffered from a lisp and an excessive flow of saliva, and I can still hear his voice above all the others bawling "Get inshide your shells!"

I was only too glad to reach the quiet of the cell and shut the door on the howling dervishes outside, and there I remained unmolested for another twenty minutes, when an officer turned the key and a prisoner with a red band on his arm presented me with a piece of bread, which I afterwards found weighed exactly six ounces, and an ounce of margarine. He was followed by another orderly, who poured a pint of foul tea into my china mug, and finally the officer appeared again, this time with an orderly carrying a bucket of porridge. I received a pint of the mixture in my outstretched plate, the officer ladling it out with a wooden spoon.

The cell was then locked and I confronted my breakfast. But I had no appetite, and the bread was coarse and unpalatable. It took some time to get used to prison bread. There was no milk or sugar with the porridge, and the only relish one could use was salt, of which there was a small quantity in the cell. I often wondered if double or treble the ordinary consumption of salt was injurious to the human organism. Some men used large quantities of it, and I often saw them pouring salt into their cocoa.

In half an hour's time the cells were unlocked again, and the men could be heard filing past. They were removing the slops after washing up the breakfast things. My door was not opened. Presently the bell rang again, and there was another rush for the staircases, with the usual clamour from the supervising warders. The prisoners were being assembled in working parties for their daily tasks. It took some little time to get them away, and then came the turn of prisoners who had arrived the previous night.

After we had disposed of the breakfast slops we were marched off to the reception-room, where we drew the remainder of our equipment and waited for the arrival of one of the Deputy Governors. He interviewed each man separately, consulted the prisoner's dossier, and questioned him about his civilian occupation, with the object, no doubt, of gaining some idea as to what he was best fitted for in prison.

I have every reason to be grateful to Commander Foster, for such was his name. He had heard of me long before I had come under the fierce blaze of notoriety, and I left his room with the assurance that I should be placed in the Library, the most coveted of all prison occupations, as soon as a vacancy occurred. In the meantime I should be posted to the Shed, there to learn the gentle art of sewing mail-bags.

From the Deputy Governor we passed on one by one to the Chaplain, who explained the nature and scope of his ministrations. He seemed to be the right type of man for the job, radiating energy and good cheer. I remember he referred to the arduous nature of his duties, and the difficulty of giving adequate attention to the individual prisoner where there were so many, and I drew a smile when I suggested that he had one great advantage over all other parsons, in that he was never likely to meet with active opposition or open criticism from his flock.

Finally, we met the Librarian, who was accompanied by a prisoner amanuensis, who entered in a memorandum-book our numbers, names, ages, religions, and cell addresses.

On emerging from the last interview I was accosted by an officer, and ordered to take a bucket and scrub the cell in which we had had our cocoa the previous evening. The room was a fairly big one, and I had to move in order to get the job finished within the allotted span of an hour. The other members of the party were scrubbing floors, forms, and tables, and when we were marched back to C Hall the reception-room was as clean as the proverbial new pin.

On reaching my cell, through a storm of yelling and howling, I found that a knife and fork had been placed on the table, with a pen and a bottle of ink, and an official letter-form on which I could write home. When the cells were opened up again shortly afterwards the warder threw me two ounces of bread, and told me to get my letter written as quickly as possible. His orderly handed in a food-tin with the day's dinner, which consisted of a stew, containing a fair quantity of fat meat and potatoes. The odour was not pleasant, but I determined to try it. My stomach, however, quickly revolted, and I had no better success with the bread. So I turned my attention to letter writing, the last means of direct communication with the outside world for twenty-eight days.

In the afternoon we were taken before our Landing Officer, the gentleman nicknamed "Horse-Face," who made us an issue of salt and toilet-paper. Without an adequate supply of the latter no prisoner ever feels at ease. He favoured us with a short lecture on prison

discipline, and breathed vengeance against any man who
attempted to break the regulations. "If any of you fellows
don't behave, you're for it. You might as well smash your
heads against this," he added, tapping the stone wall with
his knuckles. The prisoners showed no sign of fear, but
merely gazed at him stolidly. A sardonic grin flitted
across the face of the young burglar who had been
betrayed by his girl.

"Now," continued the officer, "you will return to your
cells, where you will find buckets of cold water, scrubbing
brushes, and soap, and if those cells are not a damn sight
cleaner than when you went in, there will be trouble
for somebody. And don't forget that it's not only the
floor you scrub, but your bed planks, table, chair, washstand, and bookshelves."

And so we started on the depressing and tiring job of
scrubbing a prison cell. A charwoman might have found
it easy enough, but to a man unaccustomed to manual
labour it was really fatiguing. However, at the end of an
hour I had finished, not, it is true, entirely satisfied with
the result. I felt that I might have been more successful
with hot water, but this was a forbidden luxury. The officer
thrust his head into the cell for a rapid inspection, said
nothing either by way of praise or dispraise, and ordered
me to fall in on the ground-floor.

We were then taken to another cell, a sort of show-
place, where a young warder gave us a lecture on the art
of making a prison bed, and the regulation method of
folding and hanging blankets and sheets, so that cells
would present a neat and uniform appearance. He spoke
with a pronounced Cockney accent, muffled by adenoids,
and his English was not acquired in any of the schools.

After a practical demonstration questions were invited, whereupon the young burglar broke in eagerly with: "When are we going to see the old man?" His question had no relevance, of course, to the business in hand. The warder regarded him fixedly for a moment, and then, with ominous quietness, asked him his name. "Castle," answered the youngster with engaging candour. "Ah, I thought so," said the officer, sagely nodding his head, as if suddenly receiving confirmation of a suspicion which he had entertained for some time. "Like father, like son! When will the other members of the family be coming in?" And then, noticing our blank looks, he burst into a sudden rage, and shouted in the lad's face: "And don't you call the Governor the 'old man' again. You'll see him soon enough, by the looks of you. Damned if I haven't half a mind to case you now!" What casing meant we were to learn later.

We were now equipped and ready to expiate our crimes as ordinary criminals, but it was approaching four o'clock in the afternoon, and too late to take us to the Shops, so that we were sent back to the cells with orders to shut the doors on pain of death. Here a joyful surprise awaited me. Lying on the table were two books, and a card recording my name and number, the numbers of the books, and the date of issue. And they were good modern books. One was the political reminiscences of Griffiths Boscawen, and the other a readable novel by Beverley Nichols.

At five o'clock tea was served. It consisted of a pint of cocoa, six ounces of bread, and an ounce of margarine. The cocoa looked greasy, but it was steaming hot, and pleasant enough to the taste. A mouthful of the bread and margarine finished me. I could not get on with it.

There were no further interruptions that evening, and I settled down to read the novel, but the light was dim, and the experiences through which I had passed had seriously weakened my eyesight. In the end I had to give it up. I looked through the bars of my window at the sky, which was black as velvet, and studded with stars, and wondered what my world thought of me. Life is so swift and varied that few people remember anything but the closest personal experiences. My fall would soon be forgotten, but there were some who were grieving in secret, and not a few whose regrets would be sincere and deep.

Curiously enough I experienced no sense of the "sin" of which the Schoolmen talk so glibly, nor was I the victim of remorse. I simply felt that circumstances had been too strong for me, and that I had behaved as the majority of other people in a similar fix would have done. But there was no comfort in the sky. "Look not to it for help," sings Omar, "for it rolls impotently on as you or I"; and I was very glad when a neighbouring clock struck eight, the hour before which no beds may be put down in C Hall.

The coir mattress was hard and lumpy, but a recumbent position is more restful than sitting down. If only my brain would stop working! Thought-control is difficult, and to some people impossible. Indeed, the conscious effort to secure it only makes matters worse. I could not relax mentally, and therefore could not sleep.

To add to my troubles, a prisoner on the floor above, evidently of a religious turn of mind, kept on singing dolefully and untunefully, "Abide with Me," while the man next door was snoring like a pig. The latter must have fallen asleep as soon as his head touched the pillow—an example that I would have given anything to follow.

On two occasions at least the tiny shutter over the peephole in the cell door was moved, and I knew that I was under observation by the officer on evening duty. At last nine o'clock struck, and the click, click of the switches could be heard as the night watchman started on his round on the top floor. In five minutes my light was extinguished, and I lay in the dark, wakeful and wretched. I never slept at all that night.

CHAPTER III

AT this early stage it might be as well to interrupt the narrative in order to give the reader a clear idea of the layout of Wormwood Scrubs, and of the system under which this great penal establishment is worked. The prison in which malefactors are confined consists of four long, narrow buildings, standing at intervals of two hundred yards. They are known as A, B, C, and D Halls. Between B and C Halls are the Carpentry and Shoe-making Shops, the Shed, the Baths, and the Bakery. The Brushmaking and Tailor's Shops, the Part Worn Store, the Library, the Recreation Room, the Catholic Church, and the Jewish Synagogue lie between C and D Halls. These are all low, rambling buildings, over which the Halls tower like grim warders. I believe that the prison was erected in the 'seventies entirely by convict labour. By the division into separate Halls the authorities intended to minimize the risk of mass outbreaks. At one time female prisoners occupied D Hall, the cells in which are rather smaller than the others.

The church, an unconsecrated Gothic building, runs along the front of B and C Halls, exactly opposite the main gate, and stretching towards A Hall is the hospital. On the right of the main gate is a building where prisoners meet their friends and relatives, the offices of the Chaplain, the Schoolmaster, and other officials, a small court for the trial of prisoners, and the quarters of the single warders. On the left stand the offices of the Governor, the Deputy Governors, and the Steward, and behind them the General Stores. The whole is surrounded by a high wall thirteen or fifteen feet high, with a tower at every corner. Round the foot of the wall, and in such spaces as are not covered by buildings, or used as exercising-grounds, are flower and vegetable gardens cultivated by prison labour.

The Governor and the two Deputy Governors are the chief executive and administrative officers. They are not usually recruited from the ordinary prison staff. In practice most of them are selected from retired officers of the Army and Navy, their prison pay, which is not large, forming a welcome addition to their Service pensions. They wear no distinctive uniform, and are always clad in mufti.

This book does not pretend to speak with any authority on the multifarious duties that must devolve on the administrators of a great prison, but will only deal with the Governor and his Deputies in so far as they came into contact with the prisoners themselves.

They interviewed each man on admission, and fortified by the papers relating to his trial and sentence consigned him to a working-party, a decision which was subsequently confirmed by a Board, consisting of the Governor, a Deputy, the Chaplains, and one or two other officials. Once a day they held a little court in every Hall, heard applications and complaints from prisoners, and punished offenders against prison discipline. An accused man was "cased," not crimed as in the Army.

For good behaviour every man had one-sixth of his sentence remitted, so that a person sentenced to a year's imprisonment would actually serve only ten months. The reduction of two months could be cancelled by the Governor for breaches of the rules, and in addition the

C

prisoner could be deprived of all the privileges he had acquired through good conduct and length of service, and made to undergo prison discipline as from the beginning.

At least once a day the Governor or his Deputies visited all the establishments in the prison, and assured themselves that the routine machine was functioning smoothly. They attended concerts and Church services, and in fact were on duty from early morning until the latest prisoners were bedded down at night. I always found them courteous and fair, and firm without being harsh.

The Chief Officer is the next in authority, and he is promoted from below. This man wears the ordinary prison uniform of blue, his cap and shoulder badges indicating his rank. He did not often come into contact with the prisoners, and I fancy his main duty was the preservation of discipline and efficiency amongst the warders themselves.

Each Hall is in charge of a Principal Officer, as are also the reception-room, the bakery, and the hospital. The next in order of rank is the Hall Officer, who presides on the first floor of each Hall, and supervises the accommodation of prisoners, and arranges their frequent changes of domicile. There are two Landing Officers on each floor. They serve out the rations, but on the whole their duties are disciplinary, and they are responsible for the maintenance of order and cleanliness on their respective landings.

Officers in charge of the Shops are skilled tradesmen, and as such earn additional rates of pay. There are other warders posted to the Shops for disciplinary purposes only. The Chaplain is supported by a Church Army officer, while a second Church Army officer attends to the spiritual needs of the Borstal boys in A Hall. Catholic prisoners have their own priest, a Rabbi from outside looks after the Jews, and a Nonconformist minister holds a service every Wednesday evening in the church. The Librarian, the Photographer, the Schoolmaster, the Steward, and his clerks are exempted from wearing uniform, a privilege which is not shared by the Organist.

There are approximately three hundred cells in each Hall, so that when full Wormwood Scrubs accommodates twelve hundred prisoners. In the course of a year there are between five and six thousand new entrants.

A Hall contains boys destined for Borstal Institutions. They are rarely seen, except in squads passing through the prison grounds. B Hall is divided into two parts, one for the use of ordinary prisoners, and the other for young prisoners—lads between sixteen and twenty-one, commonly known as "Y.P.s." The majority of the adults are short-term men, employed almost exclusively as cleaners in the hospital, the church, the recreation-room, and the gymnasium. On the ground-floor, however, are the penal servitude men, prisoners who have received sentences of three years and upwards, and who are waiting to be removed to Maidstone or some other similar establishment. Here also are to be found prisoners temporarily transferred from other penal institutions for the purpose of giving evidence in London Courts, or for attending bankruptcy proceedings. These are technically described as "Lodgers."

I have met all kinds and conditions of men among the

penal servitude class, even murderers whose death-sentences had been commuted to imprisonment for life. They do not mix with the ordinary population of the Scrubs. They leave the Hall only for daily walking exercise, weekly bathing parades, Church services, and Saturday afternoon concerts. At all other times they sit in front of their cells sewing mail-bags. Talking is prohibited, and at four o'clock in the afternoon they are locked up until half-past five the following morning.

C Hall is the preparatory school for the hard-labour and second-division prisoner. It is here that he is knocked into shape, and made to feel that he has broken all the rules of the game, and is an outcast from decent society. There is, of course, no such thing as physical brutality. The punishment takes the form of shouting and bullying. Men are seldom spoken to decently or civilly. This would be regarded as a sign of weakness. No detailed instructions as to the regulations governing the conduct of the establishment are given to new prisoners. That is not to say that they do not quickly learn them all, but they learn them in the rough school of experience, by breaking them ignorantly, and at some cost to their self-respect. A wise man needed only one lesson. The object of all this apparently stupid treatment is to make men feel that they have sinned, and sinned deeply, and that they will know what to expect if they are foolish enough to repeat the offence. Humiliation and fear of the consequences are the two instruments relied upon for the reformation of character.

Perhaps the most galling and irritating affront to a sensitive man is the pandemonium that breaks loose as soon as prisoners assemble for duty, or return from work.

It resembles the howling and yelping of a wolf pack. Shouts for silence are interspersed with commands to keep to the right or the left, whichever direction is in favour at the moment, and when the bewildered newcomer gets upstairs he is assailed by Landing Officers with orders to retire to his cell and shut the door. This he is very glad to do. In the privacy of his cell he is free from insults and noise, and if he feels so disposed he can curse his uniformed tormentors as deeply and as heartily as he pleases.

The purgatory of C Hall lasts for ten or twelve weeks, but sometimes longer, if D Hall, which is the next and final stepping-stone, is not discharging normally. The new arrival is lodged on the first or second floors, and his promotion proceeds heavenwards to the third or fourth.

The cell has to be scrubbed thoroughly at least once a week, and if it is not spick and span the occupant sooner or later earns a bad mark from his Landing Officer. He soon learns the advantage of taking off his hobnail boots on entering, even if they have to be put on again within a few minutes. They leave tell-tale marks on the floor which are not approved by keen-eyed warders.

Outside the cell door is a flat board with a buff-coloured sheet of paper attached, recording the man's name, his number, the total marks to which he is normally entitled throughout the length of his prison sentence, and spaces for the reports of his Landing Officer, and the officer in charge of his working-party.

Marks are awarded under the headings Fair, Good, Very Good, and Excellent. Three Fairs in succession entail a visit to the Governor, and some form of punishment. With good behaviour marks accumulate at the rate of six a day, or forty-two a week. In the early stages of prison life the sight of a total of two or three thousand, to be worked off at the rate of forty-two a week, is hardly conducive to gaiety. Periodically the sheets are removed for the entry of the officers' awards, and their return is awaited with not a little apprehension, especially if there has been trouble in the Shop, or the appearance of the cell has invited unfriendly criticism. By the side of the conduct-sheet stands a slotted board, into which is thrust a stiff card showing the prisoner's name, his sentence, and his occupation in the gaol. The colour of this card indicates the man's religion. White stands for Protestant, Red for Roman Catholic, and Blue for Jew.

Work begins at half-past eight, and continues with a break of a quarter of an hour until twelve. There is an hour for dinner. The men then start work again, and with the exception of another quarter of an hour's spell they carry on until a quarter to five in the afternoon. Prisoners, at any rate those in the first stages of their punishment, are compelled to work in their cells after tea, and this cell task usually takes the form of sewing mail-bags. The task is designed to occupy an average man for two hours. When this is finished he can turn to reading, and at eight o'clock he is permitted to put his bed down and retire from the world if he can.

At seven o'clock on Wednesday mornings a brief service is held in the church. Attendance is not compulsory, but most First Stage men prefer to go rather than sit in a locked cell. On Saturday mornings men are taken to church before breakfast to hear the news of the week, which is served out in tabloid form either by the Chaplain or by one of his assistants.

On Saturday afternoons all hands troop into the church again, this time for the weekly concerts arranged by philanthropic people from outside. The performances are limited to an hour, and bring a great deal of happiness into the drab life of prison. A man who misses a concert, either through sickness or his own fault, feels that he has been more than unfortunate.

There are two services on Sundays for adult prisoners. The morning service differs very little from an ordinary Church service, except that the singing is heartier, and there is no collection. In the afternoon a few brief hymns and prayers are followed by another concert of half an hour's duration. Occasionally a Salvation Army band supplies the music.

At all these functions the prisoners from D Hall, who of course have spent at least three months in captivity, occupy the front seats. C Hall men sit in the middle of the church. Behind them are the penal servitude prisoners from B Hall, while Y.P.s and patients from the hospital occupy the rear seats.

Warders stand on duty in the aisles, enforcing order and quiet, and when the services begin they retire to the back and keep their charges under observation. The choir consists of forty or fifty voices, and as a rule it performs very creditably. Practice takes place on Wednesday evenings under the direction of the Chaplain, who is a vocalist of no mean order. The position of chorister is eagerly sought after, ensuring as it does an hour a week of limited freedom and pleasant association with others.

On Thursday nights all the cells in C Hall are opened up at seven o'clock in the evening, and the prisoners, carrying their chairs with them, are marched to the recreation-room to listen to a lecture, illustrated by lantern slides. Some of the lecturers are women, and their talks are mainly concerned with travel in out-of-the-way parts of the world. When I was at the Scrubs there was a short series of informative talks on bee-keeping by an expert. The whole series of twelve was completed by a lecture on venereal disease by a doctor who was not in the prison service.

I well remember this gentleman's dissertation on the dread disease, from which many entrants to Wormwood Scrubs are sufferers. He spoke freely as a man amongst men, and his pointed references to the erotic inclinations and habits of the human male caused considerable amusement, and stamped him as a man who knew his business.

Towards the end of his speech he referred to the time within which the disease might appear after infection had taken place, and then, having invited questions from his audience, he resumed his seat. Immediately a prisoner with a pronounced Scottish accent, and with just a trace of anxiety in his voice, rose and said that he had always understood, his authority being a medical work, that the disease could only appear within so many days from contact. The doctor briefly replied that the man was entirely mistaken.

But the Scotsman was by no means satisfied. Would the doctor be good enough to check his statement, as it seemed to conflict with other medical authorities? At this the lecturer rather lost his temper, and ordered the questioner to sit down. He then proceeded to repeat with more detail exactly what he had said before, but he was no sooner back in his chair than the seeker after sexual knowledge was on his feet again.

This was too much for the audience, who now began to take a hand in the game. There were loud cries of "What day did you come in?"—"Why didn't you pay fourpence and have a decent girl?" and "Give him a blood-test!" accompanied by a good deal of laughter. On this the warders, who had heard the lecture dozens of times, and were probably only half awake, sprang to life, commanded silence, and threatened all sorts of penalties if the tumult did not cease at once. The little doctor also announced sternly and menacingly that he himself would stand no nonsense, and the meeting terminated quietly.

The hospital consists of two wards with thirty beds, and probably the same number of cells for sick men needing rest and quiet. The beds are good iron beds with spring mattresses, and the food, of course, is much superior to the ordinary prison fare. There are also a number of cells for mental patients, some of them padded. They are generally full.

When a man makes up his mind to go sick he reports first thing in the morning to his Landing Officer, and is absolved from attending drill or exercise. His cell is not opened up until the doctor comes on his rounds about ten-thirty in the morning. The doctor is accompanied by a hospital warder, and a prisoner brings up the rear with a wooden tray slung from his neck, loaded with medicine-bottles and drugs. A turn in hospital, provided the man was not too ill, was looked upon as a desirable rest-cure, but the thing most dreaded was two or three days in the cell. The doctors often prescribed this for men suffering from severe colds and high temperatures. So much did prisoners hate the solitude and monotony of cell life that many refused to report sick when they were urgently in need of medical attention. The prison doctors, and I think there are three permanently attached to the staff, maintain the best traditions of the medical profession. They are always decent and kind to the men; I found that the relationship existing was that of doctor and patient, and there was none of the browbeating or abusiveness of the old Army "quack."

Every prisoner is compelled to have a hot bath once weekly, an event that is looked forward to by all. There is an unlimited quantity of boiling water, and it is an easy matter to obtain a bath at any temperature. Half an hour is allowed for immersion, after which the men, who parade in working-parties, put on their weekly change of underclothes and socks, and hand in their soiled garments. On entering the baths all prisoners serving sentences of six months and over receive a clean kit with their own names and numbers, comprising shirt, underpants, vest, socks, and handkerchief. Others are handed the different articles by Part Worn Store prisoners from a stock kept behind the counter. When dressed each man has to clean out his bath, which is not difficult with the aid of paraffin, and the warder in charge inspects the result before squads are permitted to leave.

During the First and Second Stages of their Odyssey prisoners are allowed to write and see their relatives and friends once a month. Not more than three visitors for each prisoner are allowed in at any one time, and on Sundays the prison is closed to all strangers. Visitors are escorted to a room close by the main gate, where they see their friends through a glass darkly. Talk is difficult, as there are many conversations going on at the same time, and there is a watchful warder listening in. But

when the prisoner, by effluxion of time and good behaviour, reaches the zenith of prison life—that is, the
Fourth Stage—he qualifies for what is known as "open"
visits. In the summer-time he meets his friends in the
open air under a portico near the hospital, and in the
winter in a room adjacent to the Schoolmaster's office.
Fourth Stage men can converse freely with scarcely any
supervision. Third Stage prisoners may write to and see
their friends every three weeks, and Fourth Stage men
every fortnight. Outgoing and incoming letters are all
censored.

Food looms largely in the minds of men whose lives are
directed by others in a fixed routine, and who have no
intellectual pursuits to claim their attention. Prison fare
is not exactly exhilarating, and convicted gourmets must
suffer like the devil. Breakfast never varies. It consists
of six ounces of bread, an ounce of margarine, a pint of
porridge minus sugar and milk, and a pint of very inferior tea.

Tea also is a stereotyped feast—six ounces of bread,
margarine, and a pint of hot cocoa—but dinner is a vari-
able one, and offers some scope for ringing the changes.
It may consist of bully-beef and potatoes, pork and
beans, sea pie, shepherd's pie, Irish stew, and a number
of other obscure concoctions, with a very occasional
haunch of mutton. All of these messes were meticulously
weighed, so many ounces per man, according to the scale
hanging in his cell, the work, no doubt, of some dietetic
expert. Two ounces of bread completed the midday meal.

Now although this diet may be scientifically arranged,
and capable of keeping a man engaged on prison labour
in good health, it leaves him frightfully hungry, and it

is incapable of sustaining prolonged intellectual or physical effort. This was especially noticeable in the boxing contests. Very few men could last more than four rounds. At all times the younger prisoners were ravenous, and the pangs of hunger probably play an important part in the work of reformation. On the completion of a year in gaol a slight addition to the diet was allowed, one ounce of cheese for tea, and an ounce of pickles whenever bully beef made its appearance.

Shaving is a most important business in the life of the average modern man, but if he ever feels mad enough to try shaving under difficulties, let him qualify for Wormwood Scrubs. On admission, and for some weeks thereafter, prisoners are allowed to shave only twice a week. On permitted days a safety razor, which he must use in the dinner hour, is left on the prisoner's table by an orderly. The blade is invariably maddeningly blunt; only coarse, common soap may be used, and the water is stone cold. Readers can imagine what a devilish business it is to remove a three days' stubborn growth with equipment and accessories of this kind, and how excruciating the operation can be in the depth of winter.

Fortunately no one seems to care whether the face is free from herbage or not, and I never heard of anyone being penalized for not having a close shave. A month of this torture and then three shaves a week are allowed, until finally, when a man reaches the Fourth Stage, and has spent twenty-one weeks in captivity, he is presented with a razor and a new blade for his own use, and he can shave in hot water as often as he likes.

After ten or twelve weeks of C Hall the prisoner is transferred to the top floor of D Hall, and becomes a

Second Stage man with one stripe on his arm, like a lance-corporal. Men who receive such promotion are formally addressed by the Governor on arriving in their new domicile. He explains the privileges to which they automatically become entitled, and warns them against the dangers of abusing them. The prisoners are a happy crew, for they know that C Hall, with its terrorism, is behind them, and that with good behaviour and good luck they can look forward to the gradual relaxation of prison discipline.

The most important privilege is that of dining in association with one's fellows, and no one, unless he has been a solitary captive, realizes quite how much this means. Tables are arranged alphabetically on the ground-floor of D Hall. Twelve men sit at each table, presided over by a Leader, who is responsible for order and the equitable distribution of the rations. He sits at the head of the table, and his Deputy, who assists in the business of serving the food, sits at the opposite end.

Each of the other ten men takes it in turn to wash up the dishes and tidy the table, a duty known in the Scrubs as "Mary Ann." The Leader's job is no sinecure. The task of maintaining order amongst men, of whom many are resentful of any sort of discipline, without appearing officious, requires a good deal of tact and strength of character. The measuring-rod of a Leader's popularity is, of course, his fairness in dealing out the rations. Any tendency to generosity towards himself or his friends is immediately spotted, and most sensitive Leaders take a little less than their due. If a man feels that he is being "carved up," as they say in the Scrubs, there is generally trouble. The aggrieved party always has the right of appeal to the Hall Officer, but if that gentleman finds by the simple process of weighing that there are no grounds for the complaint the wretched prisoner goes before the Governor.

The bread ration was always known as a "toke." The origin of the word seems to be wrapped in obscurity. If the loaf falls short of the regulation weight, small pieces of bread are attached by means of wooden skewers. These are called "jockeys."

Promotion to Second Stage carries with it an increase in reading matter, another valuable privilege, and the abandonment of the cell task, which is replaced by educational classes. The educational syllabus covers a great variety of subjects—languages, history, economics, shorthand, book-keeping, geography, and poetry—and one witnessed the strange and moving spectacle of navvies struggling with Shakespeare, fraudulent bankrupts studying accounts, and smash-and-grab bandits toying with advanced literature and music. With few exceptions, the instructors are all London County Council teachers, and give their services gratuitously.

There is another privilege enjoyed by Second Stage men, and that is the right to remain in Hall until seven o'clock every other Saturday night. The prisoners sit at the dining-tables, and play draughts, chess, and a game called tippet, or, if they prefer it, they can read or talk.

After six weeks as a Second Stager, the good-conduct prisoner receives his next promotion to Third Stage, and sews another stripe on his arm. He can now write a letter, and receive friends every three weeks; he can talk freely to his comrades when exercising, although a warder is always present at these walks, and he finds it easier and more comfortable to shave in the cell next to the D Hall barber. When not engaged in other duties he is free to stay up until seven o'clock every night.

At the end of another six weeks, and provided he has behaved himself according to the standard set by the authorities, he has arrived at the Mecca of all prisoners— Fourth Stage, when all prison privileges are thrown open to him. A third stripe appears on his arm within an hour after the Principal Officer has announced the translation. Now he can write to and see his friends every fortnight, and, what is more, when free from attendance at the various classes he can repair to the recreation-room after tea, read the newspapers, listen to the wireless twice a week, and play games, including quoits and table tennis.

The recreation-room is situated about 50 yards from D Hall. It has a small stage, and is frequently used for concerts, lectures, and plays. In the winter time the prisoners are locked in the recreation-room, where discipline is maintained by Leaders. Occasionally the Orderly Officer unlocks the door, and the Leader in charge formally reports the number of men present, finishing with the conventional words "All correct." But there was very little interference from warders, and the men enjoyed themselves in their own way, under the guidance and control of their own Leaders.

When the summer months come round the recreation-room is kept open, and prisoners can stroll about in the adjacent courtyard. All territory beyond the courtyard is out of bounds, and it is the duty of Leaders to see that this rule is strictly obeyed.

Fourth Stage men are permitted to go to the library daily in the dinner hour and select their own books.

They are not compelled to retire to their cells until eight
o'clock in the evening, where they are followed a quarter
of an hour later by the Leaders. All prison activity is then
at an end.

The Leader system was evolved some years ago, and
marked a distinct advance in the evolution of prison
treatment. On the whole, I should judge that the experiment has been eminently successful. Approximately
twenty-five men who have reached Fourth Stage are
selected, on grounds of experience and character, to take
charge of the tables in D Hall, and to perform the duties,
without the authority, of junior officers.

They can move parties of men about the prison; they
assist in the maintenance of discipline and order in D
Hall, and they control the men in the recreation-room.
Without them all the privileges at present enjoyed by
well-behaved prisoners would be either drastically curtailed or abolished altogether; or prisoners would never
be freed from the presence and surveillance of their official
custodians.

It is a position requiring plenty of firmness and *savoir
faire*, because while a Leader might have many unpleasant duties to perform, he must never forget that he
is a prisoner himself. If he is to win the confidence and
the willing obedience of the men under him, he must
first of all be a decent fellow. He is under an obligation
strictly to observe the prison regulations himself, and to
report all serious breaches by others.

Naturally his position as a "quasi-screw" tends to
bring him into conflict with the unruly element present
in every large congregation of men drawn from all sections
of the community, but if a Leader has right on his side,

and has not imbibed too freely of the officer spirit, he generally receives the ungrudging support, and even the affection, of the better type of prisoner.

It would be idle to say that Leaders never betrayed the trust reposed in them. Many of them did, but a more careful system of selection would prevent this. Far too often Leaders were appointed solely on account of their usefulness to the officers in charge of working-parties, and not because of any capacity to control and influence men by example. One privilege enjoyed by Leaders might be mentioned here. On the day of their release they are entitled to an early pass, so that they can leave the prison before any of the others, and so, by a quick getaway, escape the attentions of any gentlemen who might be harbouring a grudge against them, as the result of the conscientious discharge of their duties.

There were also a few Party Leaders who could move bodies of men from one part of the prison to another, but who had no other powers. And there were the Red-bands, who could move their own bodies about the prison, but nobody else's. The latter were usually appointed as orderlies to the officers in B and C Halls, or were employed on work requiring the service of only one man.

One is often asked the difference between hard labour and second division men. The answer is that there is none, except that men sentenced to hard labour are supposed to spend the first two weeks in gaol without a mattress. They perform exactly the same work as second division prisoners, and in my time there was at least one hard labour man in the library.

CHAPTER IV

THE second day dawned, and after another night's sleeplessness I was feeling far from well. The clangour of the prison bell in D Hall came almost as a welcome relief, and as soon as the light was turned on I sprang out of bed with the fixed intention of shaking off the weakness that had invaded me. But the folding of the bed-clothes proved an almost intolerable task, and if I had known the proper procedure I should certainly have reported sick that morning.

However, I managed to struggle through the business of tidying up the cell, which was opened at six o'clock, with the same advice to open the windows and throw out the slops. Neglect to open the windows for ventilation purposes was a punishable offence, but in the winter the windows had to be shut before going to work, to prevent the influx of cold air into the Hall. In the summer they were kept open all day. Failure to open or shut them as required involved punishment, and many a man lost a concert or a lecture through a lapse of memory.

The morning was dark, cold, and slightly foggy, and we trudged round the exercise-ground in silence. Lights burned in the courtyard, but the depressing nature of the weather and the grimness of the surroundings, seemed to have damped the spirits of even the liveliest prisoners. The officers wore their greatcoats, and stamped on the ground to keep their feet warm. There was not much shouting; the men were too quiet, and we were glad to return to the shelter and warmth of C Hall, although Heaven knows it looked grim and forbidding enough from the outside.

When the bell rang for work I joined the crowd surging down the staircases, and found my way to the Shed party, which was drawn up with the others opposite the side entrance of the Hall. On the wall hung a large blackboard with the names of the Shops painted in the margin, in alphabetical order, beginning with the Brush-makers and finishing up with Works. Each party was counted as the men marched out, and the number chalked up on the board. The grand total, plus the men employed as cleaners and the sick, represented the total population of C Hall, and if the figures did not agree there was a great deal of commotion amongst the warders.

The Shed was a spacious building capable of accommo-dating at least one hundred and fifty men. There were about forty men in our party, and another sixty from D Hall, so that the room was not overcrowded. Each man squatted on a low wooden chair. These were backless, in order to deprive us of the luxury of reclining.

The instructor took up his position in front of us, surrounded by sewing-machines and other mechanical devices. Silence was enjoined on the men, and the order was given to start work.

The newcomers were then called up to receive their first lesson in sewing mail-bags. We were shown how to wax the threads, the use of the leather appliance or "palm" which prevented the heavy needle from wounding the hand, and then the correct method of sewing the canvas. Straight sewing was easy enough, and the mechanical exercise not unpleasant. The difficulty arose when it came to the business of turning corners.

Our instruction lasted for fifteen minutes. Then we were dispatched to our chairs to carry on. Having little mechanical sense, and being in a low physical and mental condition, I am afraid I imbibed very little of the brief lesson, but I knew enough to run down the sides of the canvas, which would, I hoped, some day do service for His Majesty's Post Office.

The man seated on my right happened to be the youthful burglar who had drawn down on his head the officer's wrath by inquiring for "the old man." To my alarm he was inclined to be talkative, and without turning his head he asked why I was there, and for how long. To the first part of his question I murmured something unintelligible, but when he learned that I had received what is commonly known as a "stretch" he bubbled over with sympathy, and drew his chair closer.

What was worse, he made not the slightest attempt to lower his voice, which was keyed almost in a conversational tone. I darted apprehensive glances in the direction of the instructor, who was now quartering the room for the culprit, and just as I turned to give the burglar a word of warning the instructor located the source of the disturbance.

Laying down his sewing, he approached us in leaps and bounds, and to my astonishment and disgust awarded me full marks for the breach of the rules occasioned by the chatter. He ordered me to take up my stool and walk to another part of the room, and threatened that if he heard another squeak he wouldn't give me a second chance. I bent to my task, and cursed the burglar for his curiosity.

But I was to learn that curiosity was one of the besetting vices of the great majority of prisoners, especially
the younger generation. They would relate with the
utmost candour, and even glee, full details of the exploits
that had brought them within the precincts of Wormwood
Scrubs. Shame, in the sense in which the word is commonly used, was conspicuous by its absence. And their
narratives were sometimes amusing, and always instruc-
tive to the student of human nature; but a sensitive
prisoner did not stay to listen. If he did he probably
remained to curse. For the tellers of criminal tales were
by no means disinterested parties. Every story was
encumbered. The author expected a *quid pro quo* in the
shape of your own life history, or at least its most dramatic
incidents, and if you failed to disclose the required information you were regarded with the contempt earned
by a man who figures in every round of drinks and never
buys one.

I well recollect a highly diverting occurrence arising
out of this almost universal prying into other people's
affairs. One day four prisoners were standing in the
library. They had been left there by the Leader of their
working party, who was to call for them a few minutes
later, and they whiled away the time recounting the mis-
adventures that had landed them in gaol.

Three of them were known to me by sight, and it was
obvious by the ease and rapidity with which they reeled
off their stories that they had done so many times before,
and that they were only preparing the way for a full
confession from the fourth man, a newcomer of a most
unprepossessing and surly appearance. They laughed and
joked at one another's expense. Occasionally the surly

individual permitted a smile to flit across his ugly features, but he never opened his mouth.

At last, when the three had exhausted their personal anecdotes, they waited silently but expectantly for the stranger to begin. But he uttered not a word. Then one said encouragingly, "Come on; tell us what you got 'lumbered' for." There was still no response, and then came another coaxing request: "Come on, mate; tell us why you're here!" And back shot the savage and unexpected answer: "For not minding my own bloody business!" The three questioners melted into the background of the library.

At half-past ten there was a welcome break of a quarter of an hour, which was spent in walking round the nearest quadrangle under the watchful eye of a warder. Then we returned to the Shed to carry on until noon. Most of the men were engaged on sewing, but there were a few cutters, and a number of ironers. Occasionally an officer would thread his way down the room, shouting a man's cell number. When the man was found, and was leaving in the company of the officer, the latter would call out the sacramental words: "One away, sir!" and when the man was returned, "One on, sir!" There were no further incidents that morning.

On the resumption of work in the afternoon I found to my consternation that the burglar had followed me to my new address. He pulled up his chair and began to chat with all the nonchalance of a lifelong friend. A general order from the instructor for silence fell on deaf ears. Had I served in the war? I nodded in the affirmative. "Why," he whispered, "you're old enough to be that young swine's father, and you were fighting for your country when he was a blinking baby!" I agreed that very likely the officer was a puling infant in 1914. "Well," said the burglar hopefully, "why don't you punch him on the bloody nose? It's disgraceful that men of your age should be spoken to like this!" Had I consulted my own interests only I should have told this boy to shut up.

Instead, I quietly reminded him that we were in prison and had to submit to treatment which would not be tolerated elsewhere. But the burglar was adamant. The humiliation of elderly men, especially those who had been soldiers, for whom he entertained a tremendous admiration, by unfledged, callow warders offended his sense of justice, and he launched into a fierce diatribe against the whole company of prison guardians.

How long this might have lasted I do not know, but the flood of invective was interrupted by the sarcastic voice of the instructor, who had stalked us unawares. "So you're at it again!" he rasped, addressing me between clenched teeth. As a sheep before his shearer is dumb, so I opened not my mouth, but I looked him steadily in the eye for a moment, and resumed my sewing.

This action seemed to disconcert him, for he immediately turned his attention to the burglar, and shouted: 'And you're no better than you ought to be! Get back to where you came from, keep your mouth shut, and don't have any more truck with this old gas-bag, or you'll meet trouble. And as for you," he said, assuming a threatening attitude in front of me, and waggling his forefinger in my face, "I have warned you once, I'm warning you again, but——," and I gathered from what followed that if ever I spoke out of my turn again, no matter where or in what circumstances, somehow or other he would hear me, and would just as certainly punish me.

And then this wretched little bully moved back to his seat, with many backward and threatening glances in my direction. In ordinary circumstances I am a fairly even-tempered man, but at that particular moment I would have liked to press that officer's carotid glands until his eyes popped out of his head.

Five o'clock came, and we were marched back to C Hall, each man carrying sufficient canvas for the making of a single mail-bag, with needles, thread, and wax to boot. That night I should probably have to sew for two hours, or possibly longer, in my cell.

A thick fog was beginning to envelop the prison, and the silent prisoners, in their grey uniforms, looked like wraiths flitting into a grey and ghostly fortress. The interior of the Hall was not much more attractive than the outside. The fog had already penetrated the building, and the lights seemed to shed a ghastly and unearthly appearance over the usually drab scene.

But there was no time for flights of imagination. Already the air was charged with raucous voices. The daily war was on again, and I sped to the cell as quickly as my burden would allow. And what a sight it was! The fog was forcing itself through the loosely closed window, almost blotting out the feeble glimmer of the electric light above the door. The confined room looked like the entrance to a ghostly tunnel full of swirling mists, in which a tiny light struggled vainly against the invader.

I stood for a moment in the middle of the cell. The canvas was still on my shoulder; a rope to go round the top of the mail-bag hung loosely from my neck. My left hand clutched needles, threads, and the leather protector. And at that moment I caught a glimpse of myself in the mirror, and the thought of what I had been, and what I was now, attired in the garb of infamy, and bearing the burdens of disgrace, struck through me like a sharp knife.

Something snapped inside, and the last vestige of self-control vanished. Hot tears coursed down my cheeks like a flood, and my body shook with sobs. Do not imagine that this sudden breakdown was the first sign of repentance, and the beginning of a new and better life. I take pride in relating that it was the only occasion during all these weary and monotonous months that I succumbed to self-pity, and it did not last long.

Throwing my traps on the floor, I cursed myself loudly and fluently for a weakling and a coward, and vowed that not all the uniformed swine in Christendom would break my spirit. Presently I recovered control of myself, and strange to relate felt much better for the paroxysm. Women know much more about these matters than men. Perhaps that is why they weep so readily.

After tea came the struggle with the canvas, but I soon reached the bottom of the bag to be, and there encountered difficulties, which for the time being proved insoluble. I tried to remember the instructor's directions, but without any success, and finally had to give it up as a bad job. I was just on the point of turning to Beverley Nichols for distraction when the key turned in the lock and the door opened.

My visitor was Commander Foster, the Deputy Governor. I rose in some confusion, not knowing the reason for this unexpected call, but he signed to me to resume

my chair while he himself sat on the table. And in this
unconventional attitude we talked, not as Deputy Governor to prisoner, but as man to man. This first meeting
was the prelude to many, which I shall ever remember
with gratitude.

We discussed my own case, and what I hoped to do
on release, and then the talk turned on prison routine
and discipline. Commander Foster had been trained in
Dartmoor, and was far happier with the old lags than
with first offenders. The old lag was a criminal, and would
never be anything else. He took his medicine as a matter
of course, he never expected favours, and he was never
disappointed. It was easy to deal with him because he
was an incorrigible social enemy, without hope in the
world.

But a first offenders' prison presented very different
problems. Many of the inhabitants had the same outlook
on life, and the same training, as himself. Not a few had
fallen from positions of great affluence. That in itself
was a punishment much more severe than any the
authorities could inflict, and the Commander's kind heart
was touched by the contemplation of so much social
ruin and misery.

"I suppose you know," he added whimsically, "that
very few of you can ever stage a come-back. Society is
too strong, and too vindictive." I might have been inclined to disagree with him then. I am not now. He was
anxious to know what I thought of the discipline in C
Hall, which I frankly described as stupid nonsense, but
with this he would not agree. The only weakness he could
see was that it was not nearly severe enough.

"But do you mean to tell me," I cried, "that all this

shouting, bawling, and insulting behaviour is going to make a better man of me? Doesn't it rather tend to raise a demon of resentment against authority and all connected with it?" "That is all right as far as it goes," assented the Commander gently, "but you must remember that you are an educated man, and that you have been somebody in the world. No treatment that penal institutions can devise is going to help you very much. Your greatest punishment lies in your known fall from grace, but I suppose that society has to show its disapproval in some tangible way, and here you are. We can't discriminate in a place like this, and our greatest and most pressing problem is the youthful prisoner—fellows who were born since the outbreak of war.

"You haven't been here long, but I dare say you have already noticed the difference between the youth of to-day and men of our age. The youth of to-day have no restraint whatever, and they treat us (meaning the prison authorities) with noisy contempt. And we can't reach them through fear, because they haven't any. You look upon the behaviour of these warders as an insult; vulgarity dressed in little brief authority. But these youngsters regard it all as part and parcel of a noisy age. Sometimes I think they even like it.

"When they leave here they have no fear of returning, and they tell their friends that prison is all poppycock. In my opinion the leniency shown to youthful first offenders is a source of crime. They ought to get it in the neck as soon as they go wrong."

Possibly there is something to be said for this point of view, though I always suspect the opinions of experts on principle. I remarked that as far as could be seen the behaviour of the great bulk of the men was excellent; in fact, quite as good as could be expected from any body of men drawn haphazard from the various strata of the community.

He concurred, but he was inclined to attribute the high level of conduct to the fear of losing the many privileges to which prisoners become entitled by effluxion of time in a first offenders' establishment. It was no light thing to be deprived of the society of one's comrades, to sacrifice a communal for a monastic life. It was a very real punishment to have to forgo concerts, or to be locked up without reading matter, and to dine only on porridge and potatoes. Even fairly tough customers would not throw away such valuable concessions, acquired as they were within a few weeks of admission, except under the strain of great temptation or great provocation. I gathered that something like 88 per cent of the prisoners in Wormwood Scrubs never renewed contact with the guardians of society. This is a very high and gratifying figure, but it must not be forgotten that the inhabitants of the Scrubs are not of the criminal type. They are only ordinary citizens who have been found out.

Commander Foster spent very nearly an hour with me, and as soon as he had gone I turned in, feeling that I might be lucky enough to secure a little sleep. The long talk had helped to lift me out of myself, and the *crise des nerfs* earlier in the evening had somehow relaxed the tension from which I had suffered for so long. And after an hour or two of turning and tossing I lost consciousness and slept until four o'clock in the morning.

CHAPTER V

IT is a truism that we never know what a blessing sleep is until we lose it. Poets, the mighty Shakespeare included, have sung its virtues, but when recovering from insomnia, and it has been a common experience, the lines in the "Ancient Mariner" always recur to me:

> O Sleep, it is a gentle thing,
> Belov'd from pole to pole,
> To Mary Queen the praise be given,
> She sent the gentle sleep from Heaven
> That slid into my soul.

Those four or five hours of untroubled sleep worked wonders. Physically I felt as if I had been dragged through a bush backwards, but mentally I had got a grip on myself at last, and felt equal to the task of facing my gaolers with equanimity, and even with interest.

It was Wednesday morning, and there was no distribution of cocoa, and no drill. The men paraded for early morning Church service. It was an unusual experience for most of us to attend church at that hour. The Chaplain preached the sermon. His style and manner were well adapted to the congregation. Forcible and humorous by turns, he never fell into the error of addressing the men as if they were in special need of salvation. His breezy cheerfulness did me good, and I felt for a moment as if I had renewed contact with the healthy and normal side of existence.

An old man sat on my left-hand side. His round face was covered with a short stubby growth of whiskers, and the top of his head was completely bald. I had noticed

him on the exercise-ground. Bald men usually wore a
prison cap of the glengarry type, to protect them from
the cold, but this old fellow defied all weathers. He was
also very rocky on his pins, and was unable to maintain
the sharp pace set up by the younger and more active
prisoners. For that reason he was always to be found on
the inside paths, marching uncertainly, but at a pace best
suited to his physical capacity.

I had also noticed that he was a target for the abuse
and satire of the warders in C Hall. Apparently he could
neither keep his cell clean nor fold his bedclothes according to the regulation method, and the lethargy of his
movements aroused universal official disapprobation. But
the shouting and the rough wit had no perceptible effect;
he simply carried on as if he were deaf and dumb.

The old fellow took no part in the singing, but as soon
as we knelt for prayers he drew closer, and I waited for
the inevitable question. Very soon came the hoarse
whisper, "How long are you here for, mate?" I told him,
and he took a moment to consider the sentence. Then
"Burglary?" he queried. "No." "Bigamy, perhaps?" I
again answered in the negative, and in order to divert
attention from myself I added: "What was the matter
with you this morning? The Officer on No. 3 Landing
seems to have you set." "Of course he has," grumbled
the ancient. "I can't do nothing right in this dive. They
find fault with my cell. I can't fold a blanket to please
them, and they howl at me on sight. I never see such
—— goings on in all my life."

The Army swore terribly in Flanders in more than
one campaign, and I had often helped in the good work
myself, but I had never heard this abominable word in

church before. Its unexpected use on this solemn occasion, and the old fellow's doleful tone of helpless futility, made me double up with hysterical laughter, and I was lucky to escape the attentions of the officers on duty. I was to learn within a very short time that it was practically the only expletive used behind prison walls.

After the service was over the prisoners indulged in walking exercise in the different courtyards, and at the end of half an hour were marched to their respective Halls for breakfast.

With the ringing of the bell for work came the usual dash for the stairs. At the foot of the stairs I noticed for the first time the Hall Officer of C Hall. He was a smart-looking fellow of moderate size, with greying hair, and a prison cap set at the rakish angle made fashionable by Earl Beatty. His back was as straight as a poker, and the narrow waist-line suggested that he might be guilty of wearing corsets. Altogether a live, dapper-looking man.

And he stood at the bottom of the stairs, his legs wide apart, and his hands clasped behind his back, while he see-sawed backwards and forwards on his feet and fiercely scrutinized each prisoner as he passed. He was searching for men improperly dressed, but Wednesday happened to be an off day. The most common sartorial faults were unbuttoned tunics and missing ties. Men attended drill minus their ties, and it was an easy matter to forget to put them on in the breakfast hour.

Woe betide the man, however, who paraded for work without one. He had committed an almost unpardonable crime against prison decency and convention. We have all seen pictures of prominent film actresses registering the different human emotions, fear, surprise, or scorn, but no candidate for Hollywood ever approached this Hall Officer when he chose to express pained amazement, outraged authority, and righteous indignation. His facial mobility was remarkably good, and I should judge that he put the wind up more freshmen than any other warder in the Scrubs.

When the Shed party formed up opposite the side door I saw the Principal Officer for the first time, a short, aggressive-looking little man with a quick, springy step and a staccato voice. As he paced restlessly up and down the lines he reminded me of a terrier on the look out for a rat against which he bore an ancient and deadly grudge. It was evident that this tense, eager little fellow was greatly feared. A man dashed on to parade late and very much flustered. He darted from one group to another in a vain endeavour to find his own party, like a calf that had become separated from its mother. The P.O. intercepted him, and what he said was nobody's business. Whenever he opened his mouth, which was not often, he looked and spoke daggers. I never saw him smile, except in triumph, when some scorner of prison government was taken *in flagrante delicto.*

On arriving at the Shed I found that the youthful instructor of the previous day had been superseded by an older man of a kindly, staid appearance. He was, in fact, the Chief Instructor. I explained to him that I had got badly tangled up on the cell task, and in a few minutes he showed me where I had gone wrong. On hearing my name he recalled my case as reported in the newspapers. He seemed interested in me personally, told me not to worry unduly about the work, and invited me to seek his assistance whenever any difficulty arose.

I was grateful to this officer. He seemed wise and kind and tolerant, but I never had any occasion to go to him for help, for a few minutes later a junior officer came threading his way down the room. He handed a chit to the instructor, who called out C2—33. It was my number. I rose and approached them. "Here's your man," said the instructor, and to me, "You're going to the library." My heart jumped with excitement. The transfer had come much sooner than I expected. "This way," said the junior, making for the road, and as he reached the door he turned and shouted, "One away, sir!" to the instructor, who gravely nodded his head, and seizing the chalk marked me off on the blackboard.

The library was a low wooden building between C and D Halls. Here I was handed over to the Leader in charge, who chalked up my admission on a blackboard. The Librarian was on duty at Reception, and would probably not put in an appearance for another hour. In the meantime I could do what I liked.

I chose to make a survey of the room. There were fifteen or sixteen prisoners, nearly all of whom were men of decent education, and who had occupied respectable and even distinguished positions in life. A long table three or four feet wide ran down the middle of the room. At the head sat the Leader, with four or five prisoners ranged on either side. In a corner were three men surrounded by boxes of index cards. Close by was a prisoner, a signwriter by occupation, who painted numbers and names on new and repaired books. There was also a cleaner, and three or four men were engaged on special jobs.

Talking was general, although loud conversation and

E

laughter were frowned upon. After my brief experience in the Shed, it was easy to understand why the
library was regarded as the El Dorado of prison
occupations.

The walls were lined with books arranged in categories
of Fiction, Architecture, Art, Belles-Lettres, Biography,
Geography, History, and so on. They were numbered
consecutively, and arranged alphabetically according to
the authors' names. In all there might have been ten
thousand volumes, covering every topic under the sun.
Some of the books, as I subsequently found, were old
and out of date, especially on the scientific and handicraft
side, but there was a good deal of interesting modern
stuff, and very few of the classics were missing. The
library boasted a large number of volumes in French,
Italian, German, and Russian; even the lesser-known
European languages were well represented, and there
were a few in Arabic and Chinese. On the whole, an extremely interesting and useful library.

In due course the Librarian arrived, and I was given
the job of selecting books for the weekly changes, and
packing the various baskets. A fixed routine was followed.
On Wednesday mornings fresh books were issued to the
hospital, and the first and second floors of C Hall. In the
afternoon the short-service men in B Hall received their
change. On Thursdays, the biggest day, issues were made
to the third and fourth floors of C Hall and the young
prisoners in B Hall, and on Fridays the library staff
supplied the inhabitants of D Hall, other than Fourth
Stage men. Saturdays, Mondays, and Tuesdays in the
library were largely devoted to a close examination of
returned books, and putting them back on the shelves.

Damaged and torn volumes were handed over to the repairing staff for attention.

Details of all new arrivals in the prison were reported to the library every morning, and within a few hours the literature was in their cells. Penal servitude men in B Hall were allowed an almost unlimited supply of books, and changes there were made every morning.

The quantity of literature issued to a new prisoner depended on his sentence. Under six weeks he was entitled to one educational book, which might be history, art, economics, or science, but a sentence of six weeks or upwards commanded two books, one educational and the other fiction. The educational book was changed every fortnight, and the fiction weekly. The supply of reading-matter to which a man was entitled grew with his promotion from stage to stage, until the time arrived when he could come to the library in the dinner hour and select whatever books he required from the shelves.

The books in a prison library are turned over again and again in the course of a year, and there is a considerable wastage as a result of deliberate defacement and ordinary wear and tear. In Wormwood Scrubs the loss was made good by a continuous inflow of new books from prisoners' friends and relatives. Men were allowed to have books sent in, provided they agreed to hand them over afterwards to the authorities for general circulation, and condemnations were more than offset from this source.

A great deal of malicious damage was done to books by foolish and bad-tempered prisoners. I have known cases where volumes were torn to pieces in a fit of insensate and ungovernable rage. More often pages were removed, and the value of a book destroyed, by gentlemen who had neglected to lay in an adequate supply of toilet paper, but the commonest offenders were those who could not resist the sight of a blank sheet of paper. All the sufferers from *cacoethes scribendi*, and the spiritual brothers of men who carve their names on trees and pews, and write filthy verses on the walls of public lavatories, seem to drift into the Scrubs. *Muraille blanche, papier des fous*, and as soon as these fellows encountered a virgin page, up bubbled the urge for composition, and down went an obscene or forthright opinion of their governors.

Of course it was an offence to deface books, which were always scrutinized on return to the library, and numbers of prisoners were cased every week for unwanted literary and artistic productions. I remember my first "find" in this connection. On the fourth floor of C Hall was an officer who went by the name of "Kaiser Bill." He was a tall man with a fierce, upturned moustache, and was rather liked for his easy-going disposition. A short, tubby warder on the third floor, who was very noisy, but otherwise fairly harmless, was a great friend of his. In a returned volume I came across a sketch of "Kaiser Bill" and his dumpy friend. The drawing was excellent, but underneath were two lines which earned the artist three days in cells:

> Whether they're short or whether they're tall,
> Bide your time, and —— 'em all.

The Librarian assessed the literary capacity of every newcomer at the interview the morning after arrival and recorded his opinion in a book, which was handed over to the library Leader. The Leader made out cards, and issued literature in accordance with the information supplied. A well-read person was marked W.R., and he received the best in the library. ILL stood for illiterate, and these poor devils were supplied with albums of pictures cut from illustrated papers and magazines. The number of adults and even young prisoners who could neither read nor write was surprising. The letter S meant that the man suffered from arrested mental development, and could appreciate only a simple book. L.P. stood for large print, and indicated that the prisoner suffered from poor eyesight.

The great majority of new arrivals had no distinguishing marks against them. They were literate, and that was all. Really good books did not come their way until the library staff had had time to assess their destructive capacity. They had to be content with the rag-tag and bobtail of the library until they had established some sort of reputation for peaceableness and good behaviour.

I remember one morning the Librarian's amanuensis came in with the record of the previous day's catch, and pointing to one name he said to the Leader: "This fellow is an Irishman, as his name denotes, and he's the toughest bird I have ever seen in this place. His face is torn to pieces, there's no skin on his knuckles, and he has two policemen's scalps at his belt. He doesn't look as if he has had his fill yet, and I shouldn't be surprised if he causes trouble."

"Oh, well," said the Leader musingly, "I suppose we'll have to do our little bit to tame him," and he strolled over to the scientific section and came back with a book entitled *Wood and What We Make of It*. I had overheard the description of the Irishman's character, and wondered what his reaction to the book would be. At the end of a fortnight the volume came back, and I took the trouble to examine it carefully. To my surprise there was not a mark anywhere; the pages were all cut, but virgin, and had obviously been read. Our Irishman had evidently abated his Celtic rage, or else his opinion of the book was beyond expression. But no. The text finished high up on the last page, and underneath were the words THE END in large print. Here he had expressed his pent-up feelings simply but emphatically in one phrase:

And a —— good job too.

I won't say that there was ever any demand for *Wood and What We Make of It*, but it was always in use, especially for drunks and disorderlies, and people with thick heads and thick ears. Strong men broke down and wept when they looked at it. They couldn't destroy the infernal book. That would have meant serious punishment, and if they were serving a sentence of less than six weeks there was nothing else to read except the Scriptures. I often met prisoners who pleaded for its removal from their cells, expecting, of course, a decent substitute. One day a man swore to me that he would either do the book or himself an injury. A great civilizer and subduer of men was *Wood and What We Make of It*. I don't suppose its obscure and humble author ever dreamt of the main use to which it would be put.

Another useful book was *Croquet and How to Play It*, by Lord Tollemache, but this generally found its way into the cells of gentlemen convicted for dangerous driving. Its soothing and restful qualities were really not quite as great as the title might indicate, judging from the remarks of prisoners who were compelled to read it. All without exception flew into paroxysms of rage as soon as the title was mentioned. A sister volume on the gentle art of putting, and one or two fragments on Michaelmas Daisies and Wild Flowers shared the same unmerited disfavour. Motorists, like poets, are an irritable race.

Frankly, I could only wish that the study of these gems of literature gave half the pleasure to prisoners that their selection did to the library staff. Never on child or on treasure was so much loving care bestowed as on *Wood and What We Make of It*. Its loss or permanent disfigurement would have ranked as a major calamity.

Books for the changes were packed in large baskets, which were pushed round the various floors in little trollies. Four men, including a Leader, accompanied each trolly. The books which the prisoner had read lay on his table with his library card. The Leader entered the cell, and handed these to one of his men, who called out the numbers, which were marked off on the card in ink by the Leader, and entered in the outgoing column of a memorandum-book by a third man, together with the cell number. A fourth man made a hurried examination of the returned books for defacements and loose pages. The Leader announced the number and nature of the replacements required. These were picked out and written up on the card and in the in-going column of the memorandum-book.

In the library itself each book was carded with its number. The card also bore the name of the book and the author. The memorandum-books recording issues and returns were handed over to the staff, who kept the

index cards and posted the particulars. A glance at a
card showed where a book was, and its movements over
a period of time.

When visiting cells the Leader had to be very careful
not to make over-issues, or to offend the religious sus-
ceptibilities of prisoners. Ardent Roman Catholics, for
instance, squealed like guinea-pigs if they returned from
work and found a copy of *Westward Ho!* lying on the
table. Half of them would not wait to ask for a change.
They rushed to the priest, with the result that the careless
Leader came in for a good wigging from the Librarian.

I well remember a gentleman in the hospital, who
had been a barrister in the Malay States, and was said to
have been a son of a judge of the Indian High Court.
This man was a particularly nasty piece of work, and was
always in trouble for petty offences. He was one of the
most voluble talkers I ever came across, and perhaps the
most voracious reader. At this particular time I happened
to be in charge of the library change-over. The ex-
barrister was a very difficult fellow to please, and expected
the library staff to supply him with everything he wanted,
and at once.

I always did my best to humour him, for I understood
that he was not quite right in his head. It was with some
surprise, therefore, that I received one day a visit from
the Roman Catholic priest, who complained that I had
been palming off on one of his flock, the ex-barrister, the
heretical productions of H. G. Wells.

I knew the man was a Catholic, and for that reason it
was most unlikely that I should have given him anything
from the pen of the great H. G. On examining the records
there was no trace of an H. G. Wells book on issue to

him. A visit to the hospital cell, however, disclosed the fact that he had improperly borrowed the book from another prisoner, and then reported to the priest that he was being bombarded with literature offensive to his religion and to God.

He wanted another book, and I deliberately chose *The Life of Edward Carson*, but within twenty-four hours the priest was back again with the news that Carson, if not so dangerous, was equally obnoxious to the barrister, who had Irish blood in his veins. This gentleman had convinced the authorities that he was slightly mental. For that reason he was not "cased" for the deception, but I gathered that the priest intended to impose some mild form of penance.

The members of the library who lived in D Hall had a very short time allowed them for dinner. As soon as the meal was over a bell rang, the staff fell in, and marched back to the library, followed by all the Fourth Stage men who wanted a change of reading matter. Three librarians attended to the long queue of prisoners. As each man stepped forward his books were taken from him. The numbers were called out, erased from his library card, and entered in a memorandum-book.

He was then free to wander about the library and make his own choice. When he had made his selection the volumes were taken from him by one of the staff, who called out the numbers, when the necessary entries were made on card and in memorandum-book.

In a corner of the library was a small counter, behind which a Leader officiated, and handed out literary dope in the shape of modern thrillers. Edgar Wallace, "Seamark," Horler, Sax Rohmer, "Sapper," Zane Grey, and Cullum were the lords of this domain. Business was always brisk at the "smasher" counter, and there was tremendous competition for the latest bargains. When all had been attended to, a Leader took the party back to D Hall, where they put their books away and joined their working-parties. The library staff then had half an hour's repose.

CHAPTER VI

LIFE in the library was as pleasant as it could be in a prison environment. The Librarian had spent the whole of his life in the service, but his method of dealing with the men under him was a complete reversal of what obtained in the Shops. He was firm, but his firmness was tempered with real kindness and courtesy, and he won the respect and affection of everyone on the staff. During the whole of my time there I never saw one serious betrayal of the trust he reposed in his "boys."

All the library staff were, of course, picked men, and were virtually on parole. They enjoyed a very large measure of freedom, and for hours at a time were subject to no supervision whatever, except that exercised by their Leaders. With few exceptions, these prisoners had held responsible positions in civil life. They had given their word scrupulously to observe the prison regulations, and although they were convicted criminals, their word was their bond. Of course, open disobedience would have meant translation to one of the Shops, but I fancy that one of the principal reasons for their excellent conduct lay in the affection inspired by the man at the top. He was too decent a fellow to let down, and any prisoner abusing the confidence reposed in him would have found his severest critics in his own comrades.

Transfer to the library brought with it a change of cell tasks, sewing mail-bags giving way to writing up the change directions on library cards, and making up files for Borstal entrants.

The staff of the library were an interesting crowd. The

law was well represented, at least four having practised
as solicitors. One of these was a lively, bustling old gentleman, eighty years of age, and another verged on seventy.
The former lived in the hospital, where he enjoyed a
decent bed and superior food. As an inmate of the hospital
he came on duty an hour later than the other prisoners,
and left an hour earlier in the afternoon. His work consisted of writing the numbers in new books on the front,
middle, and back pages, and covering blank spaces with
the prison stamp, thus reducing the temptations to which
prisoners with literary aspirations were exposed. He had
succeeded a distinguished prisoner in this job, Lord
Kylsant.

The other old fellow lived on the ground-floor of
C Hall, and although he had long been entitled to a
transfer to D Hall he resolutely refused to leave his first
prison home. It was not that he was unable to tear himself
away from C Hall. Our ex-attorney had other reasons. His
managing clerk, whom he blamed for all his misfortunes,
happened to be an inmate of D Hall, and the sight of this
man always threatened him with an apoplectic seizure.
He had therefore sought and obtained the permission
of the authorities to serve the whole of his sentence
in C Hall, and every evening he might have been seen
sitting outside his cell, sewing dilapidated books, which
was his library job, and chatting with the officer on
duty. All the other inhabitants of C Hall were, of course,
locked up.

It was commonly believed that he was on excellent
terms with all the warders, and that he was not above
passing on information about the behaviour of his fellows.
Some even went so far as to say that his resoluteness in

sticking to C Hall was determined not so much by his hatred of the obnoxious managing clerk, as by the fact that he was allowed a dram of whisky every night before turning in. As all drink was contraband, this was probably only a malicious rumour.

There were three accountants, two bank managers, a schoolmaster, an estate agent, the secretary of a well-known London club, a Merchant Service skipper, a commercial traveller, a journalist, a foreman of works, and a signwriter. The prisoner who washed up the floors was usually a short-service man of not more than three months, and was selected for his capacity to do rough work.

The Merchant Service captain was one of the most interesting members of the party. All his life had been spent on Eastern routes. He had run contraband for Enver Pasha and the Young Turks during the war with Italy. On one occasion he commanded the ship which carried the Holy Carpet from Egypt to Medina, and was the only infidel on board. During the Great War he had commanded a gunboat attached to the Australian Navy, and saw a lot of service round the Persian Gulf and the Red Sea. Not only had the Skipper led a more than usually adventurous life, but he was able to write and speak with more than ordinary skill.

The bank managers, as far as I can remember, had no claims to any special notice, except that one was the Leader in charge, and an ardent Christian Scientist. The journalist had edited a paper in Beira, Portuguese East Africa, but whether in Portuguese or English I cannot say. His spoken English was by no means impeccable.

The three accountants were true to the characteristics

of their profession—methodical and careful without being brilliant.

In the foreman of works we had a character, although not always a pleasant one. He claimed to be an Australian, and he had certainly served with the Australian Forces, winning the D.C.M. on Gallipoli. This gentleman was in prison for bigamy, and openly and sometimes offensively expressed his sense of moral superiority over the other prisoners, who had almost all been convicted for disregarding the difference between *meum* and *tuum*.

The schoolmaster, like many of his class, was quite cranky, and should have been in a home instead of a prison. He never seemed to me to have enough sense deliberately to plan and execute a crime, and his stupidity was only exceeded by his piety. After three or four months this man obtained a transfer as organist to the Catholic Church, which was adjacent to the library. Naturally no one had ever seen or heard him play an instrument, but he managed to convey the impression that he was a musician of some ability. Such was his skill, however, that the first service at which he performed had to be abandoned. As there was no other Catholic musician available in the prison, his services were not dispensed with, and we had to endure the daily agony of listening to the harmonium as it moaned, groaned, bellowed, and roared under his unpractised hands. In the end he did acquire sufficient command of the instrument to get through the service, but although we frequently fell foul of the schoolmaster as a librarian, these little passages were nothing to what was said about him as a budding organist.

While the days passed pleasantly enough at work, life in C Hall was never anything but humiliating. Nevertheless, I managed to get through the three months without attracting a great deal of undesirable notice from the warders. I did not, however, entirely escape their attentions. One day, about three weeks after admission, I returned to my cell at twelve o'clock to find that something was amiss. The bedroom utensil stood upside down in the middle of the room, and what appeared at first sight to be verses were chalked on the floor above and below it. The author must have gone down on his knees to write them. My mind immediately reverted to the "Ode to a Grecian Urn," but on peering closer I found that these were no verses in praise of jerries. They were, in fact, a very caustic criticism of my jerry's disgraceful condition and my laziness, written by an irate and uneducated warder.

On rising to my feet I found that the chair had been similarly treated. It was described as filthy, and on the table was scrawled the ominous instruction: "See your Landing Officer at once." Well, I saw the Landing Officer, who happened to be a substitute for Horse-Face. This man assumed an air of terrific indignation. During all his long experience he had never encountered a cell quite so dirty, but the jerry was in such a state that words completely failed him.

I answered meekly enough that I had done my level best with scrubbing brush and soap to keep the wretched thing in decent order, but he insisted that in twenty-three years he had never seen such a rusty, offensive vessel. *Experto crede*, I thought, and piped low, but twenty-three years! The upshot was that I had to scrub the cell. That was not difficult, but try as I would I could make no impression on the offending jerry. In despair I took counsel with my fellows in the library, and they advised me to offer a slice of bread to one of the cleaners in exchange for a lump of sandstone. That did the trick, and it was the only thing that could have done it, but strangely enough sandstone was never issued to prisoners, and had to be obtained, if at all, by surreptitious means.

After four weeks on the second floor of C Hall I was promoted to the fourth landing. Kaiser Bill, the indolent but good-tempered officer, was on duty here. I had not been long in my new domicile before a rather unpleasant experience came my way. It was a Wednesday night, and on the stroke of eight I decided to put my bed down. Arranging the planks on the floor, I shoved them up against the door with my foot. The impact was a fairly noisy one, and a second or two later the shutter over the peep-hole moved and a savage eye glared at me from the outside.

"What's the matter with you?" shouted the officer on duty, his voice quivering with rage. I was astonished at the unnecessary display of temper, and simply replied that there was nothing wrong. "There's nothing wrong!" he answered sarcastically, imitating my voice. "We'll bloody well see to-morrow whether there's nothing wrong, when you're charged with attempting to break out of your cell!" I pointed out to the man as quietly and reasonably as I could that it was my custom to sleep with my head to the door, and that I had merely pushed the bed against it with my foot. The idea of an attempted escape was ridiculous. But he refused to listen to explanations, and having informed me in blustering and vituperative language that I would be cased the following day, he closed the peephole.

There was not much sleep for me that night, and early in the morning I made it my business to inquire of the Redband if any charge had been preferred against me. He knew of none, and I was not sent for during the day. That night, Thursday, we were to attend the weekly lecture. At five minutes to seven I could hear the cells being unlocked, and the men moving about, but minutes passed and no officer's key rattled in my door.

He never came at all, and I missed the lecture. Later in the week I broached the matter to Kaiser Bill, who assured me that as far as he knew there was absolutely nothing against my character. He promised to make inquiries from his relief, who apparently never came into C Hall except on night duties from 6 p.m. to 9 p.m., but I heard no more from that quarter. Kaiser Bill was a tired man, and further questioning might only have annoyed him.

The library staff were unanimous in advocating a policy of *laisser faire*. They argued, and probably rightly, that the warder class were a close corporation, and that if a prisoner succeeded in having one of their number hauled over the coals he would make enemies of all.

But the next Thursday the same thing happened. The cell was never unlocked. I was almost tempted to push the bell, which communicated with the officer on duty on the ground-floor, but I shrank from the idea of being bullied and browbeaten by a party of warders, who might refuse to listen to any explanations, and who would probably only assure me in brutal enough terms that I was in prison, and only getting what was coming to me.

On the following Wednesday the prisoner in the neigh-bouring cell, a little fellow by the name of Jones, with

F

curiously black, birdlike, restless eyes, whispered that he would follow up the warder, if he passed my cell again, and point out that I was entitled to go to the lecture. I was grateful for his offer. On Thursday, about seven, I heard the cells on either side opened up, and the men bustling downstairs. A second later the covering over the peephole moved. It was Jones. He told me that he had chased after the officer as promised, and that the latter had threatened that if Jones himself did not mind his own bloody business he would be locked up too.

The following week I was transferred to D Hall, and delivered from the petty tyranny of a warder whose face I never saw, and whose name I never knew, and who had not only usurped the Governor's authority in punishing me at all, but had penalized me for a crime which I had never committed, and for which I had never even been tried.

During the whole of my time in C Hall, Commander Foster visited me regularly at least three times a week. It might seem unusual to people not familiar with penal establishments, but during those visits we struck up a firm personal friendship, based, I hope, on mutual respect. I, at least, shall not easily forget his sympathy and helpfulness, especially during the first week of prison life. It means a lot to realize that your Governors know the load you are carrying, and are ready to go out of their way to ease the burden.

Another welcome visitor was Colonel Hamilton, of Guildford, one time Inspector-General of Prisons in Bengal, and a member of the Society of Prison Visitors. This Society is composed of gentlemen of a charitable frame of mind, who give up a very large part of their time to visiting men whom they have never previously seen or heard of, bringing them news of the outside world, and transacting business for them with the consent and approval of the prison authorities.

The official visitors are supplied with a set of keys on entrance, and move about the prison as freely as the warders. I counted myself very fortunate to have been placed on Colonel Hamilton's list. He never missed a week, and even after my elevation to Fourth Stage, when the need for a friendly visitor is not so great, I never failed to see him.

Prison visitors were of all ages and occupations. Some, indeed, were comparatively young men, but they willingly sacrificed one evening a week all the year round, and they thoroughly deserved all the gratitude that captives felt towards them.

I came in personal contact with one other prison visitor. He was a garrulous, doddering old magistrate from one of the London suburbs, who sentenced men to imprisonment during five days of the week and came to the Scrubs to see how they liked it on the sixth. There was another gentleman of Irish or Welsh origin, who on one or two occasions attracted a certain amount of attention in D Hall through being obviously under the weather. It was said that one night he entered a cell, sat down, and promptly fell asleep. The man whom he came to see enjoyed the welcome experience of reading the visitor's *Evening News*, and at the end of half an hour woke him up, showed him out, and shut the door.

I also have memories of a new member of the Society, who was instrumental in getting a Leader dismissed and punished. This gentleman had no experience at all, and knew practically nothing of the duties and responsibilities attaching to his office. He had on his list a prisoner by the name of Shorty. Shorty's bosom friend in the Scrubs was a man generally known as Lofty, who was as tall and thin as Shorty was squat and fat. Shorty and Lofty had, in fact, worked together in civil life as the driver and conductor on the same bus. In their spare time they manufactured dud shillings and half-crowns, which were passed into circulation by Lofty, the conductor, in the course of his daily duties. Shorty was in the Shoe-shop, and to everybody's astonishment one day he appeared on parade with a Leader's band on his arm. He did not keep it long. By hook or by crook Shorty had to smuggle a letter out of the prison without the knowledge of the authorities, and he chose the latest official visitor as his instrument.

He led this gentleman to believe that posting a letter on a prisoner's behalf was an everyday affair. It was one of the reasons why they had visitors. The man consented to carry out Shorty's wishes. But although he was prepared to post Shorty's letter, he was not apparently willing to incur any expense in the matter. On the way out he applied to the Gate Officer for a stamp and an envelope. The warder smelt a rat, and Shorty's little scheme was exposed. The next time I saw him he had lost the badge of leadership, and was squatting on the floor of a cell in C Hall, on the point of beginning prison discipline all over again. His bed, chair, and books were outside his cell door, and would not be restored to him until eight o'clock in the evening, and he was living on a diet of bread, water, porridge, and potatoes.

CHAPTER VII

AT the end of twelve weeks I was transferred to D Hall
on promotion to Second Stage. It was a week or two
before a vacancy at a table could be found for me, and
during that time I had to feed as in C Hall, in the cell,
but the atmosphere of the prison had miraculously
changed. When tea was served the first night, and the
door locked, the warder on duty returned and called
through the peephole: "You all right?" I was too thunder-
struck to reply, but back he came, and shouted: "Why
the devil don't you speak when you're spoken to?" This
was more like the old home, and I knew how to deal with
outbursts of that nature. To save trouble and an answer,
I pointed to my ear to indicate deafness. He moved off,
grumbling and growling at the bad manners of the age,
but at nine o'clock, on turning off the light, he called out
a cheery good night. Things were much brighter, warders
were human after all, and I slept soundly.

At last the day came when I was posted to R table,
and I took my place at the board with eleven other
prisoners. They were all strangers to me, although I knew
a number by sight. The table had the usual quota of two
or three Jews.

On the whole my companions were a fairly motley
crew. The Leader was an ex-bank manager with a genial,
pleasing personality, and his Deputy was an ex-postman
of a swarthy and sinister-looking complexion. On my left
was a youth supposedly a public-school boy, who had
travelled all over the world in the employ of a well-known
firm of consulting engineers, and on my right sprawled

a great hulking fellow much like Carnera in build and appearance. He had been chucker-out for a firm of amusement caterers in Piccadilly.

Next to him sat a Jew who had been convicted for passing bad coins, and on his right was the old man Marshall who had spoken to me in church.

On the opposite side of the table was a quiet, inoffensive, elderly man, of whose history I knew nothing, and next to him sat another Jew who talked incessantly on almost every subject under the sun. He had been a printer in the East End, and finding himself in a bit of a mess financially had yielded to the temptation to print bogus cigarette coupons. He was supported by an income-tax collector, whose left-hand neighbour was another Jew, a little fellow with a round, reddish-brown face like a russet apple.

The eleventh man was the driver of a steam-roller called Eric; he was covered with hair, and looked like an ape, and was famed in that place where large appetites were not unusual for the ferocity with which he attacked his food. Eric had knocked a woman off her bicycle and assaulted her, and he looked and behaved as if he might tackle anything.

Very little was said to me at breakfast. I was a new-comer, and the men were quietly sizing me up, but at tea-time the public-school boy took me into his confidence and related his fall from grace.

It appears that he had come home from the East with plenty of money in his pocket. One of his first acts was to visit his old tailor and order a number of new suits. He did not bother to pay for them at the time, and was so busy carrying on a long round of frivolities in London, Paris, and Vienna, that the matter slipped his notice.

On his return by air from Paris, he was arrested in his London flat for obtaining credit with intent to defraud, or some other charge of that sort. It seems that his tailor had gone bankrupt, and that the Receiver had launched a criminal charge without even asking for settlement of the outstanding account.

The Magistrate before whom he appeared delivered a lecture on the growing and reprehensible practice of defrauding honest tailors, and sentenced him to eighteen months' hard labour. Eighteen months, when his solicitors had advised him that it was only a matter of going into the box and going home.

But he was sure to win on appeal. His father's solicitors had come into the picture, and had assured him that nothing in the world was more certain. But would you believe it? Despite the fact that his liberty for eighteen months was at stake, these doddering old fools allowed his right of appeal to lapse by one day, and there he was in the Scrubs, the victim of a vindictive receiver, a revengeful magistrate, and a hopelessly incompetent firm of lawyers.

It was a pretty thin tale, and I could see by the sceptical grins on the faces of the other prisoners that they had all heard the story before, and didn't believe a word of it. I was soon to learn that this youth, whose name was Skilton, was the most inveterate liar in the Prison. He couldn't tell the truth about anything, and he was about the only man in all that large population on whom one could put one's hand and say with certainty: "*You* will come back again!"

He spoke well and confidently, and with just that air of polish and plausibility to deceive people with little or no education. But he could not deceive the Jew who had printed the cigarette coupons. This man spent every meal time closely questioning Skilton, analysing his answers, and then gathering information from other sources to prove that he was a liar. And indeed he took no pains to conceal his opinion of Skilton, whom he openly and almost daily described as "the biggest liar God had ever shovelled guts into."

After having given me his story, Skilton let me know that his fiancée was visiting him the next day. She was coming in an Hispano-Suiza car, which had cost Heaven knows what. After their last meeting she had written to say that she was very dissatisfied with the condition of his usually glossy hair, which had become as dry and wayward as the coir in his prison mattress, and he felt that something ought to be done about it. Should he use his ounce of margarine, not on his bread, but on his head? As an old hand I strongly supported the claims of the stomach, but he had already made up his mind, and ate his bread dry. The next evening he appeared at table magnificent and in a shining crest. To such shifts is love in prison reduced.

The man on my right, who resembled Carnera, was a different proposition. Logan had no education whatever, and his table manners were deplorable. He was twenty-three or twenty-four years of age, and had been employed by one of those firms of amusement caterers which abound in the West End. But the prosperity of our friend's boss had come to an unexpected end. He had an attractive site in Piccadilly, and should have gone on flourishing like the green bay tree.

A hated rival, however, had actually had the impertinence to take a shop next door, and was succeeding in enticing his numerous customers away from his establishment. Something had to be done to stop the rot, and he took counsel with Logan.

The upshot of the conference was that one Saturday night Logan went to the Elephant and Castle, where he was born and bred, with £25 in his pocket, and returned with a dozen of the most ruthless and determined toughs in that neighbourhood. And at a given signal, at midnight, they fell suddenly upon the shop next door with bars of iron and such other weapons as they could lay their hands on. In the excitement of the scrimmage Logan split open a policeman's head, and knocked another constable unconscious.

He was arrested, with others, on the eve of his wedding, and after a remand in custody for a week he was sentenced to a year's imprisonment. His employer was not ungrateful, and paid him £3 a week during the whole period of his enforced detention. The postponed wedding was to take place on the morning of Logan's release.

I have said that his table manners were not of the best. He always lowered his body, and drank noisily from the mug of cocoa as it stood on the table. When the liquid had receded an inch or two in the vessel, then and then only did he consent to seize it by the handle and raise it to his lips. Logan's appetite was enormous. Of course, he was a big man, but nevertheless the way he set about his victuals frightened me. Eric was his only rival in that respect.

It was my second morning at table when Logan, with his mouth full of food, turned to me and said abruptly: "You're in the library, aren't you?" I admitted that that was where I spent my time, and then he went on to describe with great gusto the type of literature he liked. He preferred books about London, with plenty of murders in them. "You know: mysterious murders; strange bodies in the library, and all that."

Logan was growing enthusiastic about his literary predilections, when the Jew on the opposite side of the table mentioned something to his neighbour about Palestine. "What's Palestine?" Logan inquired of me. I told him that it was a country in the Near East—"Never heard of it," he said briefly. And then I suddenly remembered that Logan was an ardent Roman Catholic. "Palestine," I said, "was the birthplace of our Lord, and Jerusalem is the capital." "Is that so?" he replied, with an immediate show of interest. "And our Lord was born there, was He? Tell me, how many miles would Palestine be from here? You know, I would rather like to go there, if I could manage it."

I suggested, something about two thousand miles, whereupon his face dropped, but I pointed out that the trip could easily be made by aeroplane in a couple of days. He pondered this information for some minutes, and then slowly shook his head, as if the decision to give up a project on which he had suddenly set his heart really pained him. "No, no," he said; "I'll never be able to get there: it's too far from the 'Elephant.' "

The Jew who had got into trouble over the cigarette coupons was an interesting character. A voracious reader on the scientific and philosophical side, he had long ago abandoned all belief in Judaism. His grandfather was a Russian, who had fallen foul of a Grand Duke, and had chosen Shoreditch in preference to Siberia.

Our friend's name was Laski. He explained to me,

shortly after my first appearance at table, that the business of printing and selling cigarette coupons was quite a lucrative one.

After months and months of ill-health in his family, he had almost decided to sell everything up, when he was approached by a friend, one of the Chosen People, who drew a very attractive picture of the almost unlimited possibilities of making money out of the printing and sale of cigarette coupons.

Better still, the chances of discovery were so remote as to be almost negligible. Laski agreed to take a risk, and within a very short time he was making £12 to £15 a week, without any trouble. Things looked rosy. With better food and proper medical attention his wife and child quickly recovered, but at this stage the tobacco companies began to take an interest in Laski's existence.

They did not yet know that he was the nigger in the woodpile, but they were painfully aware that somebody was flooding the market with dud coupons, and they began an intensive search for the intruder on their preserves. But fortune still continued to smile on Laski and his misguided efforts. Then the companies grew desperate, and offered a reward of £50 for any information that would lead to his arrest.

No information was forthcoming, and they raised the offer to £100. In Laski's words, that tore it. One evening he returned to his press to find a broad-shouldered gentleman, with a truculent jaw and a bowler hat, examining the machinery, and behaving generally as if he owned the place. He was a detective, and he took Laski to the nearest police station, where he was locked up for the night. At the end of a week he was on his way

to Wormwood Scrubs for a sojourn of fifteen months;
but what hurt him most was the knowledge that his
friend, who had introduced him to the business of manu-
facturing bogus coupons, was the richer by £100 of the
tobacco companies' money.

His friend with the russet face was an extraordinary
little fellow in appearance. Not more than five feet high,
he was almost as broad as he was long, and in his walk
he rocked from side to side like one of those weighted
figures which you can never persuade to lie flat.

He was named after the great lawgiver, and no one could
ever have mistaken him for other than what he was—a
Jew of the Jews. And yet, on his admission to the Prison,
he had put himself down as a member of the Church of
England. It appears that he had been told by somebody
at the time of his conviction that Church of England
prisoners enjoyed very special privileges, in which Moses
intended to participate, so that when he was asked what
his religion was he promptly named the State Church.

The Reception Warder attempted to reason with him,
but Moses was adamant. He had always been Church of
England, and always would be. "But your name!"
protested the officer, weakly. "Has nothing to do with
it!" snapped Moses, and down he went on the records as
C. of E. But Moses was not long in the establishment
before he learnt that his information about the supposed
advantages of belonging to the Church of England was all
illusory, and as soon as he had convinced himself that
there was nothing to be gained by his subterfuge he
returned to the faith of his fathers.

Both Laski and Moses were fast friends at the time
I joined the mess, but when the former declined to take

any part in the Passover ceremonies, Moses broke with him altogether, and such was his hostility that for the sake of peace he had to be transferred to another table. Moses didn't mind professing Christianity if there was any material advantage to be derived from it, but to relinquish Judaism from conviction was another matter altogether.

Both these men were in the tailor's shop. It did not matter what occupation a Jewish prisoner followed in civil life. He might be a merchant, a stock broker, or a city financier, but the official eye only saw the potential tailor. "You're a Jew, tailor you!" and in nine cases out of ten he was posted to the tailor's shop.

The third Jew sat on my side of the table, between Logan and the old man Marshall. He was an undersized, sharp-faced fellow by the name of Golder, full of restless energy, and always on the move. Golder had made a comfortable living for many years by systematically debasing the currency.

Without working too hard, he turned out enough bad coins in a week to bring in £20 worth of good ones, thus reversing the principle underlying Gresham's Law. In his neighbourhood he enjoyed the reputation of being something in the City. Coining takes a man a good distance afield. Golder frequently packed his Gladstone bad, the emblem of business respectability, and travelled as far as Birmingham, Liverpool and Leeds, and other big towns in the Midlands, where he unloaded his wares on small shopkeepers.

Tobacconists seemed to be the chief sufferers at Golder's hands, and by a stroke of poetic justice smoking was the immediate cause of his downfall. Every Saturday night he and his pal left home with forty dud shillings, which were used exclusively in cigarette machines. This expenditure, if expenditure it can be called, ensured an adequate supply of smoking material for the coming week,

About ten o'clock in the evening they left a hostelry in Fleet Street, and made for the nearest automatic machines. Having rifled these of a dozen large packets, they proceeded to another site, and Golder was just putting in a second "shilling" when a heavy hand fell on his shoulder. He turned round to confront the usual type of London detective, bowler hat, black moustache, and all. A glance showed that his mate was also in custody.

They were hurried off to Snow Hill Police Station, and detained pending further inquiries, but the sleuths were dealing with a man a little more astute than themselves. Golder had always lived dangerously, and he knew that some time an end must come to his anti-social activities. For that reason he was invariably shadowed by a friend whenever he went abroad. The shadow witnessed his taking off, and dashed with all possible speed to Golder's home in the East End.

Here he hastily collected all the paraphernalia of the coiner's art, and removed it to another address. And he was not a minute too soon. A car loaded with police officers pulled up at the front door, but they were doomed to disappointment. An intensive search yielded exactly nothing, and Golder escaped by a hair's-breadth the major and serious charge of coining. It was a close shave, and he always swore that he would never return to the business of making money, except in a legitimate way.

Old Marshall was a type I had never encountered before, and never want to again. He was a man who had apparently never enjoyed even a board school education, but he had managed to earn enough to marry and bring up a large family. Although he had never been in trouble with the police before, his moral character was decidedly low, and his conversation revolting. It was a punishment to have to listen to him, and he always struck me as a man who needed a long course of expert psychological treatment.

After the death of his wife, Marshall evidently lost what little decency remained to him, and he was caught in a compromising position with a young man, one of the pests of society, underneath a London bridge. The horrible nature of his crime was known to all, and because of his age, his filthy speech, and his sexual perversion, he became the butt of the coarse and more vulgar element in the prison population.

And these men could be cruel. I frequently had to rescue the old man from his heartless tormentors, who when they had nothing better to do, emulated one another, in making his life unbearable. One of their favourite jokes was to whistle in unison "Underneath the Arches" as he came trundling down the full length of D Hall to join the exercise parade on Sunday mornings.

Marshall's general behaviour was not such as to evoke sympathy from the better type of prisoner, for he wreaked on Eric the same kind of treatment he was in the habit of receiving from other bullies. Now Eric was a man whose vocabulary was probably limited to two hundred words, and any kind of connected or sustained conversation was quite beyond him. He was a married man, and he had been foolish enough to exhibit a photograph of his wife, a young woman of rather an attractive appearance. Marshall pretended to take an enormous

interest in her welfare, and as his sentence was expiring
three months before Eric's, he spent a great part of his
time in impressing on the latter the first thing he intended
to do on his release. And in Marshall's plans Eric's wife,
who, the old scoundrel was always careful to point out,
had been cruelly wronged, figured very prominently.
To all this baiting Eric could only reply with vile threats
and curses.

The Deputy Table Leader was, as I had said, an
ex-postman. There were large numbers of these men in
Wormwood Scrubs, and I always felt sorry for them.
This man had a big family, and the scandalously small
wage which postmen receive had only kept them on the
bread line. He had therefore turned to "snobbing" to
supplement his meagre income, but his wife was laid up
with a long and serious illness, and he solved his immediate financial difficulties by robbing the mails. It was
not a large amount, something under £20, but the Judge
babbled the usual homily about positions of trust, and the
necessity for protecting the public, and sent him away
for fifteen months to reflect on the enormity of his crime.
He was gloomy and morose, and never contributed
anything to the conversation, which, as the reader will
judge by the character of the participants, never reached
a very high level.

The income-tax man was quiet and reserved. He was
not with us very long, and even his face is but a dim
memory.

I had, of course, as a Second Stage man, started in to
re-educate myself, and had joined the Economic, European
History, and World History classes. These intellectual
pursuits took up an hour a night for three evenings a

week, and although I learnt nothing, the experience was interesting enough.

An application for admission to the Debating Society was refused on the grounds that the membership was already exceeded. The men in charge were nearly all young L.C.C. teachers, and competent enough according to the book. What struck me about them—and I joined other classes at a later period—was their almost unanimous belief that the present social system had outlived its usefulness, and was fast approaching dissolution.

There was a very strong sympathy for the Russian experiment, and what appeared to me to be a great deal of muddled sentimentalism about the brotherhood and equality of mankind. There was also a tendency, I thought, to question the motives, and belittle the past performances, of the British Empire, and I often wondered what their influence must be on the formative minds of the rising generation. On the prisoners they had no effect at all. The classes were regarded more as a form of entertainment than as a school of serious instruction.

During this time my job in the library, which consisted in selecting books and packing the baskets for the different halls, proceeded smoothly enough. Naturally the work was not arduous, and on off days I had many opportunities for renewing acquaintance with favourite authors.

Morning exercise had become painfully monotonous, and although over age, I applied for and obtained permission to join B drill. It was not too strenuous, and the change was exhilarating. Besides, there was a cup of cocoa and a slice of dry bread for every man who took drill, and by this time my appetite had returned, and I felt as hungry as the youngest.

G

The instructors were not good, and there was only one officer who approached the old army men for word of command, and smartness in the detailing and execution of movements. On Wednesdays, Saturdays, and Sundays there was no drill and no cocoa, and exercise was confined to walking round the quadrangles.

Early morning service was held on Wednesdays, and on Saturdays we listened to a resumé of the week's news from the Chaplain, or one of his assistants. We always preferred the Chaplain. He had a strong, resonant voice, a cheerful, happy countenance, a nice sense of humour, and an excellent idea of what constituted news. His Church Army man seemed to think that we were all football or boxing fans, and incapable of taking an intelligent interest in the serious doings of the world.

Sunday morning was rather a trying time, as we were compelled to walk round and round the courtyards for an hour or an hour and a half, and to pursue this aimless task without talking or resting was an exhausting business. Of course, it was not always devoid of humour. An elderly Jew used to cause me quite a lot of amusement. He was corpulent, his face was rubicund and benevolent, and he invariably led the aged and infirm on the inside paths. Being bald, he wore a prison glengarry, pressed firmly down on his head, and in wet weather he was never without a grey prison cape. Perched on his nose at a rakish angle was a pair of gold-rimmed pince-nez, and if it were not for the fact that the cape and trousers were on the short side, he might have been mistaken for a Medieval bishop out for a matutinal stroll.

I passed through Second and Third Stages without any serious trouble, and on promotion to Fourth Stage was immediately appointed a Leader with a table of my own. The responsibility of looking after the welfare of others added a zest to prison experience, and although I encountered many awkward characters, I found that the very worst men responded to cheerfulness, tact, and absolute fairness. I was a Leader for a good many months, and never once had occasion to "case" a man for a serious offence, and so lengthen his time in gaol.

I was sorry in a way to say good-bye to R table. The conversation was often amusing, if coarse and vulgar, but there was very little open quarelling, and the men were quite amenable to the Leader's directions. The only serious disturber of the peace was Laski, who cross-questioned Skilton daily with all the pertinacity and shrewdness of a skilled advocate. Every statement made by the latter, and he made many, was openly and boldly challenged.

One day Laski informed me that he had been reading the City Notes in one of the papers, and he wanted to know what the Editor meant by "Kaffirs." I told him. At the next meal he was ready for his victim. "Look here, Skilton," he said ingratiatingly, "I've been looking up the Stock Exchange news lately, and I see there has been great activity in Kaffirs. I know that the Stock Exchange has nothing to do with niggers, but you say that you've spent a lot of time in Africa, and perhaps you can tell us just what it all means."

Skilton was flattered by this unexpected deference to his own superior knowledge, and promptly obliged. He knew Kaffirs very well, but Laski was wrong in supposing that they had nothing to do with niggers. They were the biggest firm operating in the Cape, universal providers in fact, and the bulk of their trade was done with the native population.

"Is that right?" inquired Laski of me sharply. I shook my head, and explained briefly that Kaffirs was an omnibus Stock Exchange term covering all the Rand goldmining shares, in which English people were the largest investors. But Skilton would have none of that. He personally knew one of the managers, and at divers times had transacted a great deal of business with the firm.

Furthermore, his own employers were not only consulting engineers, but were stockbrokers as well, and he felt that he could speak as one having authority, and not as one of the scribes. But I suggested that as members of the London Stock Exchange were debarred by the rules from carrying on any other business, he must be making another mistake. "There you are," shouted the Jew triumphantly. "Skilton, you must be the biggest liar who ever lived. You pretend to know this, and you pretend to know that, when all the time you know sweet F.A. You built the Sydney bridge, and only missed inclusion in the Honours List because you were recalled on urgent business. You drew up the plans for the Zambesi; in fact, you have had a hand in every big engineering feat during the last thirty years, and you are not twenty-five years old. When you're cornered, you resort to more lies. What's those lines you quoted the other day?" he cried to me, excitedly: "It's all right, I've got them!

> Oh, what a tangled web we weave,
> When first we practise to deceive!"

Skilton was choking with rage, but the Jew went on remorselessly: "And now I'm going to tell you something,

Skilton, that we heard in the engineer's shop on the very best authority. You were never an engineer at all; you were nothing more than a damned valet, who creased the trousers of a consulting engineer. And as for all this talk about your mother driving up to the prison gates in a Rolls-Royce, it's all bunkum. The only car your old mother has ever been in is a tram-car. You're the joke of the whole prison; nobody believes a single word from your lying mouth. Even the Chaplain has found you out, and as far as R table is concerned, you're damned, and done for!"

This outburst shattered Skilton's confidence, and within a few days he had wangled a transfer to another table, but we continued to hear from newcomers stirring accounts of his magnificent work for civilization in countries as far apart as Colombia and Cathay. In a sense, Skilton was lucky to be in prison. A constant stream of new recruits ministered to his vanity. It did not matter that they quickly passed from wonder and admiration to disillusionment and contempt. Others were always ready to take their places, and Skilton was perfectly happy as long as he had an uncritical audience.

As a Fourth Stage man I tasted once more the great joy of reading a daily newspaper. Five daily papers were received in the Scrubs for the use of Fourth Stage men: *The Times*, the *Daily Express*, the *Daily Mail*, the *Daily Sketch*, and the *Daily Mirror*; and three Sunday papers: the *Observer*, the *Sunday Times*, and the *Sunday Pictorial* The *Daily Express* was, I think, the most popular, with the *Daily Mail* a very close second. A prisoner had not a great deal of time for reading the papers, especially if there were a large number of Fourth Stage men on his table. Promptly after tea, Fourth Stage men trooped off to the recreation room, where the papers were handed out by the Leader in charge, but educational classes began at 6.30 p.m., and in practice the individual had only five or six minutes for his perusal of the day's news.

Promotion to Leadership brought with it a change of work, and henceforth I was in charge of one of the library working-parties, with access to all parts of the Prison. It also entailed attendance at committee meetings D Hall duties, control of the recreation-room, and a task known as "Visits." Friends and relatives of prisoners were admitted every day except Sunday. On presentation of their passes at the main gate they were ushered into a waiting-room. The passes were placed in a box by the gate officer, and were collected at intervals by the Leaders on duty, who ascertained the locations of the men wanted by reference to a register in the Chief's office, and brought them in. When the Leader had collected his man, he proceeded to the main gate and shouted "Friends of Brown" or "Friends of Jones," and as soon as the waiting relatives appeared they were shepherded into the closed boxes, or taken to meet their Fourth Stage friends in the open grounds.

During the week the D Hall orderly and the Chaplain's orderly spent their afternoons on visits, but on Saturday, the busiest time, two or three other Leaders were in attendance. After a certain hour on Saturday all the men were in church listening to the weekly concert. The Leaders chalked on slates the cell numbers of the men whose friends had arrived, and with slates raised aloft marched down the aisles of the church in the invervals between the items.

All these activities gave an interest to a life which

at its best is essentially grey and monotonous, and I date my happiest moments in prison from the day I became a Leader. True, there were numbers of men who resented the authority vested in a Leader, and took no pains to conceal their contempt and hostility, even at the risk of being "cased," but tact, good humour, and patience invariably won them over. On the other hand, the office provided numberless opportunities for helping fellow prisoners, and for making their lives more comfortable by little acts of kindness and consideration which were seldom unappreciated.

CHAPTER VIII

IT was a few days after my promotion to Leadership that the Digger arrived. He was deposited in the library by a Leader about ten o'clock one morning. The librarian had not returned from reception, and he was invited to take a chair by the Leader in charge. His case had received a great deal of prominence in the Press. As Fourth Stage men we were familiar with the details, and as two of our number had recently been discharged we had more than half expected that he would spend his time with us.

The newspapers had published the information that he was a New Zealander, and our Australian colleague immediately greeted him as Digger. The name stuck. He was tall, gaunt, and weary-looking, and his face was heavily lined, but his eye was bright, and he engaged in general conversation with the greatest energy.

Asked by someone the everlasting question as to how he liked the Scrubs, he replied that it was not really too bad, and that it was at any rate a safe asylum from duns, and the monstrous regiment of women. "But you, of course," he added, turning to the Australian, who had already unburdened himself of the information that he had "married" a number of women, "You prefer gazing into the bright eyes of danger, or won't believe that the female of the species is more deadly than the male." The Digger had sized up his fellow Antipodean accurately, and his bantering remarks were the opening shots in a long verbal battle between them over the question of women.

The other sex was an obsession with the Australian,

who was a man of fifty, and as white-headed as one of
his native cockatoos. The only time they yielded first
place in his conversation was when he was relating his
famous exploit on Gallipoli, another feat of arms which
brought him the D.C.M.

On the arrival of the Librarian, the Digger was given
the usual initial job of selecting volumes for the weekly
changes, and packing the baskets. He did this in association with the Aussie, and under the supervision of our
Estate Agent. We soon discovered that a man had come
into the library who knew more about books than the
whole lot of us put together, and there were two or three
who rather fancied their accomplishments in that direction.
He shouted Latin with huge enjoyment, and then trans-
lated, for the benefit of the *profanum vulgus*. His knowledge of the English and French classics was far and away
above my own, and he had more than a passing acquaintance with Spanish and Italian literatures. Of course,
all this was of no very great use in the work on which
he was engaged as a prisoner, but he confided to me that
if only he could keep clear of the screws, one of whom
had already forcibly expressed the opinion that he was
not clean about the house, he was going to have a happy
time in the library of Wormwood Scrubs.

The Aussie had no pretensions whatever to literary
taste, and lived on magazines. There was great rivalry
between him and another man called Pelling for the
limited supply available in the library. These two
practically cornered the lot for their own use. Like
jackdaws with shiny spoons, or dogs with bones, they
would conceal those not in immediate use in all sorts of
secret hiding-places.

Magazines were on issue to Fourth Stage men only. One day the leader in charge of the "smasher" counter complained that the supply had completely run out, and that there would be trouble with some of the lads at the midday change. Pelling was out of the room, and under the Aussie's gleeful directions his hoards were discovered, and half a dozen magazines dragged out.

These were handed over to Fourth Stage men, but Pelling was too busy on other work to notice what was going on, and that his beloved magazines were passing into the hands of strangers. As soon as the Fourth Stage men were marched out he seized a ladder, and dived his arm behind a mass of books on a top shelf, but the object of his search was not there. He shifted the ladder, and tried another hiding-place, with no better results. A third attempt produced another blank, and on this occasion he fearfully examined his hand as he withdrew it, as if by some infernal enchantment he had been deprived of sight.

Pelling, by the way, had only one eye. A German had accounted for the other. At last he descended the ladder, a look of baffled amazement on his features, and after glaring belligerently round the room with his one baleful eye he subsided into his chair, breathing heavily. All the time this comedy was going on Pelling had been under furtive observation by every man in the library, but when he returned to his seat they were all absorbed in their own affairs, without overdoing the part. Except the Aussie, who sat with a magazine prominently displayed before him, and a smile of ineffable satisfaction on his face. Describing Pelling's appearance later, the Digger said he looked like a gander on whose anserine intelligence the awful significance of Christmas had just dawned.

The Aussie, who was a hard labour man, had secured admission to the library by misrepresentation. He had boasted that he was an expert with the brush, and that painting numbers on the backs of books was child's play to him. So he was brought in to succeed a man who was shortly leaving. But on trial he proved a complete and dismal failure. Under any other officer he would have been sent somewhere else, but the Librarian was too kind-hearted to return him to the shops.

He was about the only man who ever got into serious trouble in the library, and it was his ruling passion that nearly lost him his privileged job. One day the Digger was passing the Aussie's chair, when he stopped and cried:

Whither, O splendid ship, thy white sails crowding,
Leaning across the bosom of the urgent West. . . .

at the same time gently passing his fingers through the Aussie's white locks. The latter had been engaged in cutting pictures from a popular illustrated paper for the benefit of illiterate prisoners. After gloating over the form and features of one of the world's most famous screen actresses, he was surreptitiously transferring the photograph to a leather case, which he carried in his pocket in defiance of the regulations.

"You mind your own business," shouted the Australian, jumping to his feet. "Don't get excited," countered the Digger; "I'm only doing you a good turn. If you're caught with a picture of that beauty in your possession you'll be for the high jump."

The Aussie, however, was not taking advice from anybody. A few days later he dropped the incriminating case,
which he had received from a man in the Shoeshop for
services rendered, outside his cell in D Hall. An examination showed that three other stars shared with the famous
Mae West the Aussie's admiration. The principal officer
of D Hall decided that the culprit must be a library man.

He knew the Aussie's weakness, and taxed him with
the "crime," but the latter at first denied all knowledge
of the case and its contents. Finally, under persistent
cross-examination, he broke down, and admitted that
he was the guilty party. He was informed that he was
for the Governor, but he had a good friend in the
librarian. The P.O. stormed and raved. No man in that
place would tell him a deliberate lie and get away with
it, but the Librarian represented that the Aussie was truly
penitent, and had given his solemn pledge to shun all
female attractions from that time onwards. In the end
the trouble was smoothed over.

"I should have thought that the anaphrodisiac qualities
of our diet in this show would have quelled all interest
in that sort of thing," said the Skipper to the Aussie
when we were discussing his lucky escape.—"Talk
English," replied the Australian sourly, "and I'll know
what you mean."—"Well," the Skipper continued
gently, "the food here is designed to reduce to a mini-
mum the trouble from which you have been a life-long
sufferer. A normal prisoner loses entirely his interest in
sex. I don't know whether it's because I'm getting old,
or getting better, but from being moderately lecherous,
I'm as holy as a monk in a hair shirt, and the general
opinion is that the food is responsible."—"It's not the

food at all," growled the Aussie, "it's the dope they put in the cocoa, and that's why I only drink half of mine."— "Well, if you're right," interjected the Digger, "you'd better drink none at all in future, and spare yourself unnecessary risks!"

It was a fact that large numbers of full-blooded men with fairly strong animal tendencies grew seriously alarmed after a few weeks of prison régime. They wondered what on earth had happened to them, and their fears were allayed only after swopping experiences with others. The Aussie merely voiced the general opinion when he declared that the cocoa was doped, but I think the diet was so devised as to reduce below normal the erotic inclinations of the average man.

Within a week of his coming amongst us the Digger very nearly got himself into a spot of trouble. Every morning the Governor or his Deputy paid a visit of inspection, but on this occasion the chief officer acted as substitute. He was a big man with an enormous chest. His face was the size and colour of a ham, and on his head was perched what appeared to be a ridiculously small prison cap. Also he had a wooden leg, and walked with a pronounced limp. Altogether the Chief was a formidable looking customer, and he was universally feared. As he stumped into the library the Leader in charge rose and reported all correct.

The Chief never opened his mouth, but having glared critically round the room, he turned his broad back, and made for the door, in front of which stood a high screen to keep out the draughts. The Digger, who had noted his resemblance to Robert Louis Stevenson's most famous character, called out to no one in particular, in a rather loud voice: "I say, what a glorious morning face!"

But the Chief had not gone: he was merely concealed by the screen. Back he came and without saying a word, fixed the Digger with a glittering eye. The latter bent his head and wrote hurriedly on a library card. The suspense was trying, and we who knew the Chief's savage tongue marvelled at his silence. After what seemed an age, he turned and went out, banging the door behind him.

"If you persist in seeing the funny side of things," said the Skipper, addressing the Digger, "they'll apprentice you to the tailoring or bootmaking trades before long!" But the Digger was shaken, and said nothing, and after an admonishing from the Christian Scientist Leader, who was cursed with a nagging conscience, the librarians proceeded in silence with their allotted tasks.

As a Leader most of my time was taken up in charge of library parties on the weekly changes, but the first duty every morning was to attend to the literary requirements of penal servitude men in B Hall, and the new arrivals in the prison. There were two or three men to carry the baskets, and I very soon attached the Digger to my party. The outing, except in wet weather, was always a pleasant change, and many of the men we met were interesting if notorious characters.

One of these was an Irishman called Molloy, who had received seven years and sixteen strokes with the cat for armed robbery with violence. He had appealed against his sentence, and was detained in Wormwood Scrubs pending the result. Molloy was a morose and savage fellow, and gave his keepers plenty to think about.

He would fly into the most ungovernable rages, but I got on very well with him, because I had always given him what he wanted in the way of Wild West stories, of which he was inordinately fond.

It was many weeks, however, before his appeal was heard, and the supply of Wild West books ran out. I explained his case to the Digger before leaving the library, and we agreed that Nat Gould would probably be a satisfactory substitute. Molloy was seated outside his cell, and greeted us with a surly nod. I opened the conversation by telling him that as he had read every Wild West book in the prison we proposed to introduce him to Nat Gould, the author of many racing thrillers.

But I got no further. Cursing me with a filthy tongue, Molloy spurned the basket with his foot, and sent our carefully arranged books flying in all directions. The Digger and the Skipper began to collect the scattered volumes, while I firmly told Molloy that because of his disgraceful exhibition of temper he would get exactly nothing that day. I was frightened, but to the surprise of everybody, Molloy suddenly quietened down, and apologized for what he had said and done.

He had just been told, he said, of the failure of his appeal, "and, you know," he continued, addressing me, "what that means." I knew only too well. He would suffer the pain and degradation of a flogging either that day or the next, and Molloy feared the ordeal. Floggings took place in the gymnasium, and when anything was afoot, Leaders were warned not to take parties that way. I was sorry for the man. Undoubtedly he was a violent and desperate sort of brute, but although he had a consuming hatred for society, there was good in him, and he was not unresponsive to kindness. I asked him if he really wanted something new to read, and he consented to try Nat Gould.

Two days later we saw Molloy again. Normally he was a big, broad-shouldered man, standing six feet high, but on this occasion he was doubled and bent, and seemed to have shrunk to half his measure. He smiled grimly but feebly as we deposited the baskets outside his cell. I had to pass between him and the cell to get his library card. "For Christ's sake don't touch my back!" he screamed, and then he poured out a stream of the vilest and most blasphemous curses against God and man that I have ever listened to. Molloy had been through it, and the dreaded experience had only hardened his savage heart.

The Officer in the Tower lived two doors away from Molloy. His case had attracted enormous public attention. He struck me as the last person in the world who ought to have engaged in the delicate and dangerous business of selling secrets to foreign agents. He confined his reading to a single author; I think it was W. J. Locke. It was typical of the man that when Locke's books ran out he started reading them all over again. A German grammar, and a translation of Sherlock Holmes in the same language, completed his selection of library volumes.

One recollection of Baillie Stewart still amuses me. Periodically a general search of the whole prison for contrabrand was conducted. Prisoners would parade for their daily work as usual, when, without any warning, the order would come to retire to cells and shut the doors, which, of course, locked automatically. The men would dash to their quarters, and the tinkle of steel in the lavatories announced that prisoners were getting rid of unauthorized razor-blades. The general search was on.

Two warders would enter the cell, search it, and, if necessary, strip the occupant. On this day my cell was opened up early. The officer in charge inquired genially, "Anything to declare, Leader?"—"Nothing," I replied, also in a jocular vein, "but I'm offering neither objection nor resistance to a thorough search."—"Come on," he answered, "the Librarian is waiting for you!" and off I went.

A general search always upset the ordinary prison routine, and I was unable to get to B Hall until the afternoon. Baillie Stewart was not seated outside his cell, but his door was ajar, and I pushed it open and entered. He was standing in the middle of the cell gazing up at the sky. The man looked harassed and worried. "What's the matter with you, Stewart?" I inquired.—"I'm in trouble," he answered, in a tone that indicated that tears were not far off. "There's been a search this morning, and I've been found out."—"What was it?" I asked. "Anything serious?"—"A couple of onions," replied Stewart, as if he were going to his doom, and for the life of me I couldn't help laughing in his face.

Apparently the poor fellow had a friend in the stores, and the latter had suggested to Stewart that a trifling addition to his diet in the shape of an onion or two wouldn't do him any harm. It was unfortunate that the gift was no sooner in his possession than the order rang out to withdraw to cells, and it never occurred to him to throw the forbidden vegetables through the window.

Baillie Stewart lived in B Hall for two months or

H

more before his removal to Maidstone. He always addressed me as Sergeant, because as a Fourth Stage man I wore three stripes on my arm. His main interest in life seemed to be what the newspapers were saying about him. On this point he never failed to make daily inquiries.

There were only two general searches while I was in the Scrubs. The first one yielded a pair of kippers, which were secreted in a mattress belonging to a man who worked in the officer's mess, and the second Baillie Stewart's onions.

One of the outstanding personalities in B Hall about this time was a gentleman by the name of Calligan. He had suddenly made his appearance in London society as an ex-general of the Peruvian army, with large silver and gold concessions at his disposal. For a few months Calligan dazzled the West End, but did not seem to make much headway with City financiers.

Finally luck came his way, in the shape of a large middle-aged woman with an ample fortune and an impressionable heart. Calligan made love to her, and like a good cavalry man he was soon in the saddle, but the course of true affection did not run smooth. Her elephantine caresses and readiness to weep for joy irritated him, and he determined to make a break for the tall timber.

There were, needless to say, other and more pressing reasons for taking the trail with secrecy and dispatch. The good lady had not only showered her affection but her gold upon the gallant adventurer from the Andes, and Calligan was impatiently looking forward to the time when he could spend without let or hindrance the

£40,000 received from her for the sale of a gold concession, which existed nowhere but in his fertile imagination.

Calligan had always acted on the assumption that love is blind. But in some things it is as sharp as a needle, and his inamorata was quick to notice the subtle change in his pretended feelings. This, combined with a diminished bank balance of £40,000, caused her great uneasiness, which she communicated to a male relative, and the relative told the police, and the police took Calligan as he was boarding the Channel boat at Dover.

He was serving a sentence of six years' imprisonment when I met him, and he had come up from Maidstone to give evidence in another case. He loathed the Scrubs, where he declared the discipline was much more severe than in Maidstone prison, but his impudent face was always wreathed in smiles, and the prospect of six years behind the bars did not depress him in the least. Brazen cheek seemed to be the main asset of all the confidence tricksters I came across. Not one of them had any education worth talking about, or any particular charm of manner. They had learnt, however, in the school of experience that an artful appeal to the cupidity of mankind seldom passes unheeded, and they had certainly acquired the ability to play upon that universal weakness.

The Leader in C Hall was a confidence-man of some fame and importance in his profession. Bill Braithwaite had travelled the world, and he was as familiar with Shanghai, Istanbul, Budapest, or San Francisco, as he was with London, Paris, or New York. I had many long talks with Bill, who was never tired of relating the difficulties, dangers, disappointments, and brilliant successes of an expert trickster's eventful career.

For quite a long time he had done very well by inducing his victims to put money on horses which always won. As soon as confidence had been firmly established they were persuaded to plunge in thousands, with which Bill decamped. One night he went to the Savoy Hotel to draw a cool £11,000 from a Lancashire business man for the purpose of investment in his infallible system. The money was handed over and Bill was entertaining visions of the Moulin Rouge and Mediterranean cruises, when two detectives jumped from behind a screen, and he was a prisoner.

He had never been convicted before, and the magistrate passed a comparatively light sentence of fifteen months, but a month or two before it expired Bill was sent for by the Governor and informed that he would be re-arrested as soon as he shoved his nose outside the gates of Wormwood Scrubs.

It appears that the Canadian police had been looking for him for years. They had tracked him down by the description and history given in the London trial. We were all sorry for Bill. No doubt he had been defrauding innocent but greedy people all his life. However, there was something very attractive about the man, and one felt that he could never be petty or mean. Besides, he was getting on in years, over sixty, and the prospect of a long sentence in a Canadian prison tried his courage.

We read the report of his case in the newspapers. The Canadian police applied for his extradition, and after two hearings the magistrate granted the application. It appeared that six years previously Bill, or somebody very like him, had defrauded a Montreal couple of £6,000, their life-savings. On that occasion the trickster had posed as the trainer of President Hoover's racehorses.

The D Hall change on Friday afternoons was an easy one. The Digger was astonished when he viewed the interior of this Hall for the first time. Cleaners were busy on the floors, some were scrubbing tables and trestles, and others were arranging flowers in vases for table decorations.

The flowers had been sent in by friends and relatives of prisoners. We stopped for a moment to survey the animated scene, and the Digger suddenly recollecting, one of his first Latin exercises, turned to me and said: "Servi mensas dominorum variis floribus ornant." When I told him that all these preparations were being made for the benefit of the prisoners themselves, and not for the officers, he refused to believe it. "Why," he exclaimed, "this is more like a home for unfortunate gentlemen; but look at the way they treat me in C Hall!"—"Ah, yes," I said, "but we've been through all that. This is your reward for good behaviour."

On reaching the top floor, where all the cleaners resided, we were besieged by men clamouring for the pick of the books in the basket, and pleading: "Give us a decent *friction*, Leader. Give us a decent friction!" When we reached the library, the conversation turned on the mispronunciation of words, and the general tendency to corrupt the mother tongue. The Skipper referred to the fact that all the cleaners without exception used friction instead of fiction, and said that it was doubtful if they had acquired the habit in prison. Indeed, the standard of speech amongst the younger men was disgracefully low, and made one feel that the millions spent on general education were largely wasted.

At any rate, the influences of the home and the workshop seem to be too powerful for the teaching profession.

"People have little respect for the spoken or written word nowadays," said the Digger. "They are content if they make themselves understood, and the man who loves words for their own sake is looked upon as a prig. Take business English, the expression of the thoughts of those great public benefactors who accumulate fortunes for themselves, and at the same time make the country rich and prosperous. If as a correspondence clerk for any one of them you were to write plain, straightforward English, you wouldn't hold your job a week. They are in receipt of favours, not letters. Cheque value is enclosed. They revel in ultimos, proximos, instants, and idems. They are always too happy to oblige, as if they were expiring in some kind of ecstasy. Any phrase or sentence that is stupid or meaningless immediately achieves distinction when it has been used once or twice by some tomfool apostle of efficiency.

"There is one word which is almost universally maltreated by Londoners. I don't know what the rest of England is like, but the Metropolis always sounds like a blasted poultry-run to me. Very soon the verb to lie will only be used in the sense of telling a falsehood. People are always going to lay down, or lay up, and even those with some claims to education fall readily into this stupid mistake. Here's a man," he cried "who has turned to thrillers as the most lucrative form of literature, and who claims to have been a Professor of Morals and Ethics. His hero, a Harvard graduate, says: 'You will find some tools laying about in the garage.' 'Between you and I and the gatepost' is another common phrase with people who pride themselves on the purity of their speech," said the Skipper; "but what are we going to do about it?"

"I don't know," growled the Digger, "except that we ought to be damned careful what we say."

CHAPTER IX

THE DIGGER was worried about his eyesight, and in a letter to his wife he mentioned that he was experiencing some difficulty in reading ordinary print. The next thing he knew, he was ordered to report sick by his Landing Officer. The censor had read his letter, and passed it on to the Medical Superintendent, a proof that the authorities were not unmindful of the physical welfare of the people in their charge.

When he appeared amongst us again he was wearing prison spectacles, but their use hardly improved an appearance which already bordered on the ugly. The Aussie, with the smug self-satisfaction which frequently belongs to men who are conscious of their good looks, had the temerity to suggest that the sooner his vision returned to normal, the better it would be for everybody. He did not succeed, however, in ruffling the Digger's good humour.

"You know, Aussie," replied the latter, "there was once a man, whom you have never heard of, called John Wilkes. Wilkes was notoriously ugly, but he was also a notorious rake, and he boasted that he only needed ten minutes' start with a lady to beat the handsomest man in England to the bedpost. And Wilkes was not lying. He had brains, and his talk would charm a bird off a tree."

"What's all this rot to do with me?" queried the Australian. "Only this," replied the Digger: "I know that I was in a back seat when faces were handed out, but Dame Nature is a shrewish mother. There's a snag about every gift of hers. If she bestows a handsome exterior, she is niggardly with her allowance of grey matter, and yours is a case in point. Granted that you have many scalps fluttering from your belt, and that you have wrought fearful havoc amongst ignorant house-maids, and guileless servant girls, but you have as much chance of adding an intelligent woman to your collection as I have of becoming King of England. Besides, you antiquated old scoundrel, your good looks are not suffi-cient unaided to carry you to victory. You've got to marry the girls before they yield their secrets, and then the law steps in to put a term to your little game."

"Has it never occurred to you," enquired the Skipper innocently, "that the butterfly is the true explanation of whatever success the Aussie has achieved with the ladies?" At this sally there was a general laugh. The Australian was tattooed from head to foot. Birds, beasts, and various love tokens covered his tough hide, but he was proudest of all of a tropical butterfly, which, so he confided, adorned the most sensitive part of his anatomy. I thought the barbaric custom of tattooing had almost vanished, but there were dozens of men in Wormwood Scrubs who had been through the tattooer's hands.

The Aussie was a trifle discomfited by this exchange of banter, but he was an incessant talker, and silence always weighed heavily on him. For a time he waded into the business of examining returned books, on which the Digger also was engaged, and then his voice was raised excitedly. He had discovered the finest book in the world, the only one that had ever made a lasting impression on his mind. "What's the name of it?" enquired the Digger casually. "*Boo Jesty*," announced the Aussie without hesitation. "*Boo Jesty*?" queried the Digger, raising his eyebrows; "has anybody here ever heard of *Boo Jesty*?"

No one was familiar with the book, and the Skipper, who suggested that the title sounded like the pet name of a chimpanzee, asked the Aussie to tell us what it was all about. "It's about the Legion of Honour, or the Foreign Legion and Africa, and the author's name is . . ."

"Wren will have to select English title for his stories in future," interrupted the Digger, on whom the light had suddenly dawned; "but *Boo Jesty* is a marvellous shot in the dark for *Beau Geste*." The Aussie, however, refused to be corrected on this occasion. One of his victims had been a Frenchwoman. She had approved his pronunciation, and on a matter of this kind a Frenchwoman's opinion was infinitely superior to a Pig Islander's.

That morning the Digger made his first find. He was turning over the pages of a book of some value—one, indeed, which he had personally selected for Jones, the little man who had tried to secure my release from the cell in C Hall. Jones was always in trouble with authority, and he had been banished for some breach of discipline to C Hall, where he lived next door to the Digger.

On this occasion Jones had almost destroyed the value of the book by writing a screed pages long, not in pencil, which could be erased, but in ink. This literary contribution was not the usual obscene diatribe against the prison, or prison warders, but purported to be a true account of Jones's conversion, of his emergence from darkness into light.

He confessed that his way of life had been unutterably evil, that he had betrayed his wife, and wronged his innocent children, but on the previous Wednesday night he had been smitten with a great light like Paul of Tarsus. From that moment the filthy rags of his unrighteousness had fallen from him, and he had become a new man. He rejoiced in his release from the bondage of sin, and hoped and prayed that the first fellow prisoner to read his confession would be moved by the spirit of God to do likewise.

The Digger read this human document aloud. "Has he gone crackers?" asked the Aussie, with some trepidation.

"It looks like it," was the reply.

"But," pursued the Aussie, "he wants you to join him. You were the first to read it."

"Well," said the Digger, "I'm sorry to disappoint Jones, and I hope he won't lose faith in the efficacy of prayer, but on this occasion he's going to be unlucky. A spiritual experience of the kind he's apparently been through though is about the only thing that will cure your besetting vice, my lad.'"

By this time the Leader in charge had joined the group. One glance at the book, and he decided that the matter must be carried to the Librarian. A little later the Librarian arrived, and he was shown the first fruits of Jones' conversion. I was sent to the Brush shop to bring him in.

He came quietly, without asking any embarrassing questions, and he was invited to write his name and address on a card. His writing was compared with the confession, and when Jones saw the book his jaw dropped. "What made you do this, Jones?" said the Librarian gently, as if addressing a naughty child, and assuming

correctly that the man would not deny his handiwork·
"You have ruined a valuable book, and spoilt the pleasure
other prisoners might have derived from reading it."

"Well, sir," replied Jones, "it was like this. I felt
so happy that I thought I ought to make a permanent
record, and I had a pen and ink in my cell to write a
letter, and there was no other paper."

"I'm afraid," said the Librarian wearily, for he had
cases of this sort to deal with every week, "that the
matter is too serious to be overlooked. You'll go before
the Governor to-morrow morning, and take his punishment. See that he's returned to the shop, Leader," and
the Librarian went out on another duty.

As soon as he had disappeared through the door, Jones
looked belligerently round the room, his little black eyes
flashing a dull fire. Gone was the Christian meekness
of a moment before. Finally his gaze rested on the Digger.

"Who gave me away?" he inquired sharply.

"Well," answered the Digger, "I'm afraid I played
an important part in your exposure. I read aloud that
account of your escape from death to life, and the Leader
here decided that it was a case for disciplinary action."

"You mean to tell me," shouted Jones, "that you're
responsible for this, when I'm already undergoing
punishment for something else!"

"That seems to be the humour of it," assented the
Digger.

"The humour of it," shrieked the demented convert;
"By God, I'll——"

And for two minutes he poured out a stream of curses,
in which one vile word predominated, like the recurring
motif in a theme song. To express his bitterest and

most savage feelings, he prefixed the approbrious word with double and treble adjectives, and he might have gone on until exhausted, had not the Leader in charge ordered him roughly to shut up, or he would be cased on the spot.

When Jones had gone, and we had recovered from our astonishment, the Skipper remarked quietly: "You seem to have annoyed that fellow, and instead of you joining him, he's back again under the devil's banner with you. It's the quickest case of backsliding I've ever seen. Why, he wasn't in the Kingdom of Heaven a week!" But the Digger was in no mood for joking. The thought that he had got a fellow prisoner into trouble worried him, although he was pledged to report all such cases of defacement and mutilation to his superiors. To add to his harassment, the Aussie related that Jones in his degenerate days before conversion had been a well-known tobacco-smuggler, and that he was not above secreting a lump of "hard" in the Digger's cell.

Later in the day old Howlett, the septuagenarian solicitor, who as a rule held aloof from the general conversation, commented on the outrageous conduct of Jones, and cited his filthy language as proof of the man's depravity. But the Digger wouldn't stand for that. Bad language, he argued, was undoubtedly a bad habit, but was no more an indication of a man's moral character than constant attendance at the pictures. It arose from poverty of thought and a limited vocabulary. The days of good talking and hearty picturesque invective were no more, and there had been a marked degeneracy in cursing even since the war.

"How do you account for the almost exclusive use of this one word?" inquired the Skipper.

The Digger replied that he never realized the word in question enjoyed such a monopoly until he came to the Scrubs. "Its constant use," he went on, "is sickening, but I think, Skipper, this is the true explanation of the phenomenon. The ancestors of all these jokers were present when King Lear went off his head, and shouted 'Let copulation thrive!' Of course, the mad monarch really used the same expression as these fellows are repeating every day, but Shakespeare's embellishment made it fit for decent consumption. The King's retinue heard and approved, and bequeathed it a rich legacy unto their heirs. If you can think of anything more plausible, I'm willing to hear it." But the Skipper couldn't, and smilingly agreed that the Digger had supplied the solution of a problem which had been worrying him ever since his admission.

Old Howlett listened dourly to all this nonsense. He had taken a strong personal dislike to the Digger, not because there had been any open clash between them, but because as an old hand he resented the general attention paid to the opinions of a newcomer. The Digger had a prodigious memory, wax to receive, and marble to retain, and a flair for apt quotation that amounted almost to genius. His readiness in interlarding his conversation with quotations from authors, ancient and modern, persuaded Old Howlett that these were the gleanings of his daily reading, and not the treasures of a well-stored mind.

And very soon it became apparent that he was reporting the Digger for inattention to his work. The old man had no right to report anybody, but his position as an ex-solicitor, his age, and his service gave him a certain amount of standing with the warders, and anybody who incurred his animosity was pretty certain to suffer sooner or later at the hands of officialdom. The Librarian had evidently been well primed. He kept on telling the Digger that if the staff were not fully employed the Governor would very likely insist on a reduction, a measure which he would deplore, but to which he would be forced to consent. One day his reference to the matter was too personal to be avoided.

To our astonishment the Digger represented that he did his work as efficiently as anybody on the staff, that no complaints had been made by any of the Leaders, and that if he had half an hour to spare he could not do better than spend it in self-improvement. To Howlett's great mortification, the Librarian was prepared to sympathize with this point of view, and it was agreed that the Digger should always present the appearance of being busy, even if he were reading for his own pleasure.

One day, during Howlett's temporary absence, the Australian asked the Digger if he really thought the old man was a copper's nark. "Sir," answered the Digger, who had been browsing in Boswell's *Johnson*, "the soul of a delator resides in that ancient carcase, but a man of sense is not to be deflected from a reasonable course of conduct by the subterraneous machinations of a pettifogging ex-attorney!"

The Aussie, however, who took an inordinate interest in other people's business, disclosed that he knew of a way in which Howlett could be put in his place. A short-term prisoner, an ex-Cambridge rowing Blue, who had been convicted for driving dangerously while under the influence of drink, acted as Howlett's assistant in sewing dilapidated books. He was a reputedly wealthy man, and Howlett spent a good many hours describing in glowing terms the fortune that awaited the investor with enough courage and vision to put a trifling thousand pounds in one of his derelict companies.

As an aid to the good work he smuggled his copy of *The Times* into the library, and allowed the Cambridge Blue to read it surreptitiously. Of course, this would count as a serious offence, should the Aussie inform the Leader in charge, who could catch him in the act almost any morning. But the Digger spurned the suggestion. "No, no, Aussie," he said, "we might forget the existence of our wives, and go on marrying other women; we might divert the balances of employers or clients to our own uses; but we are not going to emulate the tactics of this pitiful old man, and blab to our gaolers. Here are two verses, which you might ponder with profit:

> If I should ever be in England's thought
> > After I die,
> Say there were many things he might have bought,
> > But did not buy.

> Unhonoured by his fellows, he grew old
> > And trod the path to Hell,
> But there many things he might have sold,
> > And did not sell.

"None of us is going to live in England's thought. That's a stone-cold certainty, but I wouldn't sell the mean and petty secrets of this old fraudulent curmudgeon for the thousand pounds he hopes to get from the Cambridge Blue. There are some things that are not done, and this is one of them."

The following week the Digger met trouble again through his passion for reading. Instead of resuming work after the half hour's break allowed to library assistants in the middle of the day, he carried on with a book, in which he had been absorbed for some time. And the book must have been funny, for he shook with suppressed laughter. At this stage, unfortunately, the Principal Officer of D Hall walked in, and stood motionless behind the Digger, who sat with his back to the door.

Whenever the Digger chuckled, which he did frequently, the Principal Officer nodded his head sagely, as if this was just the sort of thing he expected to find in the library, while the glint in his eye indicated that it was also the sort of thing he very definitely intended to stop. The comedy went on for half an hour, but we couldn't catch the Digger's eye, so engrossed was he in the confounded book.

At length the Librarian marched in, and when the Principal Officer had unfolded his story, the band played to some purpose. We all thought that this must surely be the prelude to the Digger's departure for another sphere of prison activities. Old Howlett was never so affable and happy. Later in the afternoon the Digger was called into a small office at the back of the library which the Librarian sometimes occupied. He emerged in about five minutes, with a broad grin on his face.

Instead of the sack he had received some kind of promotion, which entitled him to read without interference in the library. The Authorities relied for the replenishment of the library on gifts of books from prisoners' friends and relatives. But these books were read by the Librarian before they were allowed to pass

I

into general circulation. Precautions had to be taken to prevent the admission of salacious reading matter, or of anything which tended to glorify crime and the criminal.

Some prisoners had a habit of explaining to the magistrates that their second or third offence was due to something they had read in a prison library, just as pictures are frequently blamed to-day for juvenile crime. And the Librarian had handed over this censor's job to the Digger. It was one that suited him down to the ground. We were all mightily pleased with the issue of good out of evil, except old Howlett, who had been as lively as a cricket all that morning, and a banker by the name of Brice, whom the Digger had offended by comparing him with Beachcomber's "Red" Mullett, the gentleman who talks such portentous nonsense about gold. The Digger's new post did not, of course, prevent him from accompanying me on the daily round of the Halls.

The Skipper was anxious to know the name of the book that had caused so much bother. It turned out to be the letters of Sydney Smith, whom the Digger regarded as the wittiest Englishman of all time. For the Skipper's benefit he related a story of Smith, who, one day, in a narrow London street, saw a pair of harridans shouting at and abusing each other from opposite houses. "They will never agree," said Sydney to a friend who was with him. "What makes you think that?" asked the friend. "It's not possible," was the solemn answer; "they are arguing from different premises!"

But what the Digger was particularly interested in at the time was Sydney Smith's indignant criticism of the defaulting Southern American States, in whose loans he had sunk such a large part of his fortune. "All the arguments," said the New Zealander, "which are expounded by Smith with such telling effects are being used by the Americans themselves against Europe to-day. We hear the same nonsense about the sanctity of contracts, without the observance of which civilization collapses and dies, regardless altogether of the fact that an international debt is wholly different from one between individuals. America rightly refuses settlement in goods and services for the sake of her own industrial economy, but she also refuses to lend her favourable trade balance abroad. Instead, she persists in demanding gold. If we comply with her wishes, our credit structure must come toppling to the ground."

I expressed the view that London, with her great traditions for honesty, and the scrupulous fulfilment of contracts, would never fall down on her payments to the United States. "Don't be a fool," cried the Digger. "Is London going to bankrupt herself in a futile attempt to achieve the impossible? Despite all the solemn nonsense talked by orthodox bankers and their jackals, the City Editors, London's problem is a simple one. She has to choose between ruin and default, and Englishmen are not fools when compelled to face reality. Perhaps then we'll get rid of the gold bug, and turn our attention to devising a more rational monetary system."

CHAPTER X

IT was about this time that Hitler swept into power in Germany on a wave of hysterical national enthusiasm, and began his persecution of the Jewish race. There were about a hundred Jews in the Scrubs, and in D Hall each table had at least a couple of representatives. Hitler's brutal treatment created a great deal of excited discussion amongst them, but the general opinion was that he would be ultimately broken by the international money power, which, they claimed, was largely in Jewish hands.

There were no Jews in the library, but their synagogue was only a few yards away, and the dismal cries that issued from this building on a Saturday morning were, to say the least, depressing. The Skipper said they sounded like a crew of drunken sailors all singing independently. "If," he cried, "the Jews carry on like this in Wormwood Scrubs, what on earth must the Wailing Wall be like in Jerusalem, where they're at it all day and every day? No wonder the Arabs went berserk!"

We were at the door when the Jews issued from the temple, and they passed the library in Indian file, with caps and praying shawls. They certainly did not look a very prepossessing lot. No body of men did in prison garb. "What a mob!" murmured the Digger, watching them intently. "A few hundred honest British burghers must sleep sounder in their beds o' nights now these gentry have been rounded up!"

We chatted about Hitler's alleged intention of completely destroying the power and authority of the Jews in Germany. The Digger thought he would rue the day when he started the persecution of minorities, especially of Jewish minorities, who would command sympathy and support from influential circles in all countries. At the same time, no unprejudiced person could deny that the Jews were unpopular everywhere.

The Jew was never a producer. Who, for instance, ever heard of a Jewish farmer? He throve on the labour of others, and was always to be found amongst the middlemen. The Skipper inquired his definition of a middleman. "Disraeli's," was the answer. "A man who bamboozles one party, and plunders the other," and he devoted an agile brain and a ceaseless energy to the acquisition of wealth. To the Jew money did not talk, it screamed, and his control over money gave him control over the lives and destinies of others. This, combined with his cosmopolitanism, made the Jew an international danger.

Then, again, the Jew was exclusive and sometimes fanatical in his religious life, and perhaps we rather resented the insurmountable barriers he erected between himself and other people. The Jews were still the greatest practisers of usury in the world, a vice condemned by every great religion, including their own. They were blatantly vulgar in their outlook and habits, and they were certainly the most unscrupulous section of the community in business matters. There were some insurance companies, continued the Digger, who would not accept a Jewish risk in any circumstances. Burke had said that it was impossible to indict a whole nation, but these insurance companies, who were accustomed to assessing risks, and were unmoved by sentiment or prejudice, seemed to have succeeded in doing so.

"Then you approve of what Hitler is doing?" said the Skipper. "No, I don't," was the emphatic reply. "The Jew has as much right in the world as anyone else. He's entitled to the same measure of freedom to pursue his own happiness, but his ways are not our ways. Whenever he gets the chance himself, he's an oppressor of the worst kind, and I can never understand why the English Press should leap to his defence, as soon as he is even mildly criticized. The chorus of praise always seems to me to be inspired." The Digger said he had had occasion to look up Borrow the previous day, and he quoted Borrow's opinion of Jewish influence on the noble art of bruising:

But the greater number come just as they can contrive: on the tops of coaches, for example. And amongst these there are fellows with dark, sallow faces, and sharp, shining eyes: and it is these that have planted rottenness in the core of pugilism: for they are Jews, and true to their kind, have only base lucre in view. It was fierce old Cobbett, I think, who first said that the Jews first introduced bad faith amongst pugilists. He did not always speak the truth, but at any rate he spoke it when he made that observation. Strange people, the Jews—endowed with every gift but one, and that the highest, genius divine—genius which can alone make of men demi-gods, and elevate them above earth and what is earthly and grovelling. Without which a clever nation—and who more clever than the Jews?—may have Rambams in plenty, but never a Feilding nor a Shakespeare. A Rothschild and a Mendoza, yes—but never a Kean nor a Belcher.

"Now, after listening to this philippic against the chosen seed," said the Skipper, "I'm going to hazard a guess, Digger. You've been in the hands of the Jews at some time or other." "Don't I know it!" replied the

Digger, with feeling. "It's an experience I'm not going to discuss, but which I am not likely to forget, and I sympathize with all people, in all lands, on whose lives and fortunes the Jews have got their mudhooks."

The Skipper was anxious to continue the conversation, which had suddenly ceased, and gently quoted:

> It's odd
> That God
> Should choose
> The Jews. . . .

But the New Zealander was not to be drawn.

On the whole, relations between Jews and Gentiles in prison were friendly enough. During my time in the Scrubs I never encountered a single Jew who disdained to eat the flesh of the pig. Once a week at least bacon and beans figured on the menu. On these occasions the Jews were served with a special dish, but the Leader who did not give them a portion of the bacon and beans, which, as a rule, was a fairly liberal issue, was highly unpopular.

During their religious festivals, which were rigidly observed, the Jews were segregated, and ate together. Religious scruples demanded at the Passover that all pots and pans in which food had been cooked, and all the table utensils, should be entirely new. These articles were donated by some Jewish charitable society, and the prison stock of crockery was replenished from this source. Much to the Digger's disgust, but not to his surprise, he soon learnt that the Jew had an advantage, even in prison, over the Gentile malefactor. If a Jew's sentence expired on a Saturday, he was released on the Friday. Jews attended the synagogue on Saturday mornings, and made up for the time lost in the tailor's shop on Sundays.

Later that morning I had a fairly large number of young prisoners to attend to, and accompanied by the Digger and the Skipper set off for B Hall. Most of these lads were in prison for failure or refusal to pay trifling fines. It seemed a pity that they should begin their careers with the stigma of a prison sentence for something which could hardly be called a criminal offence. They were all at work in the Shops, with the exception of the new arrivals, who were busy scrubbing their cells.

Y.P.s were allowed a more liberal supply of books than adult prisoners, on the grounds that plenty of reading discouraged onanism.

It was a rule of the prison that a member of the library staff should not visit an occupied Y.P.'s cell alone. If the boy happend to be in, two librarians paid him a call with his books. The Skipper cursed the regulation heartily. He had done many things, and he had been accused of many things, but in his maddest moments he never dreamt that some day he might be suspected of taking advantage of a young lad in a prison cell.

That afternoon, when Fourth Stage men had been disposed of, we were discussing a prisoner in D Hall, who had been science master in a big English school. He frequently came to the library, but always maintained an air of studied coldness and aloofness. The Digger commented on his bloodless indifference to all and sundry, and said that he looked and spoke like a man who would peep and botanize upon his mother's grave.

The Skipper inquired if this remark were original, but the Digger attributed it to Wordsworth, whom he described as the third in the greatest line of poets ever produced in any country or any age. He was, in fact, never tired of talking of Wordsworth's soothing and healing power, but on this occasion he was bent on telling a story about the bard. Wordsworth, he said, was in his day looked upon as the white-haired boy of English literature. His moral character was above suspicion, and he himself could well remember the consternation with which the news was received that William in his youth had put a little French girl in the family way.

After the poet's death the usual society was formed to honour his memory, and at the first meeting someone read a letter, in which Wordsworth admitted that he had got drunk as an undergraduate. The old ladies in the audience could hardly believe their ears—Wordsworth drunk, impossible!—whereupon a waggish Don rose and said, soothingly: "Ladies and gentlemen, I beg of you not to take this confession too much to heart. I knew my Wordsworth, and I can assure you of this, that his standard of drunkenness was disgracefully low."

When the laughter had subsided, the Skipper said: "You've knocked back a few in your day, Digger. I suppose you had a private standard of your own, which you applied to yourself, and to nobody else. Most of us have, you know."

"Yes," replied the Digger, "it was a rough and ready measurement. If I fell down, and couldn't get up, I was drunk. If I entered the wrong train, over-ran the station, or attempted to get in my neighbour's house, I was just muddy, like Doctor Johnson's parson friend at Putney. On all other occasions I claimed to be sober."

A little later the talk drifted to the machine age, and the Digger, in order to illustrate a point, tried to quote Wordsworth's sonnet beginning with:

> The world is too much with us, late and soon
> Getting and spending, we lay waste our powers. . . .

For once his retentive memory failed him, and turning to me, he inquired irritably: "What on earth were those immortal lines of Wordsworth?" The little Cockney sign-writer had been listening to the conversation, and seized a rare and golden opportunity to help. To everybody's astonishment his shrill voice piped up with: "No article in this shop more than sixpence!"

A roar of laughter greeted this interjection, and the Digger, turning round, said: "By God, Cockney, you deserve something for that remark, and you're going to have half my toke!"

"I don't want your bleeding toke," squeaked the little fellow, "and there's nothing funny about what I said! I've been in their shops hundreds of times!"

I had another amusing experience with this signwriter, who was hopelessly ignorant of anything outside his work. One day the hospital orderly brought in a patient who wanted a copy of Defoe's *Journal of the Great Plague*. The book was on the shelf, but on entering up the particulars I noticed that the author's name on the back of the volume was given not as Defoe but as R. Crusoe. The Cockney was asked for an explanation. Without any hesitation he pointed to the preface in the *Journal*, in which the name of Defoe's immortal character frequently appeared in block letters. "There you are," he said, triumphantly, "that's the bloke who wrote it; only there wasn't room to print his full Christian name, and I had to use the initial."

That day the orderly from D Hall came in to summon the Skipper before the Governor. When he returned half an hour later we learnt that the censor had held back the last letter the Skipper had written to his wife, because he had had something sarcastic and uncomplimentary to say about the prison diet. The Skipper was told that he must reserve his criticism until he left prison, and was given another letter form, on which to make a second attempt.

The Digger advised him to stick to the letter and spirit of the regulations. "Well, I'm not like some people," retorted the Skipper. "I at least told the truth about their infernal treacle duff, and what's more, I told the truth about myself when I came in here." This was a thrust at the Digger, who like Moses had put himself down as Church of England, when he was in fact brought up in the Presbyterian faith. The discovery was made by the Chaplain, who found out that the Digger had not only never been confirmed, but had never been baptized.

The reason given by the Digger for his deception was that Church of England clergymen were gentlemen, who never descended to talking about such intimate things as religion and religious experiences. On top of that, they were so much concerned with the safety of their own souls that they never worried about anybody else's, and a man in the Army or in prison was seldom embarrassed by them with troublesome questions about his inner life.

The average Church of England person still retained some of the spirit which animated Lord Melbourne, who, after listening in disgust to a rousing Evangelical sermon, in which the preacher railed against sin in high places, stumped out of church indignantly exclaiming: "Things have come to a pretty pass, when religion is allowed to invade the sphere of private life!"

On the other hand, the Nonconformist minister was too often an inquisitive busybody. He wanted others to share his experience, and in his zeal to spread the Kingdom of God was inclined to meddle unduly with a gentleman's private affairs. "For these reasons, Skipper," the Digger continued, "in times of national and personal distress I have found it convenient to describe myself as a member of the Church of England."

The Skipper ventured the opinion that the Salvation Army, if by chance they had had the spiritual administration of Wormwood Scrubs, would have brought us all to the penitential form in no time. "You know how you feel when you come in here, Digger, as if the bottom of the world had dropped out. Do you think they would have missed an opportunity to catch us bending like that? Why, we should have been converted with flags flying and drums beating, before we knew what had happened."

"No, no," replied the Digger. "We're too old to be caught by mere noise and emotion."

"Not if a pretty lassie tried to convert you?" suggested the Aussie, slyly.

"No," retorted the Digger, with some severity, "but she could make a convert of you any day at a price!"

A few minutes afterwards I took the library party to the Part Worn Store. This was a weekly trip, and any man whose shoes were worn out, or whose garments did not fit, could exchange them for others. The Digger was wearing trousers that might have fitted a man twice his size, and he had firmly made up his mind to get an entirely new pair, well ironed and creased.

The officer in charge was not there when we arrived, and we were attended to by a little Welshman, a prisoner whose sentence was shortly expiring. The exchanges took some time, and I was busy trying on a pair of shoes when I heard a great commotion at the other end of the counter, and the Digger's voice raised in anger. He was calling the Welshman a damned, luxurious, mountain goat, and there looked like the beginnings of a first-class quarrel.

I intervened, to discover that the Digger had asked for a new pair of trousers, and had been told that he could have them the following week, but on condition that he brought with him half a toke. "Isn't it damnable?" cried the Digger, "we can't escape from bribery and corruption even in prison!"

I tried to reason with the Welshman, but he was adamant. "I'm not compelled to give this man another pair of trousers," he said. "The pair he's got," and he examined the Digger's legs critically, "are good enough for any prisoner" (the New Zealander winced visibly at this), "but I'm ready to change them next week on terms which I can't discuss before you."

The Digger, whose face was suffused with blood, was preparing to settle the argument in his own way, but I shoved him outside. On the way back to the library he cursed Welshmen in general, and this man in particular, for all he was worth. No wonder they were hated by English people, whose milk they watered daily! But he would get even with this lousy little Taffy!

He didn't, and he never got a change of trousers until he was made a Leader.

CHAPTER XI

THE DIGGER treated his new job of reading and criticizing new books with great seriousness, and his reports for the Librarian were constructed with meticulous care. Some books were dismissed in a few words, as, for instance, one written by an enterprising New York journalist on information supplied by a notorious gunman and murderer. "This," wrote the Digger, "is a bandit's *vade mecum.*" With others, whose merits as literary fare for prisoners were considered doubtful, he elaborated the arguments for and against at length, and left it to the Librarian to make a final decision.

At this period the Skipper was reading the *Decline and Fall of the Roman Empire* for the first time. He was tremendously impressed with Gibbon's stately diction, and was highly amused by the grave if perhaps unconscious humour of the great historian. One morning he quoted the famous passage on the younger Gordian, in which Gibbon says: "His manners were less pure, but his character was equally amiable with that of his father. Twenty-two acknowledged concubines, and a library of sixty-two thousand volumes, attested the variety of his inclinations: and from the productions which he left behind him, it appears that the former, as well as the latter, were designed for use rather than for ostentation."

The New Zealander assured him that he would presently encounter something funnier still in the description of Zenobia, where Gibbon says that she claimed descent from the Macedonian Kings of Egypt, equalled in beauty her ancestor Cleopatra, and far surpassed that princess in chastity and valour. "The humour," continued the Digger, "lies in the inevitable note. Here it is. 'She never admitted her husband's embraces but for the sake of posterity. If her hopes were baffled, in the ensuing month she reiterated the experiment.' " This quotation raised a loud laugh, which was hardly lessened when the Skipper exclaimed with great emphasis, "What a Fascist!"

I remarked that Gibbon presented something of an enigma. He had produced one of the most monumental works in English, or for that matter in any other language, and yet he was a mean, pettifogging character with the temperament of a fish. How different from Johnson, who was so much greater than anything he ever wrote!

"Yes," agreed the Digger, "Gibbon was as vain as a peacock, and as supercilious as the devil. Surely a man deserves a kicking who, when ordered by his father to give up a talented fiancée, for whom he expressed the highest devotion, solemnly records in his diary: 'I sighed like a lover. I obeyed like a son.' "

Somebody raised a question as to whether any modern author could approach Gibbon in the treatment of a lofty theme in a lofty style, and the Digger at once replied that his counterpart to-day was Winston Churchill. Old Howlett scoffed at this, but the Digger told him with some asperity that he could sneer as much as he liked. Winston was the greatest living master of sonorous English prose, and his name would go down to posterity as much for a great writer as a great statesman.

About four o'clock in the afternoon I had a visit from the tubby little warder in charge of the third landing in C Hall. He was a tiger for thriller, and I usually kept by me three or four of the latest, which he collected every

Friday. On this occasion he was shaking with laughter. It had been his day for visits, and he had been on duty for three hours in the room where Fourth Stage men met their friends and relatives.

A diminutive Cockney costermonger known to everybody as Harry had been the cause of his unwonted hilarity. Harry was a general favourite, and a model prisoner. Clean, alert, and humorous, he was never at a loss for an answer, and his fund of good spirits was inexhaustible. Every fortnight he was visited by his wife and two children, all neatly if inexpensively dressed. Harry had been in partnership with a friend called Bill Thomas, and on Harry's forcible removal from his place of business it was Bill's job to sell the assets, and present half the proceeds to Mrs. Harry.

Harry had been in prison a considerable time, as was evidenced by the fact that he had reached Fourth Stage, but nothing had been received from his partner, and this afternoon he fully expected to hear that the long-deferred payment had come to hand. But no, the same answer met his first question.

"Do you mean to tell me that Bill Thomas hasn't paid you yet?" he asked.—"Of course he ain't," replied his wife.—"Not a penny?" persisted Harry.—"Not a penny," echoed his wife.—"You're sure of that?"—"Of course I'm sure!" cried his wife petulantly, "he ain't given me a penny, and he ain't sold the donkey yet!"—"Well," said Harry with tremendous emphasis, pounding the table with his fist, "when I get out of this —— place, I'll gnaw his —— toenails off!"

As I said before, Harry was a model prisoner, and as far as we knew eschewed bad language altogether, but

Bill Thomas's procrastination, combined with the prison atmosphere, had got him down at last. When the warder had finished his story the tears were streaming down the Digger's face. "Is Bill Thomas a pacifist?" he inquired, wiping his face with his handkerchief. "I don't know," replied the officer, "but I couldn't see him sitting through that performance!"

After the warder's departure Howlett expressed surprise that we could find any cause for amusement in such a vulgar story, but both the Digger and the Skipper insisted that it was one of the funniest they had heard for a long time. The former said that it reminded him in some ways of one of the numerous stories told about W. S. Gilbert. Gilbert, who was something of a martinet, was present in the stalls at a rehearsal of the *Mikado*. Suddenly he shouted out: "There is a gentleman in the left set who is not holding his fan correctly!" A fussy Stage Manager came forward to explain that the symmetry of the set had been destroyed by the absence of one of the actors through illness. Gilbert listened patiently to the Stage Manager's rigmarole, and when he had finished remarked dryly: "Yes, yes, but that is not the gentleman I am referring to!"

The Digger said that the thought of a sick actor sitting by his fireside and holding a Japanese fan in his hand always amused him, but the picture of Bill Thomas undergoing a course of primitive chiropody was funnier still.

K

THE DIGGER passed through all his grades without a hitch, and a fortnight after reaching Fourth Stage was promoted to Leadership, and placed in charge of R table. There had been one or two changes, but most of my old associates were still there. I accompanied him to the Governor's office in D Hall to receive his Leader's band. The Governor, following the usual custom, informed the Digger that he had been recommended for promotion, and then said a few words on the responsibilities of Leaders, and the necessity for reporting all breaches of prison discipline without fear or favour. When the Hall Officer had placed a Leader's band on his arm, the ceremony was complete.

His first job in the new rôle was to take a party from D Hall to the tailor's shop, and I was told that when he arrived with his charges he bellowed "Three on, sir!" in such a stentorian voice that the disciplinary warder nearly fell off his high stool.

On his return to the library he was congratulated by everyone except Pelling, Howlett, and Brice—Pelling because he thought he ought to have been preferred on account of longer service, and the other two for personal reasons.

I was to succeed the Leader in Charge, whose sentence was shortly expiring. He was not a popular man, owing to his over-conscientiousness, a failing which the Digger declared was common amongst Christian Scientists. Our discussions on various topics outside the half-hour allotted for rest worried him. He could not bear to waste prison time.

One day the Digger picked up a *Christian Science Journal*, glanced at it, and quoted Dean Inge's observation that Christian Science was neither Christianity nor science. This elicited the retort that the worthy Dean was notoriously deficient in spiritual understanding, and could not be expected even dimly to comprehend the deep truths of being as revealed by Mrs. Mary Baker Eddy.

At this point the Digger was sent for to conduct a prisoner from B Hall to the Catholic priest's room. On his arrival at the Hall the officer on duty said that he would have to wait a few minutes, as the prisoner was attending bathing parade. The warder suggested that the man in question was a queer sort of customer. "He's a Norwegian Catholic," he added suspiciously, as if that accounted for any peculiarity.

"Well," replied the Digger, "he bears the prosaic name of Smith, which doesn't appear to have any connexion with Norway, and for all I know a Norwegian Catholic holds the same views as an English or an Irish Catholic."

But the officer insisted that Norwegian Catholics were in a pen by themselves, and were different in some mysterious way from any other brand of Catholic.

"You don't mean, I suppose, that this fellow is a Swedenborgian?" inquired the Digger.

"That's it!" cried the warder, slapping his thigh. "I'd clean forgotten his head-line. A Swedenborgian, that's what he is!"—and his tone of voice indicated that a Swedenborgian must be a good deal more peculiar in his outlook than a Norwegian Catholic. The officer wanted to know the basis of the Swedenborgian faith, which the Digger explained readily enough. As a result of their

talk he returned to the library with an order for Sweden-
borg's *Heaven and Hell*. "If the screw can read this
without skipping, and understands only half of it, he
deserves a better job," commented the Digger.

With the departure of the Leader in Charge, I moved
up to the top, and the Digger took over my duties. He
retained his job as reader of new books, and had charge
of the "smasher" counter during the daily change for
Fourth Stage men. I can remember his first day on the
smasher counter, which was always besieged by jostling
men.

A prisoner pushed his way through the mass and confronted the Digger, who was being assailed from all sides.
"Huh, huh, huh," he began, but he could get no farther.
An inquiry for his name produced the same result. It
was obvious that the poor devil was a confirmed stam-
merer. The Digger demanded his library card, ascertained his name, and invited him to put his request in
writing. Harris snatched a piece of paper and wrote painfully and laboriously upon it. He handed his effort to
the Digger, who read it with eyebrows raised. "Well, I'm
damned!" he exclaimed. "After all this trouble he wants
Bunyan's *Pilgrim's Progress*, and from the smasher counter,
too! Here, Harris, my lad, you're in the wrong department.
You'll find this book in the Travel Section." And off
Harris would have gone, to make a prolonged and futile
search of the books on travel had I not intercepted him
and shown him where to find what he wanted.

Two librarians left at the same time as the Christian
Science Leader, and their places were taken by a young
man from the Part Worn Stores, and an ex-Salvation
Army captain, who was known to everyone as the

General. The Digger had taken an interest in the young-ster from the Stores, who had a taste for serious reading, and had gone to some trouble to select the right type of book for him. In return he received every week in his clothing change, not a clean pair of socks, but a brand new pair, and when the vacancy arose he spoke to the Librarian and the transfer was arranged.

The young man, whose name I have forgotten, very soon gave us a full account of the affair which had brought him to Wormwood Scrubs. He was born in the provinces, of churchgoing people, and at an early age he sought and obtained a job in London.

He regularly attended church in the suburb in which he lived, and before long became friendly with a middle-aged widow, who took an interest in the younger members of the congregation. Every Sunday afternoon he visited the good lady's house for tea, after which they attended the evening service together. One day the banns were read out for two young people, who moved in the same set, and during the ceremony the widow turned and whispered that she did not see why their names should not be coupled together in the same way.

The idea of marriage with anybody had never entered the boy's head, but he was far too nervous and inexperi-enced to tell the old fool where she got off, and when she repeated the idea he was afraid of hurting her feelings, and foolishly nodded his assent. The lad was nineteen and the woman fifty years of age.

Within a week or two the parson was reading their banns, and in due course the marriage took place. But just before the ceremony the boy plucked up courage to tell his people what was happening. They were too late to stop the wedding, but they saw their son's employers, who arranged to transfer him temporarily to another branch in the country. As soon as the ceremony in church was over the bridegroom packed his bags and caught a train from Paddington.

"Do you mean to tell me," the Aussie intervened, "that you went straight home, packed your bags, and then got on a train, your wife expecting you to join her later?"

The youth nodded in the affirmative.

His father met him at his destination and took him home. He never saw his employers again, nor did he ever see or communicate with his wife. A month or two later he secured another post in a small town near London, where, after three or four years, he met and fell in love with a girl of his own age. They were quietly "married," but when a child was about to appear he decided to make a clean breast of his past.

The girl promptly forgave him, but, like a sensible person, insisted that he must go farther, and tell the police. The police, of course, charged him with bigamy, but they were certain that if he pleaded guilty the sentence of the court would be a purely nominal one, and should the old baby-snatcher prove amenable to reason the couple could marry and live happily ever afterwards.

The police were good enough to explain matters to his employer, who promised that whatever happened his job would be kept open for him. And so everything seemed set for a quick and happy solution to all his troubles.

His wife appeared in Court, and gave evidence as to the marriage. He disappeared on the wedding day, she declared, and had never supported her since, but there was nothing malicious or vindictive in the old lady's attitude. She behaved and spoke as if she realized that she was in a very large measure responsible for the boy's regrettable position, but to everybody's surprise the Judge professed to take a very serious view of the case. The crime of bigamy was far too prevalent, and the leniency extended to offenders in the past had no doubt encouraged many people to take risks.

It was true that there was a great disparity between the ages of accused and his wife, and that he was only a boy when he contracted marriage, but he had grown to man's estate when he committed bigamy, and the Judge did not intend to let sentiment interfere with his duty. The young man would go to prison for twelve months in the second division.

It was a stunning sentence, and his first act on arriving at the Scrubs was to interview the Governor with a view to lodging an appeal. The latter pointed out that the outcome of an appeal was prejudiced by the plea of guilty. However, before our friend had recovered from the shock, or could take any steps to have his sentence reviewed, word came through that the Judge of his own volition had reduced the term to nine months, which was still a pretty savage punishment, considering the circumstances of the marriage.

One of the strongest impressions acquired through contact with all sorts of men in Wormwood Scrubs was that the police were far too prone to advise accused persons to plead guilty, even when there were grounds for a reasonable defence. It was alleged not by one prisoner, but by dozens, that they had been persuaded to plead guilty, not only as the result of representations that the strain and expense of a lengthy trial would thereby be avoided, but because the police had guaranteed that only the lightest sentences would be inflicted. I do not know how far police officers are personally interested in securing convictions, but it seems to me that they should be prohibited from offering advice to accused persons as to how a criminal charge should be met. And I think it is wrong to induce people to plead guilty by holding out the hope of the lightest punishment.

A propos of this practice, a little Jew in D Hall frequently amused us with the story of his conviction. He had stolen a trombone from a Salvation Army bandsman, and on the issue of a warrant he had disappeared from his usual haunts in the East End. As a matter of fact, he eluded capture for nearly two years. The crime was not a very serious one, but he had unfortunately been in the hands of the police before for minor offences. The arresting officers advised him, however, that if he pleaded guilty the case would be dealt with leniently, owing to the lapse of time: he might be imprisoned until the rising of the Court, but certainly not longer.

For some reason or other the Jew had also founded great hopes on the magistrate, who two days before the disposal of the case had married a girl young enough to be his daughter. The trial was soon over, but the newly wedded magistrate did not behave with the generosity one usually associates with happy bridegrooms. He spoke severely of the Jew's past, and to the latter's consternation sentenced him to twenty-one days' hard labour— twenty-one days, when he thought he would be returning home a free man that evening! But the shock was nothing to what he received on arrival at Wormwood Scrubs, where he learnt for the first time that the magistrate had imposed a sentence not of twenty-one days but of twenty-one months! This little fellow had an extraordinarily mobile and comical face, and he used to send us into fits of laughter when he depicted himself taking the knock at the hands of the Reception Warder.

The General was a man of unusual type. He was always cheerful and polite, and his desperate eagerness to please everybody was really embarrassing. We knew, of course, from the newspaper reports, what had brought him to the Scrubs. He had occupied an administrative post with the Salvation Army, but had acquired a taste for night clubs and loose women.

These dubious amusements had driven him into debt, a situation from which he endeavoured to extricate himself by helping himself to Army funds, and falsifying the accounts to cover up his trail.

The General spoke quite freely of his escapades, and with such gusto that there was little doubt he had thoroughly enjoyed his experience of the world, the flesh, and the devil. At the same time he was one of the most devout worshippers in the prison. The Digger was particularly interested to hear from the General's own lips of his association with women of easy virtue, declaring that Army people were, as a rule, so immaculate that this sort of thing restored one's faith in human nature.

When the General came to the point where a warrant was issued for his arrest, the Digger suggested that drastic action of that kind against an erring brother was surely contrary to Army principles. "Instead of taking it to the Lord in prayer," he said, "they seem to have taken it to the charge-sergeant in the nearest police station!" But the General was nothing if not fair. He had, he said, not only falsified the books, but had kept them in his possession, and refused or neglected to give them up after repeated demands. Had he been sane and reasonable there would have been no prosecution.

I have said that the General was an enthusiastic church-goer, joining heartily in the singing, and reciting the prayers with all the fervour of a convert. He took Communion with the Nonconformists, but his religious outlook recognized no boundaries. Before very long he had joined the Church of England, and was confirmed with seven others, including a Zulu Chief, by the Bishop of Willesden. The confirmation took place at a special service in the church one afternoon at four o'clock, which all prisoners were free to attend.

The Skipper asked him if he looked upon his confirmation as a double assurance against damnation, but the General was really not anxious about the safety of his own soul. His wife, it appears, was a lady of gentle birth, and had never been quite at home in the fold of the Salvation Army. Like Huxley, she rather despised this corybantic form of Christianity. They were all too matey and noisy for one of her training and education. She had been deeply wronged, and the General thought that the least he could do by way of reparation was to become a member of a Church which, whatever its faults, had the great merits of gentility and respectability.

Some of the General's Army friends nearly got him into trouble soon after his admission to the library. They were members of a visiting brass band, and when they spotted the General amongst the audience there was much excited whispering, and a great waving of hands, to which the General enthusiastically responded. Presently a burly

warder stood at the end of his pew. "Come on, you!" was
the gruff order, and to the consternation of the band the
General was led away to his cell, and told that if he did
not behave as a prisoner he would never see or hear an
Army band for nine months.

He worked under the Digger's directions, and the only
hitch in their relations occurred through the General's
anxiety to please. If he were asked to get a book from
the other end of the library he did it at the double, and
if a chair happened to be in the way he would have no
hesitation in knocking it down. "Look here," growled
the Digger irritably, "this isn't an Army prison camp.
Take your own time, as long as you don't take all day,
but for God's sake stop this bull-in-a-china-shop
business. It's not dignified enough for the Scrubs!" But
the General was incurable.

Prisoners generally traded on his good nature. He was
the willing prey of all those who wanted the latest and
most popular books, and the whole of his spare time in
the evenings was spent in booking orders on toilet paper.
The Digger soon found that his ordinary sources of
supply for the smasher counter were running dry, and
when the cause of the deficiency was located the General
was on the mat. The Digger recommended that he should
limit his good turns to one or two a day. "If everybody
in the library imitated your example," he said, "the whole
organization would collapse." There was an improvement
for a little while, but the General could not resist an
appeal from any source, and all the time I was there he
was constantly in hot water for infringing the library
regulations.

The General was a great advocate for keeping out of

debt. He traced his downfall to the time when he began to spend a little more than his income, and hadn't the courage to change his mode of living.

Debt, according to him, was the great disintegrator of morality, and the worst and most humiliating of all the tyrannies that plagued mankind. The Digger heartily agreed with him, and declared that if a man failed to grasp the nettle boldly at the beginning he was bound to get badly stung in the end. "I have known the time," he said, "when I had to look cautiously out of the front window, and then out of the back one, before pulling the lavatory chain. It was a state of siege. If there are children the situation is worsened ten thousand times. They hear their parents telling lies to pressing creditors of the tradesman class, and they might even be called upon to play a part in the same dirty business."

The General related how, when his financial affairs reached a stage of acute crisis, he was compelled to adopt all sorts of petty subterfuges in order to avoid people who were calling for money, such as leaving by the back door and making long, roundabout detours to the railway-station. Even then he might spot a bailiff's man waiting to waylay him, and he would be compelled to duck and dive down side streets to escape being accosted. "We've been through it, too, General," said the Digger sympathetically.

The General was soon on the friendliest terms with Holy Joe, an officer who had recently been transferred to Wormwood Scrubs to act as understudy for the Chief Officer. Holy Joe, as he was known to everybody, was the mildest mannered and most benevolent fellow that ever donned a warder's uniform, and the consuming

ambition of his life was to bring his fellows to a knowledge of the love of Christ. Holy Joe treated all prisoners
with kindness, even affection, and he never missed an
opportunity for pressing the claims of his Master.

He was universally liked for his gentleness and his
transparent sincerity, but sometimes his forbearance was
actually the means of getting men into trouble. I remember one occasion, when half a dozen Fourth Stage men
were cased for toasting bread on the hot embers outside
the bakehouse, which flanked the quadrangle where
Fourth Stage men exercised. They had done this many
times under the eyes of Holy Joe, but this Sunday morning
they were sighted by the bakehouse P.O. Back they went
to C Hall to start again at the bottom rung of the ladder.

The General and he were always swopping religious
experiences, and frequently we were drawn into the
discussion, for Holy Joe was always ready to snatch a
brand from the burning. He belonged to a sect called the
Four Square Gospellers, whose adherents apparently
believe in the literal truth of the Scriptures.

A big convention had been held at the Albert Hall.
Large numbers of supporters came up from the provinces, and the train in which they travelled collided
with another train on the outskirts of London. There
were a good many casualties, and some fatalities, but
although Four Square Gospellers were in a numerical
majority, strange to say not a single one was injured!
Holy Joe proudly ascribed their immunity to the special
protection of God.

"Do you really think, sir," said the Digger, "that they
were saved because they were Four Square Gospellers?"

"Well, Leader," replied Holy Joe, "it's like this. God

has a plan of salvation for man as revealed in the Bible, every word of which is true. We accept the salvation so freely offered: we believe with all our hearts, and by so doing we escape the wrath to come."

"Yes, I see all that," answered the Digger, "but apparently you also escape from the calamities which every now and again overwhelm the ordinary run of mankind!"

"Not altogether," admitted Holy Joe. "These were true believers on their way to a great demonstration of the true faith, and God in His goodness would not deprive them from sharing in such a blessing."

"And so," continued the Digger, to our horror, "He said: The Four Square Gospellers must get to Albert Hall, and it's wooden overcoats for the R.C.s, the C. of E.s, and the others."

But Holy Joe's feelings were unruffled. He pitied the Digger and those like him who had not made their peace with God, and he went on to emphasize the shortness of our earthly journey, and the necessity for repentance before it was too late. And when he had finished his say he gazed benignantly round the room, as if hoping for some evidence that our hardened hearts had been touched, said "Good morning, everybody!" and continued on his rounds.

"He's not so well," said the Aussie, as soon as Holy Joe had gone. "I don't know," answered the Digger. "The main thing is that he's supremely happy and supremely confident, and that's a frame of mind that most of us would give anything to acquire."

The Skipper suggested that somehow Christianity had the strange and unique power of transforming some men's lives, and the Digger agreed. There was something in the life and death of Christ, he argued, which gripped the imagination and the hearts of men, something which could change sinners into saints almost in the twinkling of an eye. No other great character had the same influence. Socrates, for instance, was both great and virtuous. His death, as described by Plato, was one of the noblest episodes in human history, but no one has ever given up the world because Socrates lived and died gloriously.

The Skipper sought an explanation of the phenomenon that while the Church as a whole had practically no influence on the conduct of men and affairs to-day, the Founder of Christianity still remained the most tremendous and interesting personality of all time. Ten thousand years hence, he said, men would still be asking the question, "What think ye of Christ?"

The Digger's idea was that once you began to organize religion the spirit of the thing departed. Christianity to-day was organized into a vast business, which had far too much truck with the world and the devil. Its leaders spent the best part of their time in fighting over the words of Christ, and they all differed to such an extent that Nietzsche was justified when he said: "There was only one Christian and He died on the Cross."

"Or Tom Paine's gibe," interjected the Skipper, "Christ died on the Cross, and thousands have lived on it ever since."

The Skipper suggested that the Digger, with all his latitudinarianism, was really a confounded Puritan at heart. But the Digger protested that Puritanism was as obnoxious to him as to the Skipper. The Puritans had only substituted one tyranny, a good deal bleaker, for another.

Butler, in his *Hudibras*, had accurately portrayed the unchanging character of the Puritan:

> Compound for sins they are inclined to,
> By damning those they have no mind to,
> Still so perverse and opposite
> As if they worshipped God for spite.

Hell must be infinitely preferable to a Puritan heaven, but he suspected that the Almighty had some use for them in small numbers as a check on licence and libertinism.

"Well," observed the Skipper, "you're as big an enigma as the General. He's a member of the Salvation Army, takes communion with the Nonconformists, has now been confirmed in the Church of England, and is casting longing eyes at Holy Joe's fraternity. I'll defy a bush lawyer to determine his exact status in the Christian picture: he is, in fact, a sort of composite Christian; but you seem to believe in the Founder of Christianity, while condemning all his followers.

"Perhaps that is a fair statement of the position," the Digger assented, "but no one can study the New Testament without realizing that its teaching is the most revolutionary thing in the world. On the other hand, who has ever met a revolutionary Christian?"

CHAPTER XIII

EVERY man who sat at table in D Hall had the right to bring any grievance to the notice of his table Leader, whose duty it was to lay the complaint before the Leaders' Committee, which met every Sunday afternoon. The Skipper was in something of a dilemma, because he nursed a grievance, apparently shared by others, against his own Table Leader, who could hardly be expected to report himself.

This gentleman worked in the carpenter's shop. He was middle aged, and had spent all his life in the City as a company promoter. His appetite was prodigious, and the prison fare which tickled his palate most was treacle pudding, which appeared on the menu every eight or nine days. This treacle pudding was as sticky as the composition used by a dentist for taking an impression. I have seen men with something like fear in their eyes after they had closed their teeth forcefully on a slab of treacle pudding, and found that they were unable to open their jaws again. But it was filling, and it was sweet, and the Skipper's Leader invariably dealt himself the most liberal share. Nobody had the courage to point out the obvious disparity, and the Leader himself was blandly indifferent to the indignant glances of the table generally, who felt that they were being "carved up." Would the Digger or myself bring the matter to the notice of the Leaders' Committee?

The answer, of course, was in the negative. The Skipper's only remedy was to appeal to the officer on duty in D Hall. The only snag lay in the certainty that he would be cased if his ration came up to the regulation weight, and he was not prepared to run the risk.

The Digger declined to take the complaint seriously, and suggested to the Skipper that he ought to treat the situation as Gilbertian. "Here's a fellow," he said, whom the newspapers describe as a City magnate. He attended palatial offices in tail coat and top-hat, and he's spent the whole of his life in the legitimate but rather ludicrous business of snatching intermediate profits. Even in prison there are opportunities in a small way for the exercise of his peculiar talent, but because you see the trick done before your eyes, you adopt this dog-in-the-manger attitude. If he netted £100,000 from the public in exactly the same way, you would call him a clever fellow, a Napoleon of finance, but when it's a question of treacle pudding, you cut up rough." The Skipper, however, could not see the analogy, and refused to be comforted.

There was another Leader in D Hall from the City, who periodically aroused the ire of his fellow-diners in much the same way, but his weakness was carrots, for which he had the inordinate fondness of a donkey. The sight of these one-time financiers, who had lived in affluence, and had been envied by many, taking advantage of their position as Leaders to deprive their fellows of treacle pudding and carrots, certainly had its amusing side. In prison, however, such behaviour was regarded as a serious lapse from decency, and caused much grumbling and discontent.

The Digger had lost one or two men at R table, but their places were, of course, immediately filled. In the re-shuffle he had taken the opportunity to appoint as deputy table Leader a man in the bakery known as

Scotch Bob. Scotch Bob was of Herculean proportions with a great hairy chest like a baboon. I don't think anybody ever understood his speech, not even the Digger, but the latter always swore that Scotch Bob was the best and most diligent Deputy in the Hall, and that he wouldn't change him for a thousand pounds.

But Bob did not reign many weeks in his new post. He was a fighting man with a fiery temper, and in all the prison boxing championships Bob entered amongst the heavyweights. One day a new man, also of a truculent and reckless turn of mind, joined the baking squad. There were words between the two, and words led to blows.

In a few minutes the newcomer was being carried off to hospital with a broken jaw, and Bob returned to C Hall to start life afresh, and with a fortnight more to serve. The man with the broken jaw, however, had every reason to thank Bob for his attentions, for he spent the whole of his three months' sentence in the infirmary next door, where there were no restrictions on smoking, and where he could see his friends almost every day.

In due course Bob returned to D Hall, and was immediately reinstalled as the Digger's Deputy, a position which he kept—precariously, it is true—during the remainder of his term.

Another newcomer to the Digger's table was a professional smash-and-grab raider of the Jewish persuasion. He was quite young, and in addition to a twenty months' sentence for his part in the raid, in which a policeman had been overawed with a loaded revolver, the Judge had also ordered him a birching.

This Jew was a man of small stature, with a face as

yellow as a guinea. He was tremendously active, both physically and mentally, and a constant source of trouble to the prison authorities. Time and again he was stripped and searched for contraband. We all knew that he was smuggling tobacco. He openly boasted of his ability to outwit the warders, but although he was under constant observation, and was stripped after nearly every open visit, the officers could find nothing on him.

However, their persistence at last had its reward. One morning two warders suddenly pounced upon him in the shoe shop, and there was a quarter of a pound of tobacco in his pocket. He was returned to C Hall, and lost two weeks' remission.

About this time the newspapers were full of reports of a case in which a firm of diamond merchants were implicated. One of their travellers had been assaulted by two bandits, and robbed of £7,000 worth of stones. The insurance companies had refused to pay the loss, alleging that the robbery was a frame-up, and that the whole business had been staged by the traveller.

The Jew assured us that the allegation of the insurance companies was correct. He himself had been approached through a third party to carry out the job, and, in his own words, he had "submitted a quotation" for £600. The traveller considered this price too high, and he eventually found two men who were willing to rob him for £250.

The Jew ran two cars, and his working day began at midnight. A younger brother, a lad of sixteen, assisted him, but he was captured in the same smash-and-grab raid, and was serving a sentence as a Y.P. in B Hall. I inquired once if the birching was a very terrible experience, but he affected to treat it as child's play, and assured me that it need cause no worry to a man of ordinary physique. The Digger was not sorry to lose the Jew from his table. His general behaviour was good, but his contraband activities were a constant source of worry.

I myself was not altogether happy with my own table companions at the time. A gentleman by the name of Australian Marshall had recently joined the board. He was a boxer by profession, and could use his fists to some purpose, but he was the best-tempered fellow in the world, with a grin on his face which never came off. Marshall's weakness lay in his complete disregard for everybody in authority.

The first time I saw him he was being marched by a warder from Reception to C Hall. Marshall was not familiar with the route, and when he arrived at two cross-roads he turned to the officer and casually asked: "Which way, brother?"—"Don't call me brother!" roared the warder.—"Now don't get all hot and bothered," replied Marshall, with the air of a nurse reproving a naughty child, "I'm new to this neighbourhood, and if you don't know the way, we're lost!"

Within six months Marshall had lost all his remission marks. He was neither vicious nor violent, but wherever there was mischief afoot, there was he to be found also. One of his favourite dodges was to set up an infernal cacophony during the singing of the hymns in church. He would sing hopelessly out of tune, and break into little trills up and down the scale, with occasional bursts of yodelling, to the great delight of prisoners in his immediate vicinity.

The general laughter and sniggering naturally had the

effect of attracting the attention of the warders seated
at the back of the church. Down the aisles they would
come, searching for the master of discord, but by the
time they arrived within striking distance, Marshall
would be singing as sweetly and innocently as an angel.

He caused a great deal of fun when he appeared before
the Prisoner's Aid Society, just before his discharge.
He was asked if he had any money, and answered in
the negative. The Committee intimated that they would
be prepared to pay his fare home. Marshall at once
became all interest, and asked for confirmation on
that point.

The Chairman assured him that it was their usual
practice with prisoners who were destitute, or had
brought no money in with them. "By the way," he continued, "where do you live?"—"Melbourne," replied
Australian Marshall, and the offer was hastily withdrawn.

It was my painful duty to administer daily reproofs
to Marshall, who habitually acted on the principle that
regulations were made for slaves, and that barring prison
walls he was the freest man alive, but somehow or other
he managed to escape serious trouble whilst under my
tutelage. His happy-go-lucky attitude to life made him
extremely popular with the men, and we were all pleased
to see in the newspapers that he had won an important
fight a few weeks after his departure from the Scrubs.

Another and more serious problem was a Zulu Chief
who had been posted to my table. The introduction of
a black man to D Hall was, I gathered, an innovation,
and I doubt if the experiment was successful enough to
warrant a repetition. The Zulu was a person of some
education, at least, he spoke English fluently and cor-

rectly. He boasted of his literary knowledge and taste, and ranked Mrs. Henry Wood as the greatest of all literary artists.

His contempt for the white illiterates around him was unbounded. Normally he would have begun and ended his sentence in C Hall, but owing to his superior education, and possibly to the fact of his confirmation by the good Bishop of Willesden, the authorities permitted his transfer to D Hall to live in association with whites.

The Zulu proved an unmitigated nuisance. The men resented his gratuitous attempts to teach them their own language. He wasn't quite skilful enough to detect every grammatical error, but none within his own compass was allowed to pass uncorrected, and he took no pains to conceal his supreme contempt for his unwilling pupils.

Very soon there were murmurings that the "black bastard" would have to mind his p's and q's, or run the risk of assault and battery. I judged the moment opportune to remind the Zulu that even if he were a master of English there was an equally important subject about which he apparently knew nothing, and that was politeness. As long as he sat at my table he would respect the feelings of others, or take the consequences, and if he wanted to play the part of pedagogue, he might do it in a South African kraal, but not in Wormwood Scrubs.

The upshot was that he transferred his attentions to me, and from that time onwards he pretended that his rations were always short, and that an unfair discrimination was exercised against him on account of his colour. Unfortunately I could not persuade him to carry his complaint to the Hall Officer, but he daily voiced his indignation against the unjust treatment he was supposed to receive, and when the men advised him to put a sock in it he threatened one or two with physical violence.

Our South African journalist associate in the library was particularly pleased with the way things had turned out. According to him the only good niggers were dead ones, and he had predicted from the start that if the Zulu were treated on an equality with white men he would lose his head and get out of hand.

His usual question to me was: "Well, how's your nigger? Does one black make half a white?" And in the end I had to confess that it didn't. Before he came to D Hall I had been much impressed with the Zulu's reverential behaviour in church, a piece of *naïveté* which greatly amused the Digger.

At every service the big negro was the last man in the C Hall queue. All the other inhabitants of the prison were already in their places. Instead of following his comrades down the aisle, he turned sharp left, halted before the altar in full view of the whole congregation, and then made a most profound obeisance, after which he took up a position in the middle of the church.

Candidly I admired the man's courage, but the Digger told me not to be a fool. "Self-consciousness," he said, "is the curse of civilization. It hardly exists amongst natives. This fellow isn't plucky in the sense that we use the word. Don't run away with the idea that he's standing up for Jesus. The probabilities are that he has no convictions in the matter at all, but what *is* of the utmost importance to him is that a thousand pairs of eyes are trained on him the moment he makes his genuflection. And he's as proud as Punch about it. As soon as the audience loses interest in his antics, he'll drop this

bowing and scraping, and behave like the rest of us."
And sure enough, within a month, his obeisances had
degenerated into mere nods, and within two months he
was walking straight to his pew. I had to endure the
presence of this black man until his release.

There was another man at my table with whom it was
difficult to preserve friendly relations. He was convicted
for a series of frauds on the Post Office Savings Bank,
in which the whole family took a hand. The Judge held that
his wife was the moving spirit in the crime, and she was
sentenced to a longer term of imprisonment in Holloway.

This man was the foxiest-looking customer I have ever
seen, and with his mutton-chop whiskers he bore a strong
resemblance to the butler on the Kensitas cigarette packets.
His conversation was always filthy and disgusting.

One evening, a night or two before this man's discharge, the Digger visited my table after tea, and was
just in time to hear a very lurid account of what he
intended to do on his first visit to Holloway Prison.
The Digger listened, disgust written all over his face,
and then he observed dryly: "You evidently expect
a very open visit!"

There was a loud laugh at this from the other men,
but the gentleman with the mutton-chop whiskers
jumped to his feet, and exhorted the Digger to mind his
own bloody business, or he would have the extreme
pleasure of punching a Leader before he left Wormwood
Scrubs. "Courage is the last quality one expects from
cads," replied the Digger quietly, "and the threats of
a man who can talk as you do about his wife wouldn't
put a louse in fear. Come on!" he added to me, "let us
get away from this atmosphere."

Curiously enough, Nemesis overtook this man the very next morning. He lived two cells away from me. Between us was a burly individual named Whittington, with the disposition of a rogue elephant. A few minutes after opening up, the butler fellow passed my door, jerry in hand, on his way back from the washing-place. The next door cell was ajar, but instead of going straight to his own cubby hole he rapped smartly on Whittington's door, pushed it open, and ceremonially announced in a firm and precise voice, after the approved fashion of butlers, "Your coffee, sir!"

There was a sound of muffled curses and scuffling within, and the next moment my table companion appeared with startling rapidity, as if he had been propelled from a gun. His jerry was flung after him. Before he could pick himself up there was a shout from the officer on the opposite side of the next landing. "Stand fast, you," roared the warder. It was a fair catch. Entering another man's cell was considered a very serious offence, and this man, instead of going home in two days' time, was returned to C Hall for another week. We never saw him again.

One of the most picturesque men in the prison was a gypsy by the name of Smith, who sat at my table. Smith wore an enormous quiff, which came well down over the bridge of his nose, and then curled upwards like a wave breaking on a coral reef. He was tremendously proud of this hirsute decoration; how he had trained his hair to keep its position was a mystery to everybody.

The love of Smith's life was horse flesh, and he talked horses from morning till night. He was, of course, in Wormwood Scrubs for giving free rein to his fancy for other people's horses. The picture of a thoroughbred would send him into ecstasies. The Digger, who was also an expert horseman, insisted that Smith was merely the victim of imagination, and quoted Josh Billings in support of his contention:

Imaginashun, tew much indulged in, soon is tortured into reality: this is the way that good hoss thiefs are made. A man leans over a fence all day, and imagines the hoss in the lot belongs to him, and sure enough, the fust dark night, the hoss does.

Smith was a man of exemplary behaviour, and the close confinement, which is popularly supposed to break a gypsy's spirit and health, had no perceptible effect upon him.

Life in the library proceeded with all the regularity and monotony of fixed routine, but cheerfulness kept breaking in, and every day brought its amusing interlude. Pelling had been removed from us temporarily through illness, and had returned to find that his job with the paste-brush had been filled by another man. This caused him quite a lot of heartburning. Curious how trifles assume such gigantic proportions in prison!

I have forgotten what Pelling's occupation was in civil life, but amongst other things he had been chairman of a branch of the British Legion, or some other kindred organization.

Pelling had passed the half-century, but instead of settling down to the humdrum existence of the middle aged, he began to sow a belated crop of wild oats, and even indulged in the luxury of a mistress. Monetary difficulties inevitably supervened, and rather than abandon an illicit and expensive love-affair, he conceived the idea of paying out benefits to non-existent members of his Society and putting the money into his own pocket.

In this little scheme he was aided and abetted by an obliging secretary, also a denizen of D Hall, who was known to everybody as Tom. Mrs. Pelling was fully cognisant of the illegal methods by which their slender income was being augmented, but as she fondly believed that the proceeds of the fraud were being put away for a rainy day, she did not raise any active opposition to her husband's delinquency.

But her attitude changed electrically when she discovered that Pelling, instead of leading a sober and thrifty life, had actually been pouring his treasure into foreign laps: that he had, in fact, squandered the whole of his ill-gotten gains on a little lady with whom he had been in the habit of spending week-ends in Boulogne.

Without waiting for explanations or appeals for forgiveness, she dashed to the nearest police station and uncovered the whole conspiracy. Pelling was positively ugly in appearance. He was bald, deaf, and short of one eye, so that he must be accounted fortunate to have captured the heart of a pretty woman of twenty-five.

He was so proud of his conquest that he welcomed any reference to it, a sport in which the Skipper and the Digger frequently indulged. On fine days the Skipper, when he felt in the mood, would rise stiffly from his chair, walk to the window, and gaze for a moment or two at the cloudless sky. Addressing nobody in particular, he would remark: "Perfect day for a little sea-trip."

This was the Digger's cue. "Can't imagine anything better than a trip to Boulogne," he would say. "A nice little bit of fluff, the weather, the motion of the ship, the pressure of a little hand, and the prospect of favours to come. Well, ask yourself."

Pelling was deaf to most things, but his ears were attuned to the magic word Boulogne. As soon as it had penetrated to his brain he would sit up smiling, and would chide the Skipper and the Digger for being gay dogs, and no better than they ought to be.

Tom's attitude to Pelling was highly amusing. He bore him no animosity, although Pelling's love-affair was the proximate cause of his downfall, but he would gaze at him fixedly for a quarter of an hour at a time, vainly endeavouring to understand how a man of Pelling's age and experience could sacrifice a comfortable home and an assured income for the sake of what he vulgarly called an empty-headed bag. And having reflected on the baffling nature of the problem, of which there was apparently no reasonable solution, Tom would shake his head and walk away, gently but efficiently cursing the whole tribe of women in words that would have filled a large, unprintable book.

The persecution of the Jews by the German Nazis continued to be a daily theme of conversation in prison. The Jews were wildly excited and indignant at the treatment meted out to their co-religionists, and prophesied that Hitler was riding for a heavy fall. The Skipper suggested that as Hitler had a fiercely united nation behind him, he would be a very hard man to shift.

"Politically, yes," assented the Digger, "but the abject submission of a whole people to one man, and the cruel persecution of defenceless minorities, are conclusive proof that the Germans are not civilized."

"They're a damn sight better than the French,"

growled the Aussie, "and the next war will find us fighting alongside them!"

"Not if we retain our traditional love for freedom," replied the Digger. "The French temperament is difficult to understand, and their everlasting cry for security in every department of life gets on our nerves. Perhaps the trait in their character that offends us most is their damnable meanness. By and large I suppose the French have expended more powder and shot than any other people in Europe. They have been prodigal enough with human lives, but stuff a Frenchman's pockets with gold, and he behaves like an old maid with a man under the bed. It is better to be in hell than owe a Gaul money. He'll camp on your doorstep, and to an Englishman meanness and a minute concern for money are the unpardonable sins. But the Frenchman has this in common with us, that he prizes intellectual and political freedom, and what is of more importance, will lay down his life for them."

The German people, the Digger argued, suffered from all the faults of national adolescence. A violent self-assertiveness was the direct result of their lack of experience in free institutions, and they were willing to swallow any tomfool theory that German blood, German soil, and German culture had some peculiar and superior virtue of their own.

"Wait a minute," interrupted the Skipper; "you must admit that English people believe they are the salt of the earth!" The Digger agreed that they did, but there was this vital difference. The constant exaltation of the German character in political speeches and in the Press was an unconscious admission of inferiority. The English not only believed they were the best people: they knew it. Why talk about facts which were tacitly acknowledged and understood by all? If you could not accept the English at their own valuation, they didn't mind in the least. You were simply a damn fool who might know better some day.

Someone suggested that the Germans were our intellectual masters. The Digger agreed that this might be true, but the English had learnt in the rough school of experience that there were no substitutes for courage and cheerfulness. "Do the thing and you shall have the power" had been their motto, and they were doing worthwhile things when the Germans had barely emerged from a semi-barbarous tribal stage. The English were never overwhelmed by events. Poise was their greatest asset.

Indeed, the more terrible the situation the more cheerful they became, like Wordsworth's Happy Warrior. Other nations steeled themselves to face catastrophes: the English broke out into fatuous and meaningless songs. They knew in their own bones that whatever happened the world would be much the same a hundred years hence. Things were what they were, and the consequences would be what they would be, so why worry? And in practice they confronted situations and accepted responsibilities under which the more imaginative and better-educated foreigner simply wilted and faded away.

Howlett expressed the opinion that Hitler was only a poor imitation of Mussolini, who at any rate had not made the fatal mistake of attacking Jewry. The Digger answered that we did not yet know what Mussolini was made of. It was difficult to separate the real man from the histrionic artist. There was not a shadow of doubt, however, that he was a very dangerous element in world society, because he looked upon war as a biological necessity: as essential for the development of manhood and nationhood as childbearing was for women.

Mussolini very firmly denied that perpetual peace had any place in the Fascist creed, and the time might come when Italy would be launched into a war, not for the sake of territorial expansion, or through acute economic distress, but because in the Dictator's opinion his people needed a drastic purge.

"Well," interjected the Skipper mildly, "life is a campaign and not a bed of roses."—"That is true enough," assented the Digger, "but man is only truly civilized in so far as he attempts, and in a measure achieves, the conquest of nature. If he cannot subdue the ape and tiger, then he is not much better than a wild animal, and infinitely more dangerous. Macaulay says somewhere that the cause of nearly all great human calamities lies in the union of high intelligence with low desires, and there is a cloud of witnesses to prove that the acquisition of knowledge and mechanical progress are of far less importance than the growth of the sentiments of freedom, toleration, and sympathy within a community. Mankind would never submit to the brutish law of the survival of the fittest."

He went on to say that our poet Shirley had long ago exposed the weakness of that stupid philosophy. The Skipper was not familiar with Shirley, so the Digger recited the noble lines:

The garlands wither on your brow;
　Then boast no more your mighty deeds!
Upon Death's purple altar now
　See where the victor-victim bleeds,
　　Your heads must come
　　To the cold tomb;
　Only the actions of the just
　Smell sweet and blossom in their dust.

"We know that Shirley was right," he continued, "and we know that war is a mad, bad, and sad business, but although we all support those conditions in the business and industrial world which make war possible in the international sphere, the Hitlers and Mussolinis believe that war is a cleansing fire, which only cowards and weaklings avoid."

At this point the Leader from the Part-Worn Store entered the library with one of his men for a change of books. The latter, on hearing the Digger's observation, said: "Well, more power to Hitler's arm. He's the only statesman in Europe with any guts. We're all afraid of the Jews, but he's giving them just what they've been asking for for centuries."

I knew this man well by sight. His features were of a mild and benevolent cast, and he wore a perpetual and rather foolish smile, which singled him out from the rest of the prison population, but on this occasion he looked positively fierce.

The Skipper asked him if he had a grouse against the Chosen People. "Grouse!" exclaimed the man. "Oh, no! No. I love them so that if I had the power I would remove them all from this wicked world at one stroke!"

"Sit down," pressed the Digger, scenting a story; "loosen your stays, cut yourself a piece of cake, and tell

M

us all about it!" The newcomer took the proffered chair, and without more ado plunged into the tragedy of his life.

He was a married man living in one of London's suburbs, and held a respectable post with a commercial house in the City. There were no children, but married life had been quite happy from his point of view.

His wife apparently had everything she needed except his society, for he had long ago acquired the habit of visiting a public-house immediately his day's work was ended, and staying there until closing-time.

As the years went on he received hints from well-meaning friends that his devotion to beer was losing him his wife's affection. It was even suggested that he might wake up one day to find that she had vanished, but he scouted the idea as ridiculous. Someone even went as far as to whisper that there was a lover in the offing; and more, that the lover was a Jew—a rumour so obviously fantastic that it only moved him to laughter.

He had such faith in his wife's honour that he never even troubled to repeat to her these scandalous inventions, much less make any attempt to verify them.

But one day he received orders from his firm to go to a town in the Midlands to examine and report on the business of a branch office there. His wife packed his bag, they kissed each other good-bye, and off he set on a week's business trip.

On arriving in the City, however, he learnt that the visit had been postponed for another month. When the day's work ended he repaired to his usual hostelry and arrived home, complete with bag, about midnight, and, in his own words, "more or less sozzled."

The house was shrouded in darkness, and, fearing to

waken his patient partner, he entered the back door very quietly and removed his boots in the kitchen. It was his intention to occupy a spare room, a course that would save him a lot of explanations at that unseasonable hour.

But something impelled him to visit his wife's room to see if she were all right. He crept to the bedroom door, opened it, and turned on the electric light. To his horror there was a man in bed with her, and he had a conk like a macaw. It was a low, usurping Jew.

There were the pair of them, so deep in slumber that the blaze of light failed to waken them, a faint, mocking smile on their lips, which was not the smile of innocence. The outraged husband was too dazed to raise an outcry, but he switched off the electric light almost automatically, locked the door from the outside, and retired to the kitchen, there to meditate an ample and effective revenge.

His brain, which was none too active, as the result of the night's potations, needed a livener, so he pushed his head under the cold water tap, and as he did so he noticed a tin of petrol on the floor beneath the sink.

That gave him an idea, and within a few seconds he had splashed the house with petrol in three or four places, and set alight to it. He then withdrew to an out-house in the garden, and from that point of vantage prepared himself to view the holocaust with savage if gloomy satisfaction.

The thought that he was probably committing murder never occurred to him. Rage and hatred blotted out every feeling, even the fear of consequences. Within a few minutes the house was a blazing inferno. Neighbours quickly appeared on the scene, and screams were heard from the interior, but fortunately for the incendiary the worst did not happen.

His wife and her lover wakened in the nick of time. After vainly trying the door they made for the windows, through which they escaped, and to the amazement of the assembled neighbours the two adulterers scuttled across the lawn in their night attire.

The house did not belong to the gentleman who had so suddenly razed it to the ground. He was only the tenant, and when the insurance company had to pay the owner for the destruction of his property they declined to regard the husband's injury as an extenuating circumstance. In fact, they insisted on prosecuting, and having lost his spouse, the man also lost his liberty for a period of eighteen months, on the charge of arson.

When he had gone, the Skipper observed that the story we had just listened to seemed to provide another argument in favour of prohibition. But the Digger would not concede that. It simply proved that a woman would not brook a rival. Hadn't one of our poets said:

> Love is of man's life a thing apart,
> 'Tis woman's whole existence.

A woman might be as strong as an ox physically, and built on the same lines, but once she gave her heart away she must have love in return, or she died, or fell into a decline, or ran away with Jews. "And if you don't believe me," he continued, "let us refer to an authority on these matters. Harry," he said, addressing the Aussie, "have you ever let drinking interfere with pleasure?"

As soon as the Aussie heard his Christian name he

knew that there was trouble in the offing, but after a moment's pause he admitted that although he was not a total abstainer, there were times when he never touched a drink at all. "I know," intervened the Digger soothingly, "in the hunting season." The Aussie glowered.

CHAPTER XIV

THE highest and most responsible position to which a Leader could aspire was that of D Hall orderly. This man acted as assistant to the Principal Officer, and his duties were multifarious. He dealt with all applications for letters and for requests to interview the Governor; allocated cells for the new arrivals in D Hall, posted men to tables, and made arrangements for the Governor's orderly room in the morning. His afternoons were generally spent in attendance on visitors, and in addition to his work as factotum for the P.O. he acted as Secretary to the Leaders' Committee.

The prisoner who occupied the post in my time was an ex-naval commander, who had been secretary to the Admiral Commanding the Mediterranean Fleet. He was a very decent, conscientious fellow, but was not popular with the men owing to his aloofness and the sharpness with which he was inclined to treat frivolous or irregular applications.

A good story was told about his appointment. When his predecessor was due for discharge, Commander Foster, the Deputy Governor, had made up his mind that the ex-naval officer would fill the post admirably. It happened that the P.O. had other views on the subject. The personality and ability of another Leader had won his approval, and he raised various objections to the proposed appointment, but Commander Foster brushed them aside with the remark that "If —— was good enough to be secretary to the Admiral Commanding the Mediterranean Fleet, he is a good enough secretary for you." In due course he was made D Hall orderly.

The Chairman of the Leaders' Committee was a youngish man who had occupied a high post in one of London's leading stores. He had vanished into the blue with a considerable sum of money belonging to the firm. After a prolonged search a reward of £100 was offered for any information that would lead to his arrest, and as soon as the embezzled funds petered out, his wife collected the £100, and he went to prison.

The Chairman was a man of great business ability and unusual energy. He worked heart and soul to make the Leaders' Committee an effective organization for the redress of grievances, and for securing a larger measure of participation in the working and discipline of the prison. I well remember his valedictory speech. He spoke with such deep sincerity that one almost felt that he was laying down his office with regret.

For a long time the Digger, although a voluble and entertaining talker, never made any attempt to address the Leaders' Committee or to take part in the discussions, I was rather surprised at his unusual silence, and one day asked the reason. His answer surprised me still more. "You can put it down to sheer funk," he said. "I have never been able to face an audience with any degree of equanimity, and on the few occasions when I have been forced to make a public appearance, the ordeal has nearly killed me. It is a form of neurosis, which seems silly to the ordinary healthy man, but although you mightn't be able to see the connexion, I feel sure that if I had not been the victim of this cursed thing I wouldn't be in Wormwood Scrubs to-day, and might have cut a decent figure in the world."

I suggested a hidden streak of morbidity somewhere

which made him underrate his powers, but he insisted
that whatever the obscure trouble was, it was incurable.
"Whenever the imagination and the will are in conflict," he said, "the imagination always wins." I ventured
the opinion that functional disorders were amenable to
proper treatment to-day, and that he might be a fit subject
for the psycho-analyst. He had no direct experience of
psycho-analysis, but he had some second-hand information.

A great friend of his came to the conclusion that he
was drinking too much, and after voluntary treatment
in a private institution for dipsomaniacs, he consented to
undergo a course of psycho-analysis. For about six months
he went twice a week to a mental specialist in Harley
Street. The Digger did not know what form the treatment took, but he knew that his friend always shrank
from the ordeal. Indeed, he found it so trying that he
always had five double whiskies before he went to the
doctor to enable him to face the mental inquisition,
and five more when he came away to pull himself together.

I suggested that this hardly looked like a cure, but
the Digger replied that at the end of nine months his
friend, for some inscrutable reason, gave up drink
altogether, and never touched another until he died.
"And so he passed away," I said. "Yes," was the answer,
"the treatment was entirely successful, but—you know
the rest."

A few weeks later, however, the Digger was compelled to make a speech, and although he began very
nervously, he warmed to his subject after a burst of
applause at one of his sallies, and concluded an effective performance with force and eloquence. It happened in this way.

Two Leaders were appointed every week to Hall duty.

As soon as tea was over, they took up positions at either
end of the Hall, near the staircases. The men left the
tables in rotation. Fourth Stage men were the first to
rise, and after having taken their mugs to their cells,
they trooped downstairs again and were marched to the
recreation room.

Then, on the warning note of a bell, Second Stage
men withdrew to their cells, and those who were not
due for educational classes shut their doors for the night.
A second bell, and Third Stage men mounted the stairs,
but returned again to the tables to play draughts and
chess until seven o'clock, or to wait for their classes.

It was the Leaders' duty to see that the various Stages
marched off at the appointed time, and to supervise the
behaviour of the men left in the Hall. The Digger's
colleague was a man called Franks. Rumour had it that
he was a converted Jew, and the cast of his countenance
was markedly Jewish.

On the score of education and character he should
never have been a Leader. Franks was in Wormwood
Scrubs for committing petty thefts on a large scale.
He was a rifler of telephone boxes, and looked the sort
of person who might take pennies out of a blind man's hat.

It was commonly reported that he was in league
with most of the dealers in contraband, and that if he
did not get the lion's share, he "shopped" the offenders
without mercy. He had more men cased than all the
other Leaders put together, and although as a consequence
he stood high in the estimation of the authorities, he was
loathed by the men and despised by the Leaders generally.

Every week one would encounter notices chalked up
in the lavatories and washing-places such as: "Franks

is a bastard" or some other equally uncomplimentary remark; but the authors were never caught. If he spoke indiscreetly or disparagingly of the warders, and he was much given to this practice, his observations would be conveyed anonymously to the Principal Officer through the medium of the box standing in D Hall for the reception of prisoners' letters. But no notice was ever taken of these anonymous contributions. Franks was doing his duty as a Leader, regardless of fear if not of favour, and it was only natural that malicious prisoners should do their best to injure him.

It must not be thought that anonymous letters were always ignored. They were frequently acted upon, with surprising results, and I should say that the vast majority of the secret breakers of prison regulations were discovered, not through the vigilance of the officers, but through the treachery of their associates.

At any rate, such was the character of the man with whom the Digger shared Hall duty. A few minutes after the Second Stage bell had rung, Franks called the Digger to his end of the Hall. A Second Stage man had refused to budge, alleging that he had been promoted to Third Stage, but had forgotten to put up his second stripe. That, of course, was not a valid excuse, as there was no means of verifying his statement until the following day. In any case, it was a prisoner's bounden duty to sew on the stripe the day of his promotion.

After explaining these facts, the Digger requested the man to go quietly to bed to save further trouble, but he resolutely declined to move for anybody. "Well, in that case," said the Digger, "you give us as Leaders no option but to report you to the officer on duty."

"You can go to the devil," retorted the man, a wild and excitable Irishman, glaring at Franks ferociously, "but by God, I'll have this man's blood, if I have to do ten years for it."

Even at this stage matters might have been settled amicably, but Franks chose the moment to demand the man's name. There was no necessity for anybody to know his name, as he carried his cell number on his tunic, but the request, and the imperative tone in which it was made, drove the Irishman to fury. Losing the last vestige of self-control, he leapt on Franks like a wildcat.

The Digger seized the attacker, and threw him heavily to the floor, but he was on his feet in a second, dancing round with the agility of a prizefighter, and vainly endeavouring to get at Franks, who was standing, greatly alarmed, between the Digger and the wall.

"If you don't get out of the road I'll floor you," shouted the Irishman.

"I'm going to fight until I'm knocked out, Paddy," retorted the Digger, breathing heavily, "but you're a damn fool. You'll get a month for this."

The Irishman jumped in like lightning. The Digger warded off the blow, closed with his opponent, and, seizing him round the waist, drew him across a suddenly outstretched right leg and threw him heavily again.

They were both struggling on the floor when the Hall Officer and a second warder arrived on the scene. The Irishman, with head lowered, rose sullenly to his feet. "Get back to your cell," ordered the Hall Officer. The man stood his ground, and for a second it looked as if he might be mad enough to assault the officers.

The order was repeated, and he turned and walked slowly to his cell, both warders following.

The next day the incident was investigated by the disciplinary Sub-Committee, which reported to the Leaders' Committee the following Sunday. Both Leaders were invited to give their version of the affair. Franks spoke first, and then the Digger was called on to address the meeting.

He began haltingly, and seemed very ill at ease, but having related what happened up to the point when the Irishman lost control of himself, he said: "I am sorry for this man Cassidy, for I feel that if he had been spoken to as one prisoner to another there would be no incident to report. That was the first mistake. The second was to demand his name, when his address was plainly visible on his coat. Prisoners are entitled to resent harsh and abrupt orders from Leaders, and any attempt to bully them is certain to lead to injustice. The system of Leadership can only survive by persuasion and example, but if we are to behave as warders, the sooner the Leaders are disbanded the better."

At this point Franks rose and said that he had no wish to parade as a junior officer, and that in everything he had done he was only obeying the promise made to the Governor when he was promoted to Leadership.

"I cannot agree with that," continued the Digger, quietly but firmly. "If you are doing your duty, then your brother Leaders are failing lamentably in theirs, because you case more men than the other twenty-four combined. Personally I find these men very tractable. On the whole their behaviour is as good as one could expect in a mixed company anywhere, but they will not put up with stern commands from prisoners expiating offences possibly a good deal more serious than their own. A good Leader neither sees too much nor hears too much. If he intervenes, it is as a friend. He should case a man only for a serious and deliberate breach of the regulations. Even then the offender is entitled to fair warning."

The Digger then sat down, but Franks jumped to his feet and objected emphatically to the Digger's remarks. "You were asked to describe what happened between Cassidy and us," he shouted, "and you take the opportunity to make a personal attack on me. I want an apology from you, and if I don't get it——" Before he could finish the sentence, the Digger rose hurriedly and declared just as emphatically that Leader Franks need expect no apology from him.

"I did criticize your handling of the Cassidy business," he said, "because I am convinced you are responsible for this man's loss of self-control. Even now you don't seem to appreciate that another month has been added to his sentence, but since you have seen fit to threaten, allow me to express regret for the part I played in the scuffle. My only regret now is that Cassidy did not at least get a run for his money."

The Chairman then rose and ordered both Leaders to avoid personalities. Franks was livid with rage, but he kept his seat, and the Chairman was succeeded by half a dozen Leaders who, without mentioning names, stressed the necessity for treating the men with sympathy and understanding, and deprecated the use of the case weapon, except as a last resort.

When the meeting was over, the Digger and I went for a stroll on the D Hall exercising-ground before the after-

noon service began. I asked if Cassidy had hurt him,
and he said no, although he felt sure that if the Irishman
had been able to get one good blow home, it would
have been all over with him.

I remarked on the impulsive nature of Irish people
generally. He agreed, and said that the Irish were one of
the most backward races in Europe. They could not
reason or argue, or behave with dignity when their
prejudices or opinions were attacked or ridiculed. They
had only one answer, a blow, and they were not particular as to how the blow was given.

The traditional stage Irishman, with his irresponsible
gaiety and romantic melancholy, was a figment of the
imagination. When the Irishman's deepest passions were
aroused he revealed a streak of cold-blooded ferocity
which made the ordinary Englishman shudder.

He could be as merciless as a killer, and even if there
were no political feuds to inflame his animosity, he
seemed to drift naturally into the killing business. The
gangsters, the gombeen men, and the corrupt political
bosses of the United States were nearly all of Irish origin,
and although John Bull must be held accountable for
a good deal of Irish devilry, he was by no means responsible for all of it.

Ireland's real trouble was that she had missed the
civilizing influence of Rome. If Domitian had only
granted Agricola that extra Legion, Roman staves would
have knocked sense and order and discipline into those
thick-headed kerns, and Ireland would be a much saner
and safer place to live in than it is to-day.

As we walked round the quadrangle we were joined
by Laski, of cigarette-coupon fame. He was always

lively and entertaining, and he amused us with an account of his fruitless efforts to patch up the quarrel with Moses, who had never forgiven his secession from the Jewish faith.

A very tall, big, loosely built fellow, whom I knew well by sight, passed us repeatedly, and whenever he came abreast of us he poured out a stream of obscenity, apparently directed against the world in general. As he was alone, his behaviour suggested that there was something wrong with him mentally.

By and by the Digger noticed his antics, and when the man passed us again, with another outburst of profanity, he turned and asked if the fellow was addressing himself or us.

"Oh," said Laski, cheerfully, "he's talking to me: he always does that when there's nobody with him."

"What on earth for?" inquired the Digger, in astonishment.

Laski explained that although he did not know the man from a bar of soap, he had made inquiries since the campaign of abuse started, and discovered that he was in the Scrubs for selling uncustomed tobacco. Furthermore, he had also found out that the man's wife ran a little cigarette shop. "What has all this to do with this fellow's peculiar conduct to-day?" asked the Digger. "Well," replied Laski, "I happened to sell his good lady £6 worth of excellently printed cigarette-coupons. He knows who I am, and this is his way of showing his displeasure."

The Digger asked how long this nonsense had been going on, and Laski told us that he had had to put up with it ever since the man came on Fourth Stage, two months before. "Well, it's two months too long," growled the Digger. "When he passes us again, you walk on, and we'll tackle him together. He might be awkward."

The man presently appeared and repeated his little performance, but before he had gone a couple of yards the Digger and I had wheeled and confronted him. "Why all this bad language?" inquired the Digger mildly.

"It's not intended for you," was the gruff answer.

"So I gather," replied the Digger, "but you've been subjecting the man I've just left to this sort of treatment for two months past. He's paying for what he did, and so are you, but there's no one here to remind you daily of your crime. Don't you think you are just a little bit foolish, and a little bit cruel?"

"No, I don't," retorted the man, angrily, "and in any case, it's none of your business. My quarrel is with Laski."

"Well," said the Digger, "whatever you think, may I take it that in future you will leave Laski severely alone?"

"You can take what you damn well like," shouted the man, now thoroughly roused, "but whenever he crosses my path, I'll tell him exactly what I think of him."

"Oh, so that's the way the wind blows," was the Digger's answer. "Just take notice now, that if you dare to say another word to Laski on this matter you will have me to deal with. I am joining him presently, and if I hear any more of your filth you won't see the inside of a church this afternoon, and I can promise you an interview with the Governor to-morrow morning."

We picked up Laski again, and his tormentor passed

us many times before the service began, but he never opened his mouth, and, as far as I know, never troubled him again.

The business at Leaders' meetings was transacted with great decorum and dispatch, but there were occasions when the proceedings were enlivened by a little humour. A perennial joke had its origin in the behaviour of the sparrows in D Hall. Hundreds of these birds had their home in the Hall itself, roosting on the rafters at night, and picking up a substantial living from the tables during the day.

Almost every new Leader would make his first speech on the following theme, though not necessarily in these terms: expression naturally varied with education and temperament:—

"Mr. Chairman, I have been asked by a member of my table to bring to your notice the advisability of asking the prison authorities to remove the colony of sparrows from D Hall. Prisoners generally would welcome the presence of these little fellows if they could only be persuaded to obey the most elementary rules of sanitation, but unfortunately their busiest time seems to coincide with our meal hours. Last night the man who asked me to voice this complaint had to go without his cocoa, which happened to be in the direct line of fire: this morning the same man sacrificed half his porridge. I . . ."

And then the Chairman would rise, amidst general laughter, and explain that although the same grievance had been aired a hundred times, the authorities had laid it down that they had no intention of interfering with the sparrows in any circumstances whatever, and that it was useless to carry the matter any further.

N

One Saturday afternoon the Skipper, who was as bald as Caesar, fell a victim to these feathered sharp-shooters. After dinner he was standing talking to the Digger and me as we were waiting to go on visits.

"What's that?" he rapped out suddenly, a look of genuine alarm in his eyes. "What's what?" asked the Digger. "My head!" gasped the Skipper. We both looked, and the Digger exclaimed: "God bless my soul: you've been hit plumb centre by a sparrow!"

The Skipper cursed fluently, and reached for his large prison handkerchief. He couldn't understand why the authorities permitted these filthy little brutes to have the run of D Hall. It was unfair to the men. Prison diet was lean enough, God knows, but to be deprived of it altogether through these little blighters was too much of a good thing. No one was safe from them. The Leaders——" He got no further. A convulsive shudder ran through his frame. "You've been hit again," cried the Digger, "in exactly the same spot, and if the news is any good to you, by another bird using a slightly larger type of ammunition!"

I thought the Skipper would have had an apoplectic fit. He raved and stormed, and to save him from a third salvo we led him under the shelter of the staircase.

Business at committee meetings followed much the same lines as a company meeting. The minutes of the previous meeting were read and confirmed, after which the Chairman welcomed new members, briefly explained the constitution and procedure of the committee, and emphasized the secrecy of all their deliberations.

He then called for reports from Leaders, who the previous week had been in charge of the recreation-room, and on duty in D Hall. The Chairman of the Games and Disciplinary Sub-Committees gave a brief outline of their activities, and their reports were thrown open to full discussion. After this any member could bring forward complaints from prisoners, or make suggestions for improvements in the routine working of the prison. During the meeting a list of duties for the ensuing week was passed from hand to hand and noted. The proceedings terminated with speeches of farewell from those who were leaving us.

Committee resolutions were forwarded to the Principal Officer of D Hall, who in turn transmitted them to the Governor for consideration. The Committee formed the channel through which the Governor made known his wishes and commands on matters of prison discipline to the inhabitants of D Hall.

Contraband was the subject of numerous messages. The discovery of more offenders than usual invariably produced a warning to the effect that unless a much greater degree of vigilance and supervision was exercised by Leaders, the privilege of open visits would be withdrawn from Fourth Stage men.

A threat of this sort always galvanized the Committee into a great show of activity. The first step was to draw up a letter, signed by all the Leaders, assuring the Governor that they were equally concerned at the growth of the illicit traffic, and that they would spare no efforts to collaborate with the authorities in detecting offenders, and bringing them to book.

Having done this, each Leader addressed his own table, pleaded with the men strictly to obey the regulations in the interests of Fourth Stage men as a whole, and warned them of the consequences if they were caught.

It must be confessed that the sincerity of the Leaders' memorial to the Governor was occasionally vitiated by the almost immediate arrest and degradation of some of the signatories themselves. This happened twice in my time, and I can remember when two Leaders were deprived of their rank in one week, and returned to C Hall. They were men whom we had always suspected of improper practices.

A comparatively small percentage of men engaged in the hazardous business of smuggling. In a few cases they were aided and abetted by officers, who, of course, ran the risk of instant dismissal, and a prosecution into the bargain.

The bulk of the contraband was obtained from prisoners' friends and relatives on open visits, although a certain quantity was thrown over the wall wrapped up in packages, and occasionally transported in footballs. With the latter the donors had perforce to take pot-luck as to whom the recipients might be, and I fancy the gardening party enjoyed practically a monopoly in the air-borne freight. "Manna from Heaven," I heard one man call it.

A favourite point of delivery was the incinerator, the smoke of which could be seen by people on the Common, and in the vicinity of which Fourth Stage men were accustomed to promenade in the warm evenings.

On open visits in the summer months, Fourth Stage men sat with their friends under the portico opposite B Hall. They were supervised by an officer who occupied a chair on the lawn some thirty or forty feet away. It was impossible for this warder to keep an eye on the movements of fifty or sixty people, and unscrupulous visitors found it comparatively easy to pass contraband goods without being seen.

The craving for tobacco and sweets was one of the most painful of prison experiences. The new arrival's appetites were all blotted out in the loss of liberty, but as soon as he became resigned to his fate and accustomed to his surroundings, the desire for tobacco made life almost unbearable. There were times, and I fancy the half-hour's respite after the midday meal troubled me most, when I could have bartered my soul for a cigarette.

Some men experienced an overwhelming need for a stimulant. The Digger would often rise from his chair, and parody Wordsworth's lines on Milton:

> Woodhead: wouldst thou wert coming at this hour,
> The Digger hath need of thee.

Woodhead happened to be his local off-licence man. Sometimes he would vary this with a quotation from the Skipper's favourite poet:

> I often wonder what the vintners buy,
> One half so precious as the wares they sell.

"By God," the Skipper would interject eagerly, "that's just the way I feel!" And then we would all fall to talking of English inns, of beer, and bread and cheese, and the flavour of Virginia tobacco.

To most men the smoking habit is the hardest in the world to break, and in view of the facilities offered by the open visit system, it was surprising that the traffic in contraband was kept within such narrow limits. But apart from the penalties of detection, which were severe enough, it was impossible to enjoy a smoke with one's

head swathed in blankets, and ears straining to catch a
warder's approaching footsteps. Most men preferred to
endure the agony of going without.

The suppression of open visits, in an effort to check
smuggling, would have been a great blow to prisoners
and their friends, but an even greater blow to prison
warders themselves. Deprived of the opportunity to
track down law-breakers, and catch them with the stuff
on them, their otherwise dull and monotonous lives
would have been hardly tolerable.

One day—it was the King's birthday—the Digger
remarked: "Well, Skipper, I think that in the words of
Theodore Hook, when he was situated much as we are,
we ought to be allowed to drink the health of our august
detainer!" The Skipper suggested that as we had not
a bean amongst the lot of us, the drinks would have to
be on His Majesty, but for the moment he could not
think of any better purpose to which the King's bounty
could be applied.

A Jew, who was in the Scrubs for preaching sedition
amongst His Majesty's Forces, happened to be in the
room at the time, and he had something uncomplimentary
to say about all monarchs. This Jew had spent two years
studying Communism in a Moscow college, and was
known throughout the prison as Lenin.

"You're a fanatic, Lenin," replied the Digger; "possessed of one idea, and I was nearly going to say, that
the wrong one. The English people certainly dote on
kings, but they refuse to put up with any nonsense from
them. They had the courage to roll off a king's head,
when regicide was considered the most terrible crime
of all. Fortunately they did not dispense with monarchy

altogether: they merely set limits, beyond which no king could go without losing his throne, or his life, or both."

"But surely you, as an educated man, must agree that kingship is an anachronism to-day," urged the Jew. The Digger would not agree with anything of the sort. Since the war, dynasties had fallen right and left, but the British monarchy was more essential than ever to the welfare of the scattered nations of the Commonwealth, and was more firmly established in the hearts of the people.

The Head of the State must be represented in a single person, and was it not better that that person should be raised above all political parties, with a life devoted to one object, the service of the people?

The Crown was above all personal ambition, and nobody envied the King his job.

There was another point about our form of kingship that was frequently overlooked. Some people thought that monarchy and true democracy could not exist together, when as a matter of fact it was the presence of an impartial monarch which enabled a free people to govern themselves with the maximum degree of justice and toleration.

Again, the Throne was one of the few places where a man could rise and shine, and shed an enormous influence, without high intellectual gifts. The qualities required in a king were sympathy, toleration, and a deep sense of public duty, and King George had them all in abundance.

Wireless had greatly extended the King's influence. People all over the Empire, who perhaps thought of him as a very lofty and remote peak in the social Alps, could now hear his voice speaking as if he were in the next room: and they found that he was a man like themselves, with similar hopes and fears, and sharing their common humanity. The House of Windsor had the great merit of flexibility, and a gift of intelligent anticipation that amounted almost to genius. Who was there more modern and up to date, and a better mixer, than the Prince of Wales?

The Digger thought, however, that a large section of the popular Press in this country tended unwittingly to bring monarchy into contempt. These papers seemed to live in a perpetual dither of astonishment that members of the Royal Family could say or do anything sensible at all, and they reported commonplace incidents and remarks with a sickening wealth of adjectival adulation.

When Lenin had gone, the Skipper remarked that he never thought the Digger was such a stout royalist. He didn't by any chance make the annual pilgrimage to Whitehall to mourn the memory of the Martyr King? The Digger replied emphatically that he did not. Charles deserved all he got. He had been praised often enough for his private virtues, but he had no monopoly of them. As a king he was the biggest washout who ever held the sceptre, and his career simply proved that virtuous men with rigid views were far more to be feared in high places than loose men with no fixed views at all.

"But," pursued the Skipper, "haven't you said again and again that solitary confinement for a week with nothing to read but Queen Victoria's Letters must be the worst form of punishment that Wormwood Scrubs can inflict, and haven't you more than once issued these Letters to the speed merchants and fighting drunks of this circus?"

"Yes," replied the Digger, "but all this has nothing to do with my support of a monarchical form of government. Queen Victoria's Letters must be judged by literary standards. As for putting them in prisoners' cells, it is always possible that an obliging drunk will go mad, and do them in. Up to now I've been unlucky."

The Digger's reference to the possible destruction of Queen Victoria's Letters reminded me that the Librarian had handed me a mutilated book for investigation. It was a history of Charles XII of Sweden. Not a great deal of damage had been done, but the commentator had foolishly used ink instead of pencil.

Describing the course of an engagement, the historian said: "The King surveyed the field of battle leaning on his sword." This sentence the prisoner had heavily underlined, and in the margin, in large capital letters, he had recorded his opinion of Charles: "LAZY BARSTED!"

The offender was brought in and questioned, and smiled so broadly when the accusing History was opened up that there was little doubt his handiwork afforded him the highest gratification. He admitted authorship at once, but proceeded to plead justification. "It's like this," he said: "here's the soldiers doing all the dirty work, fighting and killing, and all that, and the King, instead of cutting and thrusting with the rest, leans on his sword. Don't you think I'm right?" he inquired eagerly.

"These books are given you to read, not to disfigure," replied the Librarian. "You'll go before the Governor to-morrow," and the man was taken back to the shop, smiling even more happily than before.

The illiterates of the prison and the foreigners, for whom the Librarian acted as amanuensis, were a constant source of entertainment to us. Chinamen provided the most fun, as the conversation on both sides was carried on in pidgin English. The Oriental would be ushered in by a Leader, and presented to the Librarian, who sat at his desk with an official letter form in front of him.

"You wantee lightee letter?" the Librarian would begin.

"Yes, yes, velly much," the Chinaman would reply, breaking into a broad smile, and nodding vigorously in the affirmative.

"Who you wantee lightee to?"

"My wifey."

"Where she live?"

And having obtained the address, the Librarian would begin by question and answer to indite the precious message. A time-honoured question, which always brought a laugh, was: "You likee this place?" The quick change in the face of the blandly smiling Celestial and the vigorous shaking of his head indicated plainly enough that he knew of many better holes than Wormwood Scrubs.

One day a squat little Japanese was brought in. He could not make himself understood at all, but after much fruitless questioning he brightened up at the sight of the Digger, who had just entered the room. We then discovered that he was there not for the purpose of letter writing, but to make a complaint about the type of literature with which he had been served.

The Japanese was a Shintoist, but the Digger had supplied him with the New Testament, which was the only work in Japanese in the library, and he had been struggling with the New Testament for a month. The little yellow man went back to his cell comforted with the knowledge that the New Testament would be removed forthwith, and that in future he would revel in the delights of picture-books, which, having been prepared by the Aussie, were not lacking in the ample charms of popular actresses.

Through the association of ideas, a visit from a China-man one day turned our conversation to the question of opium, about which the Skipper had much first-hand knowledge. The Digger ventured the opinion that its injurious effects had been grossly exaggerated in the public mind, and quoted Thomas de Quincey to show that the drug was at one time valued as a cure for consumption.

This was news to the Skipper. The Digger gave him the actual passage, and then went on to repeat the famous apostrophe, with its sonorous opening: "Oh, just, subtle, and all-conquering opium, that to the hearts of rich and poor alike, for the wounds that will never heal, and for the pangs that tempt the spirit to rebel, bringest an assuaging balm!"

"How the devil do you remember all that stuff?" inquired the Skipper.

The Digger replied that it was at least twenty years since he had handled the *Opium Eater*, but there were certain passages in it which were unforgettable, and he happened to be able to retain without effort anything that appealed to him. In his opinion De Quincey's *Levana* and the *Ladies of Sorrow* was perhaps the finest piece of impassioned prose in the English language; and to the Skipper's astonishment, and our own, he recited the whole of that noble essay without a stop, his voice gaining in strength as the narrative moved to its tremendous climax.

He had, however, his memory failures like everybody else. The word brilliantine was, he alleged, his greatest foe. As soon as he went into a barber's shop for a hair-cut, he began to think of brilliantine, in preparation for the inevitable question: "What will you have on it, sir?"—and in nine cases out of ten he left the shop without it.

I remember one occasion which showed that the Digger's memory was equally at home with the French classics. A French sailor was brought into the library in order to make his own selection. He was literate, but he could not speak or read a word of English. Despite this handicap, he managed to make us understand that he had no love for the older French classics, and that if he saw another Montaigne or Racine he would do something desperate.

"You're a sailor," said the Digger, "and perhaps you have heard of Pierre Loti?" The man disclaimed all knowledge of the author, and the Digger proceeded to tell him in halting French who Loti was, and the type of book he wrote. He advised the man to start with either *Pêcheurs d'Islande* or *Le Roman d'un Spahi*, and he detailed the plot of each story, quoting as freely from the text as if he had the open volumes in front of him.

When the Frenchman had retired, with voluble expressions of thanks and regard, the Skipper announced that he intended to undergo that evening the ordeal of a hair-cut. And, believe me, the business of having one's hair cut in D Hall was hardly a soothing experience.

As happened so often in the Army, the barber's sole qualification for the post appeared to be complete ignorance of the hairdresser's art. He was, in fact, a

Cockney greengrocer, and had never used a pair of scissors in his life.

His assistant was a Jew, whose experience was as limited as the greengrocer's, and both these men were just as efficient at the end of six months as when they began. They used the clippers confidently enough round the back of the neck, but for some reason which I could never fathom, nothing on earth could persuade them to cut the hair short on the crown of the head.

The result was that all of us had mops of hair like beehives. I well remember my first hair-cut after release. The barber looked at me as if I had been some strange animal out of the Zoo. Unable to restrain his curiosity, he insisted on knowing the name of the artist who had performed on my head. I explained that I had been ill for some months, and had to rely on the services of an amateur.

Even then the professional could not understand how any amateur outside a lunatic asylum could have made such an unholy mess of the business, and he questioned me with such persistence that I was very glad to escape from his cross-examination.

Apart from pulling out hair by the roots in bunches, a form of torture to which one never grows accustomed, the greengrocer had the irritating habit of pushing and punching our heads about as if they were so many bags of potatoes. One day I was seated in the chair squirming under the tender ministrations of the Jew. The green-grocer was attending to another customer, talking volubly and cheerfully as was his wont, and indulging in the usual practice of thumping the poor fellow's head when-ever he wanted a change of position.

I noticed a nasty glint in the victim's eye as he received a particularly vicious jab in the nape of the neck. Presently he was out of the chair, the towel still round his neck, and crouching in a fighting attitude. "You can knock your old woman about as much as you like," snapped the man, "but if you punch my head again this afternoon I'll have your guts for garters!"

The greengrocer was full of apologies, and the man climbed back into the chair; but the reference to his wife hurt. The barber had received a three years' sentence for stabbing her with a knife. On appeal the term was reduced to eighteen months, and he managed to escape penal servitude by a whisker.

The next morning the Skipper related his experience in the barber's cell. When he arrived there after tea, the Digger happened to be occupying the next chair. The Digger rather prided himself on his heavy growth of hair. "It's not too bad for a man of fifty," he said, eyeing himself complacently in the glass.

The greengrocer agreed, and inquired his exact age. "I shall be forty-seven in two months' time," was the answer. "Well, you're just three and a half years younger than I am, Joe," replied the tonsorial artist. "And what's more, I became a grandfather last week. Yes," he continued reminiscently, "I've been married thirty years, and would you believe it, that during all that time my old woman and I have never had a serious quarrel. We've had words, you know, like all married couples, but nothing to write home about."

The greengrocer was very popular with everybody on account of his cheerful Cockney temperament, but as the Skipper remarked, it was rather difficult to understand his conception of a quarrel, seeing that he had been convicted of a murderous assault on his wife by plunging a knife into her body.

While the business of haircutting was going on the barber kept up an unbroken conversation with the Digger, whom he continually addressed as Joe.

The following afternoon, when the Digger entered the library on his return from C Hall, he found on his desk an ancient scientific manual, in the front of which was a drawing of a Neanderthal man and woman, the work of some bygone artist. The woman, with her long tresses, bore some resemblance to humanity, but the man differed very little from a gorilla.

In the book was a loose sheet of paper addressed to "Our darling Joe, with love from his Great, Great, Great, Great, Great, Great, Great, Great, Great, Grand Dad and Grand Ma." The Digger gave the inscription a hurried glance, and then, looking towards the Skipper, who was deeply absorbed in his work, inquired: "Is this the brightest heaven of your invention, you damned old shell-back?"

"What do you mean?" growled the Skipper in affected surprise.

"What I say," answered the Digger. "This writing looks suspiciously like yours, and you were the only one to overhear that infernal barber calling me Joe last night!"

"Well, don't you like the name?" asked the Skipper innocently, with a grin on his face.

"No, I don't," retorted the Digger emphatically. "In the first place, it doesn't belong to me, and in the second place I always thought that Joe was the exclusive prerogative of low comedians, breezy bookmakers, and the Levy family."

"I'm glad you mentioned low comedians," sniggered the Skipper, turning to his task again, but the entry of the Librarian prevented the Digger from making an effective reply.

CHAPTER XV

THE arrival of Maundy Gregory in Wormwood Scrubs caused quite a sensation, as his trial and conviction had been well featured in the newspapers. We were all agog to see the gentleman who was reputed to have made such a profitable business out of the sale of honours, and after a day or two in the Shed he was posted to the library, together with a young ex-Army officer, who had been convicted for dangerous driving.

Gregory did not look the sort of man who had played a big part in the political game behind the scenes. His appearance was insignificant, and there was nothing striking about his conversation.

He appealed to me as being a vain little fellow, rather proud of his association with the Ambassadors' Club, and of his intimate relations with the leading political figures of the day, but without any claims to personal magnetism, or high intellectual gifts.

Gregory was undoubtedly possessed of a native shrewdness, which had stood him in good stead when dealing with gentlemen anxious to be distinguished from the common herd. I fancy he was rather admired for his skill in taking advantage of a particularly English form of snobbery, but it was difficult to imagine a man more unlike the popular conception of the political intriguer.

He worked under Howlett's immediate supervision, and spent the whole of his two months in sewing dilapidated books. Naturally our talks took a political turn, and we encouraged Gregory to tell us something of the public personalities with whom he had been brought into contact.

O

I am afraid we learnt nothing very informative, but I remember that he entertained a very violent dislike for the Prime Minister. This was about the only subject on which the Digger and Gregory agreed. The former could never understand how MacDonald had reached the highest position in the land. Here was a man, he said, who brought to every public question the atmosphere of the Mothers' Meeting and the Conventicle. He always brought to the Digger's mind the political opponent of whom Canning said: "That fellow reminds me of the fly in amber. Nobody cares a damn about the fly. The only question is, how the devil did it get there?"

"By your sentiments," said Gregory to the Digger one day, "you are obviously a Socialist, but do you think that any Socialist Government of the kind we have experienced could safely govern a great Empire like ours?"

The Digger replied that he did not, and although he believed that Socialism was certain to win universal support in time, none of the present-day political exponents of the creed could be entrusted with office for any length of time. They were bound hand and foot by catchwords and phrases. In order to be true to their theories of the brotherhood of man, they dismissed war as a relic of savagery, and therefore declined to make any preparation for defence against possible aggression. This was Carlyle's ostrich with its head stuck into fallacies, but an ostrich which, as Tom said, would be awakened one day in a terrible *a posteriori* manner, if not otherwise. Pious gentlemen like George Lansbury, who flaunted the Sermon on the Mount as a political manifesto, should not be entrusted with anything more important than a whelk stall.

"But," objected Gregory, "then you get back to the position when wars breed wars, and armaments breed rearmaments."

"Not at all," said the Digger. "If you are adequately protected the thief and the robber give you a miss." We had, he said, the same argument advanced against tariffs, that if this country, which had for so many years quixotically followed a policy of free imports, should dare to protect her own domestic market, other countries would inevitably adopt retaliatory measures. Nothing of the sort had happened, or was likely to happen. The chances were that for the first time in our history the foreigner would show a willingness to lower his trade barriers. In our mad pursuit of an impossible ideal we had very nearly allowed free imports to destroy us, and we were driven, not by logic, but by force of circumstances, to use economic weapons.

In the same way, no Socialist State could hope to stand against a world of enemies unless it was armed from head to foot, and ready to fight to the death when attacked. Pacifism was a doctrine of despair, and as long as Socialists advocated it they would never win the confidence of Britishers, who did not ask for trouble but could make a very respectable showing when it came to a rough house.

Gregory suggested that the Digger probably had a great deal of sympathy for the Russian experiment. "As a matter of fact, I have," replied the latter.

"What, with a gang of brutal murderers, who have destroyed the intelligentsia, broken every treaty, and done their utmost to embroil the whole world?" queried Gregory.

The actions of revolutionaries were always open to criticism, according to the Digger. We were apt to forget that Communism was not like an ordinary political creed. It was a religion. Its professors were missioners and Crusaders, and preached the Gospel to every creature, openly if possible, but *sub rosa* when necessary.

"They are a damn bloodthirsty crew," growled the Skipper.

"Well, let us admit that they were brutally efficient," was the reply. What was of the greatest importance now was that the Russians had accomplished wonders.

He invited us to throw our minds back, and recall the shouts of derision in the English Press at the Five-Year Plan. The Russians, the Press declared, were the most backward people industrially in the world—which was very likely true—and their grandiose schemes of reconstruction would end in tragic failure. But had they?

The Russians had recruited and trained one of the largest, and on paper at all events, one of the most efficient and formidable armies in the world. Russia was returning to the comity of nations, not because her social and political ideas were regarded with any more favour than when they were first introduced, but because she could now be a dangerous enemy or a useful friend.

The proceeds of her exports had been devoted to the purchase of capital goods, and very soon she would be as well equipped technically as any country in the world, and free from dependence on capitalist nations. The Russians had done much with very poor material, and without money. What sort of result would have been achieved in England under a similar system, with her skilled workmen and vast industrial experience?

"You don't mean to suggest that we are going to imitate these whiskered Bolsheviks?" demanded the Skipper.

"Not in their methods," replied the Digger. "Englishmen are not egoistic enough to commit wholesale murder for political or any other ideals, but the time is coming when production for profit only will be violently attacked." Science had placed at our disposal the means of turning out four or five times the goods that were being consumed to-day, and yet there were millions compelled to live below the subsistence level, and world-wide unemployment. Production was curtailed, crops were destroyed in order to maintain prices at a payable level, and farmers were subsidized to refrain from growing food, while millions could not get enough to eat. The only poor devil who was not subsidized in this cranky world was the consumer.

It was not good enough, and we might presently be compelled to experiment with some form of government on the Russian lines, and to surrender a measure of personal liberty in order to secure the economic well-being of all. Besides, if man was ready to take advantage of the facilities open to him, we stood on the threshold of an age of leisure, in which the serious problems would be ethical and moral, not economic.

All this sounded Utopian to the Skipper, who said so with appropriate emphasis, but the Digger insisted that the problem of getting a living should no longer worry us unduly, if we exercised common sense.

We prided ourselves on living in a scientific age, but we never used the scientific method, otherwise these glaring anomalies would never be allowed to exist. And with increased leisure, and security from want, we could devote the bulk of our time and energy to waging war, not on our fellows, but on the forces of ignorance, fear, and disease.

Mankind was not man yet, and could never become man by fighting for its own hand. In Browning's words, he hadn't yet begun his general infancy, and he thought that without talking idealistic nonsense, it was not visionary to picture humanity as a mighty army, freed from the original curse, obeying the co-operative effort, and advancing on Chaos and the Dark.

"There's nothing to choose between you and Lansbury," said the Skipper, "except that you refuse to offer a cheek to the smiter."

"No, I don't suppose there is," agreed the Digger.

Gregory had been in the library a week when he reported that for two days running the bread which he had saved from his morning's ration, and had secreted behind his slate in the cell, had mysteriously disappeared. Like old Mother Hubbard, he had returned each dinner hour to find his meagre cupboard bare. He sought an explanation of the phenomenon. Did the prison authorities deprive men of their savings?

"No," said the Skipper, "the cleaners have lighted on your little hoard, and they'll never leave you alone now."

Gregory suggested that he might defeat the robbers by hiding the bread in his mattress. "No good," replied the Skipper. "You're a marked man now, and they'll search every nook and corner of your cell, with all the skill and cunning that comes from daily practice. Once you are discovered as a man with a delicate appetite, the only way to beat these fellows is to devour the whole ration, or bring the remains to the library, and run the risk of being accosted by a warder for carrying an unauthorized article on your person."

The Digger suggested that if the portion was not too large, Gregory ought to be able to carry it in his tunic pocket under his handkerchief without attracting official notice. These cleaners were all young fellows, he said, and hungrier than the sea. They reminded him of the story of a mother who was worried about her daughter's moral welfare, and warned her repeatedly against the dangers of associating too closely with men.

The girl was one of those bright, confident young things who are so numerous to-day. "Don't you worry about me, mother," she replied airily, "I've got it all here," and she tapped her forehead to indicate that all was well upstairs.

"It doesn't matter where you've got it," the mother answered wearily, out of the wisdom acquired from long experience, "they'll find it. And that's just the way with prison cleaners, Gregory."

One day Gregory was asked if he did not find the weekends in C Hall very trying. The men there were locked up every Saturday and Sunday at 4 p.m. He replied that the confinement would be tolerable if only there were enough to read, but he did think that the Working Men's Club in the neighbourhood might show some consideration for captives, and refrain from making such a din on Saturday and Sunday nights. He could not understand why they broke into song at seven o'clock with unfailing regularity, and finished abruptly about eight o'clock. Their favourite chorus, "Happy days are here again," which they shouted like maniacs, nearly drove him crazy.

There was a roar of laughter at this, and Gregory looked round for an explanation. The Aussie said: "That's not a Working Man's Club, that's the Fourth Stage men in the recreation-room!"

Gregory could hardly believe his ears, and the knowledge that the noise was caused by fellow-prisoners hardly tended to alleviate his feeling of irritation. "If you were here for twenty-one weeks, you would enjoy the same privilege," said the Skipper, "and you would probably sing 'Happy days are here again' as heartily as the others, but to a newcomer mewed up in C Hall with one educational book and a mailbag, it does seem a refinement of cruelty."

Maundy was an ardent Roman Catholic, and was always in deep conversation, conducted *sotto voce*, with the Schoolmaster, who, as a convert, was crazy about his new faith. One of his first actions after release was to send the Schoolmaster a beautifully decorated Missal.

I happened to be on duty in C Hall the afternoon prior to his discharge. It was nearly five o'clock, and the men were returning from work. I don't know what Maundy had done to offend, but I saw him scuttling up the staircase like a rabbit, while an officer bawled after him, "You might be a gentleman to-morrow, but don't forget you're a prisoner to-night, or it will be the worse for you!"

A Rolls-Royce was to meet him at the prison gates, and he was to be entertained by his friends at the Ambassadors' Club in the evening. We envied him.

Gregory's place in the library was taken by one of the

queerest personalities I met in Wormwood Scrubs. He did not remain with us very long, but his appearance caused quite a lot of speculation. I have completely forgotten his name, which was aristocratic and hyphenated. For the purpose of this narrative he can figure as Bruno de Belleville-Fitzmaurice. De Belleville-Fitzmaurice had spent some months in one of the Shops.

He spoke with a cultured accent, but unlike the average Englishman of good family boasted openly of his genealogical tree. His people had come over with the Conqueror, their exploits were legion, and all his living relatives had distinguished themselves in one way or another in the public services.

A mere wisp of a man, but as cocksure as the devil, de Belleville-Fitzmaurice, with his swank, soon achieved a certain measure of unpopularity. A few days after his arrival the Skipper asked him what he thought of the library. "Charming, charming," replied the little fellow, rubbing his hands together, which was a confirmed habit with him. "Do you know, I haven't heard that disgraceful word —— for forty-eight hours! And," he added, "what a relief it is to a man with any upbringing!"

"Yes, I suppose it must be," answered the Skipper drily, eyeing him up and down with obvious disfavour. "Prison must be a very trying expereince for one of your caste."

Thus encouraged, de Belleville went on to tell us about his illustrious ancestry, and spoke freely of mottoes and crests and coats-of-arms. Looking at the diminutive braggart with contempt in his eyes, the Digger observed casually: "Coming from such a fighting stock, I suppose your family motto is *Aquila non capit muscas* or *Cave adsum*, or something of that sort?"

"Curious you should have guessed it the first time," was the pleased rejoinder. "It happens to be *Cave adsum*."

"And a very appropriate motto for Crusaders, Knight Templars, and doughty fellows with sword and lance," continued the Digger, a broad smile on his face.

"What's it mean?" inquired the Skipper.

"Beware, I am present!" answered the Digger; and the Skipper burst into such a fit of laughter that even de Belleville-Fitzmaurice began to suspect that his leg was being pulled.

About this time we lost the company of the little Cockney signwriter. Before he went, he figured in a rather absurd incident. It was during our respite, after Fourth Stage men had been finished with, that something cropped up about music, and the Cockney informed us with some pride that he played the bass viol.

"Oh, you are one of the drones of the orchestra," said the Digger. "I am always tickled by the studied nonchalance of the basses. They make a few passes with their bows, and promptly sit back and take their ease. A little later they might be persuaded to make another tired stroke, only to lapse into a state of semi-consciousness, and so on. The only time I have ever seen them work hard is in the Hall of the Mountain King, and then they move like the devil in a gale of wind."

"Do you know that thing?" asked the Cockney excitedly.

The Digger nodded in the affirmative.

"Well, you hum the air, and I'll play it," cried the excited musician, and without more ado he jumped into the middle of the room, seized an imaginary instrument and the performance began.

The Cockney moved with the agility of a trained acrobat, and as the tempo increased he attacked the instrument with all the fanatical fervour of a mad dervish. His hair was long, and kept in place by liberal applications of margarine. On this occasion, however, the violent head movements soon jerked his locks free. Sometimes they were hanging half-way down his back, the next moment they covered his face like a veil, and all the while the enthusiastic musician, with nothing clutched firmly in his left hand, performed prodigies of mechanical skill with his right arm.

It was a ludicrous sight, and even Howlett and his friend Brice could scarcely forbear to smile. And when the climax came the Cockney flung his head back until his hair almost swept the floor, raised his bow aloft with a splendid flourish, and just as he was preparing to strike a mighty chord from the waiting strings, he froze in his tracks, and remained there rigid, like a breathing image.

We all turned, and there stood the Chief, his little cap looking smaller than ever on his enormous head, his eyes glinting with hostility.

"What's the meaning of all this?" he growled.

As the senior Leader I explained that we were enjoying the half-hour's respite allowed to librarians, that a friendly argument had arisen as to how a certain piece of music should be played, and that the Cockney, as a skilled violinist, had offered to demonstrate how the thing should be done.

"Huh!" he growled again. "Well, just remember that you're all on parole, and that Leaders' jobs are not permanent."

And with that he wheeled and stumped away.

CHAPTER XVI

THE Saturday and Sunday nights' entertainments in the recreation-room were always looked forward to by the Fourth Stage men. As soon as tea was over they were lined up and marched out of D Hall. Men who wanted to read queued up, and after the Leader in charge had handed out the day's newspapers to the tables entitled to them, he distributed previous issues, on the principle of first come, first served.

This work took some time. A note was taken of the men to whom newspapers were issued, it being most important that they should all be accounted for at the end of the evening.

Chess, draughts, and dominoes were booked out in the same way. In the meantime the ping-pong tables had been fixed up in the middle of the room, and games were run off in regular order under the direction of two or three Leaders. Other men engaged in quiet contests at quoits.

As soon as the B.B.C. began to announce the football results all play was stopped, and silence enjoined. The names of the competing teams had already been chalked on a blackboard, and as the scores were announced a Leader wrote them down on the board. When the results were completed the men carried on with their games.

At seven o'clock sharp the ping-pong tables were dismantled and put away, and under the chairmanship of a Leader a concert was held, finishing with the choruses of which Maundy Gregory had complained. Any man who felt inclined could contribute an item, and providing there was a competent pianist in the crowd the concerts went off very successfully.

Sometimes we were lucky enough to have professional singers in our midst. I remember one man, a tenor, who sang beautifully, and would respond to encore after encore, but on the whole the musical items were contributed by gentlemen of the type that grows loudly vocal about closing-time.

Scotch Bob, the Digger's deputy, generally started the ball rolling, and once he had got a footing it required not a little patience and tact to persuade him to desist and give place to someone else.

Bob would sing sentimental Scotch ballads until we rolled off our chairs from sheer exhaustion, and whenever I was in charge I always made a point of satisfying his vocal aspirations first. But he never budged from the piano, in the hope that another opportunity would present itself before eight o'clock arrived. His closest friends were similarly constituted, and they could always be relied upon to provide us with musical fare of a sort.

On Sunday evenings the men due for release during the week had to follow prison tradition and supply the bulk of the entertainment. The performer could sing, recite, make a speech, or tell a story, and although I never saw a refusal, it must be confessed that many of the efforts were simply excruciating.

It was a common thing to see the audience rolling on the floor racked with helpless laughter, while the pitiful artist went stolidly on to the bitter end. The Digger managed to escape this little ordeal, but that was only because the Zulu Chief was leaving the same week, and had so captivated the audience with his war dances and shouts of "Bayete" that they declined to let him go.

The wireless was not very popular. The instrument was frequently out of order, and the noise of the ping-pong players made hearing difficult. One Saturday afternoon the Skipper listened to a crooner for the first time. "How the devil can a man lower himself to disgusting behaviour of that kind?" he growled when the performance finished.

"I don't know," said the Digger, "but as soon as a youngster shows a tendency towards that sort of thing, he ought to be emasculated *pronto*. He would then at least have something to croon about, and his caterwauling could be explained, even if it could not be altogether excused."

Saturday afternoon concerts in the church, which were attended by the whole prison population, lasted from three until four o'clock. A Deputy Governor had a seat on the platform as a compliment to the visitors, but took no part in the proceedings. The items were announced by a member of the concert party.

Naturally the audience was not a critical one; in fact, any item, good, bad, or indifferent, was warmly applauded. There were, however, one or two songs which had become stale by constant repetition, and whenever a spokesman announced that "Miss —— will now favour us with "Cherry Ripe" or "O Sole mio," a great sigh would go up to the vaulted roof.

Nevertheless the men would sit back prepared to be amused at the antics of fat and thin ladies as they trilled and chirruped their way through "Cherry Ripe."

Some of the performers were frequent visitors to the

Scrubs. One of these was a gentleman who ran a small orchestra, and it was obvious from the way he wielded his baton that he was a musical enthusiast. Older hands used to declare that on one occasion he threw himself off the platform and rolled amongst the audience in his excess of zeal, but I was never lucky enough to see him repeat that performance.

At the end of his show the orchestra would break into old favourites, in which the whole audience joined heartily, a form of entertainment which was always greatly appreciated. As the strains of "Tipperary" or "There's a long, long trail a-winding" died away a burst of tremendous applause would rise from the assembled prisoners, and the little man would approach the front of the platform, bowing profoundly at first, his bows becoming shorter and shorter until they became a succession of jerky nods, and he resembled nothing so much as a pigeon crossing the road. We were always delighted by this gentleman's musical efforts to please us, as well as by his diverting mannerisms.

There was another performer who always sticks in my memory. His appearance was seedy, but what he lacked in sartorial decoration he made up for in the superb confidence of his platform manner.

The first time he appeared on the stage, the Digger, who happened to be sitting next to me, whispered: "He hath waxed old as a garment: the moth hath eaten him up," a remark which was beaten by a little Cockney behind us, who said hoarsely to his mate: "Gawd blimey, Bill, he must have been brought up in the Part Worn Store!"

And when the cocksure vocalist opened his mouth a

titter ran round the church. Men twisted and squirmed in their pews. The man could not sing a note in tune, but he stood and poured out the most wonderful stream of discord I have ever listened to, his face wreathed in smiles, sublimely confident of his musical prowess, and thoroughly enjoying the experience of doing good.

The song was "Mother o' Mine," and the rendition was so singularly bad that another item was vociferously demanded. The vocalist gladly responded with the information that he would be enchanted to sing again, "this time," he added, "in Italian."

And he did, but what it was all about I don't know. He was too good a turn to lose, and the obliging artist announced that he would endeavour to charm his hearers a third time with a song in French, thus demonstrating his versatility.

Perhaps the shows put on by Miss Margaret Yarde, the well-known West End actress, and her helpers will live longest in the memories of the inhabitants of D Hall. Once a month on Sundays evenings a play, Shakespearean or Shavian, was staged in the recreation-room.

The Leaders and men who by reason of infirmity could not see or hear well sat on chairs in the "stalls." Behind them sat Fourth Stage prisoners, then came the Third Stage, and the Second Stage men brought up the rear.

Miss Yarde endeared herself to all by the warmth of her nature. She radiated happiness and good cheer, and the sight of her smiling face made us forget for an hour at least the pangs of captivity.

The men doted on her, and even if she took no part in the play, as sometimes happened, the honours of the evening went always to Margaret. We realized how much it must have cost her in time and trouble to keep up these entertainments month after month, and year after year, and I would like her to know how deep was the impression she made on the prisoners by her unselfish devotion to the cause of happiness.

On one or two occasions her shows were postponed through indisposition, and we Leaders were pestered by inquiries as to Margaret's health, and when she would be fit to visit us again. People who work quietly and unobtrusively rarely come into the limelight, and the benefactors of lawbreakers are not likely to figure in honours lists, but if anyone deserves public recognition for faithful services to suffering humanity it is Margaret Yarde. God bless her!

More often than not the plays were read from the book. I remember one occasion when a young and pretty actress came flying through a door in the wings, to be brought up violently, face foremost, against a table on the stage. In making her entry, and scanning her lines at the same time, she had tripped over a piece of wood on the floor. Fortunately no damage was done, but a wag in the audience caused loud laughter by shouting out, as she made her sudden and unexpected appearance, "One on, sir!"

When the performers took the curtain, one of the Leaders would present the leading lady with a bouquet of flowers. There were always resounding cheers for Margaret.

Sports meetings were held at Easter and Whitsun under the direction of the Games Sub-Committee, and the events were run off with all the speed and precision that one would expect at a regular athletic gathering.

P

The day's sport terminated with boxing contests, which were refereed by officers. Only D Hall prisoners were allowed to participate. Competitors had to be passed as fit by the doctors, and were compelled to sign a declaration that they would not hold the prison authorities responsible for accidents.

Public holidays were not occasions for rejoicing amongst C Hall prisoners. When they were not exercising they were locked up in their cells. There was plenty of time for reading, if they had the literature, and they could listen to the shouts of their D Hall companions as they cheered the competitors in the athletic events.

The Skipper was an inveterate reader of Wells. Every morning it was his custom to bring to the library a list of unusual words, which had stumped him during the evening's reading, and before consulting the dictionary he always submitted the list to the Digger, who, as far as I can recollect, was never beaten.

One day he flourished the paper with the remark, "I think I've got you this time." The Digger asked what the trouble was. "Insussurate," was the answer, but the New Zealander gave the meaning without the slightest hesitation.

Asked if he had seen the word in English before, the Digger replied that he hadn't, but that he was familiar with the Latin word *insussurus*. "It's no use asking you anything," growled the disappointed Skipper; "you're a bloody book on two legs!" But the Digger declined to be regarded as a book, alleging that the ability to construe obscure words was only one of the minor advantages of a classical education.

Only on one occasion had a classical training led him

astray. He had gone to Gloucester for a holiday, and on his way to the house where he was staying he passed a small greengrocer's shop daily. On the window were printed the words "T. Jones, Fruiterer & Greengrocer," and underneath, in much larger letters, "S.P.Q.R."

S.P.Q.R. worried him, and nobody could tell him what the letters meant. The only explanation he could think of was Senatus Populusque Romanus, but what had the Senate and Roman people to do with a little greengrocer in Gloucester?

At the end of a week the Digger determined to make a small purchase and inquire at the source. As the fruit was changing hands, he asked Mr. Jones what S.P.Q.R. meant. Before that bucolic gentleman could reply a door at the back of the counter opened, and a lanky, spindly-legged girl of sixteen shrilled at him: "Small profits, quick returns!" She closed the door as quickly as she had opened it, and the Digger went out on to the street with his apples and the translation.

After telling us this story he advised the Skipper to give up the intensive study of Wells in the scientific mood, otherwise his sesquipedalian language would cramp the Skipper's style. I passed some observation on H. G.'s astounding industry. "Yes," commented the Digger, "whichever way you look at them, the old hands, —Wells, Shaw, Rudyard Kipling, and Chesterton—knock these perky youngsters of to-day sideways."

The younger generation was noisy and crude without being convincing: infants crying in the night, and bawling not because they were bewildered or afraid, but because it paid to make a row. There was little intellectual basis to their revolt.

The Skipper remarked on the declining popularity of
Indian tales. "Yes," agreed the Digger, "but Parkman
is always interesting. As an historian he beats both
Prescott and Motley, and if ever you have the opportunity you ought to read *The Jesuits in North America*.
Parkman had no sympathy whatever with Roman Catholi-
cism, but the story of the lives of the two martyr priests,
Fathers Jogues and Brèboeuf, who lived and died amongst
the Hurons, is one of the noblest epics ever written. The
maimed priest in Conan Doyle's fine book *The Refugees*
is drawn from Jogue's life."

The Skipper wanted to know what Parkman thought
of the Red Indian. "He knocks most of the romance out
of him," answered the Digger. "You won't find an Uncas
in his pages, but then the scientific or philosophic mind
never finds anything to admire in savagery."

He went on to say that Darwin had recorded similar
opinions of the Maoris. He looked upon them as dirty,
lazy savages, but he did pay a grudging tribute to their
warlike qualities.

When Darwin visited the Islands he stayed with a
missionary, whose name the Digger had forgotten. Two
neighbouring tribes were bickering about the ownership
of land, and indications pointed to a speedy resort to
arms. To avoid that calamity the missionary called the
two tribes together, and pleaded the cause of Christianity
so effectively that the Maoris agreed to submit the matter
to arbitration. But just as the conference was breaking up
a sub-Chief made a hurried entry, and whispered in his
War Chief's ear. A dozen kegs of powder recently pur-
chased from the traders were going bad. It had to be used
before it got too bad, and war was declared on the spot.

The Skipper remarked that that was as good a reason as could be adduced for most wars, and asked if there was anything in the library dealing with the early history of New Zealand. Apparently there was nothing of any value.

The Digger declared that far and away the best book on that subject was Manning's *Old New Zealand*. Manning, he said, went to the colony as a young man. He was adopted by a native tribe, and became a Pakeha Maori. His job was much like that of a business manager's, a position rendered necessary by the pressure for modern arms and equipment. The natives would dispose of thousands of acres of land for a few muskets or hatchets, and quickly disclosed their ability to assimilate Western methods by selling the same land to half a dozen buyers, only one of whom could get any sort of title in the long run.

Manning understood and loved the native character, and possessed literary gifts of a high order. His book showed that Spiritualism was no new thing. The Maori Tohunga, or Medicine Man, called up spirits from the vasty deep with the same zest and ease as he might slash a trussed prisoner's throat, and gulp the blood of the victim as it spurted from the gaping wound.

The Skipper wanted to know if the Tohunga influence still remained. "It is dying," replied the Digger, "but it is not yet dead." During the war, he said, the authorities had a lot of trouble with an old scoundrel called Rua. Rua started a religious movement, a crude mixture of Christianity and Mormonism. His followers wore their hair long, and loafed about in their palisaded *pah* in the King country waiting for the end of the world, when they all expected to be snatched up into heaven.

On one occasion he pledged himself to repeat the miracle of our Lord, and walk on the water. The excited natives were assembled on the sea-shore, quite certain that another record was about to be equalled if not broken. Rua kept his tent, but as the fateful hour struck he appeared to his followers, who received him with loud shouts of acclamation. "Do you believe that I can do this thing?" he demanded. "We do," was the unanimous reply. "Well, seeing that there are no doubters amongst you," said the old humbug, "there is no real necessity for me to make the attempt"; and he retired to his tent with his *mana* unimpaired. *Mana*, the Digger explained, was one of the few Maori words that had been locally assimilated into the English language, and even serious journals preferred its use to the English word prestige.

"And what happened to the old boy?" asked the Skipper.

It appeared that Rua backed the wrong horse in the war. He prophesied that the Kaiser would win, and made no secret of his intention to conclude a treaty with Wilhelm as soon as he had taken his place in the sun. The prophet's open expressions of disloyalty annoyed the authorities, who discovered, or pretended to discover, that he was trading in liquor, the sale of which was prohibited in the King country. An armed police force was sent to arrest Rua, but on their approach to the *pah* the younger warriors opened fire, which was returned by the police. The stronghold was rushed, six of the defenders were killed, and Rua was captured and sentenced to imprisonment for fifteen years. Rua, according to the Digger, would probably be the last Tohunga to cause the Government any serious trouble.

Later in the afternoon news was brought to the library that a prisoner in C Hall had attempted to commit suicide, but had been cut down in time. During my stay in Wormwood Scrubs I think there were three cases of attempted suicide, all by newcomers to the prison, and in each instance the man had tied the mail bag rope to the bars of his window and jumped off the chair in the cell.

The Digger maintained that a man had a perfect right to take his own life if he found it insupportable, and that interference by the State was an impertinence. In England, he contended, the way they dealt with suicides was simply ridiculous. If a man succeeded, a coroner sat on him and found that he was of unsound mind. If he bungled the job, and recovered, they put him in the dock, and if they felt like it packed him off to Wormwood Scrubs.

No question of his sanity ever arose if the man survived, and the Digger asserted that he would not rank suicide as a much worse offence than gate-crashing. Perhaps a wife might be allowed to bring an action for attempted desertion, but no more.

From suicide the conversation turned to murder, and the Skipper, who had just finished reading a book on the history of Wormwood Scrubs, was asked if any condemned man had ever been executed there. As far as he knew he said, the Scrubs had never suffered that disgrace.

The Digger remarked that he was very glad to hear it. Old Howlett, however, protested against the spread of modern sentimentalism, which strove to deprive the community of the most effective and only practical deterrent to capital crimes. The administration of British Justice had achieved its high reputation as a result of the speed and certainty with which crime, including murder, was detected and punished. Abolish the death penalty and we would immediately sink into the disgraceful position in which America found herself to-day, with private citizens at the mercy of gangsters, and armed bandits taking life indiscriminately.

But the Digger would not listen to this. America's history, constitution, and the temperament of her conglomerate population, were wholly different from ours, and in European countries where the death penalty had been abolished there was no evidence at all to support the contention that serious crime had increased. Howlett mentioned Germany, but the Digger answered that Germany had re-introduced the axe as a useful political weapon for the extermination of the critics of the present régime.

Could anyone honestly say that in the vast majority of these crimes the murderer was in a mental condition to weigh and consider the consequences of his act, or that vast numbers of potential murderers owed their existence to the fear of the rope?

Our penal history was one of the most ferocious in the world. A hundred years ago, nearly two hundred offences were punishable by death, and boys of eight were sentenced to death for stealing from a dwelling-house to the value of five shillings. There was no connexion or analogy whatever between crime and punishment, and the brutalities of the law excited not the slightest comment in the Courts or in the Press.

"What about the Church?" inquired the Skipper. "The Church!" ejaculated the Digger. "The Church does not trespass on Caesar's kingdom: it simply prepares candidates for Heaven, and reads the Burial Service. The

Church claims to be a great stabilizing factor in society. In other words, it stands for the perpetuation of things as they are. The Church has never raised its voice against legalized savagery."

If his memory served him, even such a good fellow as Doctor Johnson defended the Tyburn executions on the grounds that these degrading exhibitions had a chastening influence on the criminal population of London.

Howlett retorted that His Majesty's Judges were surely the most competent people to express an opinion as to whether penalties prescribed by the law were too harsh, and there was no doubt that the majority to-day favoured the retention of the death sentence.

The Digger emphatically declared that they were the last people in the world who should be asked for an opinion on the matter. Every vital penal reform had been opposed by Judges. The proposal to abolish the death penalty for stealing trifling sums from the person was violently attacked by the famous Lord Ellenborough, who prophesied, out of the fullness of his vast judicial experience, that if it were allowed to become law society must inevitably disintegrate.

Nothing of the sort happened. There was no unusual increase in the petty crimes for which death was the then penalty. Hanging was the fate of the forger, but that punishment was removed at the instance of the bankers, not out of any sympathy for their enemies, but because they were unable to secure convictions owing to the humanity of the jurors.

Questions of that kind should always be judged and decided by ordinary citizens, who did not bring to their consideration the mind and outlook of the avenger. And talking of the most extreme form of punishment, what was the attitude of society to the hangman? We treated him as an outcast, as something unclean. No decent person would associate with an executioner, or knowingly remain in the same room with him. He was smuggled into prison to do his dirty work, and smuggled out of it again. He had never known of a hangman being congratulated or honoured for public services well and faithfully performed, but if the job was necessary and decent why should the man be overlooked? The truth was, of course, that we were heartily ashamed of him, and the less seen or heard of him the better.

"Well," observed Howlett, "the majority of the people in this country still stand for the principle of an eye for an eye, a tooth for a tooth."

"I don't believe it," replied the Digger. "It is difficult to get a law altered in which most people are only very remotely concerned, but I would start by abolishing the official hangman, and drawing the executioner by lot from the ordinary jury lists. Many people boggle at serving on juries at all. How would they behave if in order to serve the ends of justice they were compelled to draw the bolt, and launch a condemned murderer into eternity? We should very soon have a nation of conscientious objectors to capital punishment."

The Skipper slyly suggested that the Digger's criticism of Judges was based on an unfortunate experience of them, but the latter stoutly denied the accusation. He had numbered Judges amongst his friends, but on large matters of public policy they were not the right people to appeal to.

He could never get it out of his head that society was

frequently mad and bad and utterly wrong, but a Judge could never hold that view. A Judge was solemnly pledged to administer the laws as they stood, and in course of time he tended to look upon himself as a divinely appointed agent for the punishment of crime.

Besides, the main motive underlying punishment was revenge. Sir James Stephen, one of our highest authorities, said that the criminal law proceeded upon the principle that it was morally right to hate criminals, and it confirmed and justified that statement by inflicting upon criminals punishment which expressed hatred. Lord Bacon said that a popular Judge was a deformed thing, and that plaudits were fitter for players than for magistrates.

A Judge would be more than human if he did not assimilate something of that spirit. The Digger said that he once dined with an ex-Judge, and in the course of their talk he plucked up courage to ask him what his feelings were in sentencing a fellow-creature to death. The old man replied that the experience never affected him in the slightest. The prisoner had been found guilty by a jury of his peers. He, the Judge, was only a cog, an important cog it is true, in the elaborate machinery for bringing a criminal to book, and the mere formality of pronouncing the dread words was not a thing to disturb a man with a well-controlled imagination.

"And I thought," continued the Digger, "as I surveyed the genial features of the old gentleman: 'In another environment, what a gangster you would have made!' "

He then went on to tell us a story. Two old boys, once schoolfellows, met after many years of separation, and were discussing the merits of their respective professions.

One was a Bishop and the other a Judge. The Bishop argued that his was a greater and more important job, because while the Judge could say "You are hanged," he could say "You be damned."—"Yes," tittered the Judge, "but if I say you be hanged, you *are* hanged!"

The Skipper laughingly agreed that the Judge had made a good hit, and the conversation veered round to the foundations of our legal system. The Digger had something to say about the severity of the penal laws of Rome, and finally of the qualifications required for distinction in the Roman Forum. Cicero had enumerated them in great detail, and they represented a range of practice and study which would make most of us shudder.

The Skipper lamented the fact that he knew nothing at all of the ancient languages. "You wouldn't believe it," he said, "but I know the meaning of only one Latin phrase, *lex talionis*."

"Oh, yes?" said the Digger casually; and then the Skipper favoured us with his translation: "The lion's claws."

The next moment the Digger had given him a tremendous whack on the back. "You've made history this day, Skipper," he cried. "A howler to delight the hearts of schoolboys and pedagogues!"

"What the devil do you mean?" demanded the Skipper angrily. "*Lex*, law," said the Digger, "*is* something like *leo*, lion, and *talio*, retaliation, might pass with a beginner for claws or talons!"

When the Skipper discovered his error he was greatly mortified, but quickly regained his spirits, and to make the best of matters he remarked how true it was that a little knowledge was a dangerous thing.

"Speaking of howlers," said the Digger, "here's one which you, Aussie, will appreciate. A schoolboy, writing on the Black Hole of Calcutta, said that Surajah Dowlah threw one hundred and fifty Englishmen into a dark dungeon with one small *widow*: in the morning only twenty-three staggered out alive. Had you had the misfortune to be there you would no doubt have been one of the survivors, you tough old libertine!" But the Aussie chose to be offended, and retorted angrily that far too many allusions were made to his ruling passion, and if he liked to retaliate by speaking of the treasons, stratagems, and spoils of other people, life in the library would become unbearable.

The Aussie had a bosom companion in one of the Redbands of C Hall, who frequently came to the library with messages from C Hall warders. This gentleman's sole topic of conversation was the war. He and the Aussie had first met in Egypt, and they talked of Gallipoli and the Battle of the Wazir until our heads ached.

Although there were many old soldiers in Wormwood Scrubs, one heard surprisingly little of the war, which is fast becoming a faded memory.

Armistice Day was celebrated with appropriate solemnity. The men attended Church service, and the two minutes' silence was reverentially observed, after which a prominent visitor delivered an address. On the occasion I have in mind Major Boyd Carpenter was the speaker.

A magnificent cross of flowers stood in front of the altar, and when the service was over the prisoners passed the cross in single file, each man turning to his front and making a profound obeisance. Some of the younger men drew themselves erect and saluted smartly. Probably they

238 PRISON   FROM   WITHIN

had lost their sires in that cataclysm. Altogether it was a solemn and moving spectacle.

Later in the day we were discussing the ceremony, and the Digger argued that the time must soon come when the celebration of Armistice Day would have to be abandoned. A generation was growing up which knew nothing of the war and its agony, and they could hardly be expected to keep alive the memory of what was little more to them than an episode in history. Besides, he said, we might be building another Cenotaph before very long, and the million men who fell in 1914–18 would be completely forgotten for another army of the dead.

We could understand the feelings that prompted a grateful nation to employ the text "Their Name Liveth for Evermore," but he could not for the life of him see that it was true. It was no truer than that wonderful slogan "A war to end war," which spurred a jaded people on to make the supreme effort.

The Skipper reminded him of Doctor Johnson's observation that in lapidary inscriptions a man was not on his oath. The Digger agreed, but held that something equally noble and dignified with a closer relation to reality might have been used. The Greeks did the thing better, as witness the lines on the heroes of Thermopylae:

> Go tell the Spartans, thou that passest by,
> That here obedient to their laws we lie.

He could not follow the reasoning that a man was a hero because he was dead. Many of our comrades had fallen in battle. They were men like ourselves, no better and no worse, but their memory was said to be enshrined for ever in a nation's heart. What happened to those who came through the furnace? They sold poppies for them on one day in the year, and the ex-soldier who could not get a job was not a hero but a damned nuisance. Besides, in these days of business efficiency it soon would not pay to say that you had been a soldier, for service in 1914 would prove that you were well over forty, and therefore on the down-grade.

"I suppose," said the Skipper, "that it's easy to erect monuments and write lofty eulogies in brass, but when a war is over and the noble band of brothers is demobilized, we revert to the principle of each for himself and the devil take the hindmost; or in other words, business as usual."

"Yes," said the Digger; "there is one side of war which will always appeal to generous hearts. No man who has not fought knows what true comradeship means, when men are united, a band of brothers, in a common object. In a front line trench all artificial barriers are swept away. A man is loved and admired for what he is in himself, and not for his position in the world. And for fellows like you and me, Skipper, the men who served will always be our true brethren, living or dead."

CHAPTER XVII

THE evening educational classes took the place of cell tasks for Second, Third, and Fourth Stage men. As a serious preparation for a trade or profession which a prisoner might enter on his return to civil life, they were, I think, a complete failure. As a means of diversion and recreation they were greatly appreciated by all.

Short-sentence men dropped out almost as soon as they had started their educational training. Not the slightest attempt was made to assess a man's intellectual capacity, and to determine, by reference to his character and acquired knowledge, a course of training which might enable him successfully to face the world again.

The consequence was that men applied for admission to the most popular classes—i.e. those where they were assured of the most fun and enjoyment. Their ability to take up any course of study, utilitarian or otherwise, was restricted only by the limitation imposed on the numbers in any one class. The Aussie, for instance, solemnly recited poetry once a week, about which he knew nothing and cared less, but the teacher had the reputation for being easy-going, and his pupils were under no obligation to read up the subject in their cells.

The most popular class of all boasted the resounding title of "Advanced Literature and Music," and met once a week in the church. Its membership was limited to sixty. The lecturer was popularly supposed to be the musical critic for *The Times*, and he was undoubtedly an expert in his profession. This lecturer's method was to give a short description of the life and work of any eminent musical composer, after which he would sit down at the piano and play a few characteristic productions.

All the prisoners had to do in this class was to listen to a very pleasant talk and concert, and they could even ask for special items, to which the lecturer would respond without the slightest hesitation, revealing simultaneously a very remarkable memory and brilliant execution.

This gentleman provided us with one of the few thrills I experienced in the Scrubs. The class had been marched into the church, and sat waiting for the lecturer's arrival, but nearly a quarter of an hour elapsed before he put in an appearance. We noticed that his left wrist carried a bandage, and he explained that that afternoon he had been thrown from a horse in Richmond Park, but that fortunately his injuries were slight, and would not prevent him from carrying through the usual programme.

The class clapped him and settled down to listen. At a quarter to eight he had something to say about Beethoven, and presently was deep in one of the Sonatas. The class was always marched back to D Hall at eight o'clock sharp, but five minutes past eight came, and the pianist was only half way through the composition.

At that moment Holy Joe entered the church, but a very different Holy Joe from the one we saw every morning. Gone was the benevolent smile and the kindly eye. His face was set in rigid lines of determination, as became a man who had been ordered by a higher authority to carry out an unpleasant task at any cost. Looking neither to the right or the left, Holy Joe strode up to the platform, and without a "by your leave" or a word of protest to the engrossed musician, he firmly closed the piano.

Q

The lecturer leapt to his feet as if he had been stung by a hornet. "You can do what you like with prisoners," he cried, "but by God, if you take a liberty with me you'll find your match!" and he proceeded to tell Holy Joe what he thought of his unmannerly interruption, in language and style that could hardly be bettered. To all of which invective Holy Joe kept on repeating like a trained parrot: "It's after time, it's after time!"

The class listened fascinated. Men squirmed with excitement and pleasure, but after a particularly blistering volley of abuse Holy Joe signalled to a warder to move off, and we filed out of the church, straining our ears to catch the sweetest music our skilful pianist had ever produced.

The general opinion was that we had seen the last of the man who had afforded us so much delight, but on the following Thursday, at seven o'clock, a stentorian warder's voice rang out "Men for Advanced Literature and Music," and we trooped back to the church and waited on tenterhooks for the arrival of our friend.

In he came at last, as dapper and cheerful as ever, and when he mounted the platform a storm of applause broke from the assembled prisoners, and continued without intermission for some minutes.

We were proud of him, and more than grateful for the way he had trounced Holy Joe. It did not matter that the latter was the kindest and most popular man in the prison. He represented authority, and authority had been told just where it got off, and told in a way that we should have loved to emulate ourselves if it could have been done without reprisals.

The Digger belonged to two classes of which I was a member, World History and the History of Europe.

Both the teachers were capable and enthusiastic young men, and one of them was something of a martinet.

I can remember that he threatened to report the Digger for laziness. Students were supposed to take copious notes of his lectures, and he insisted on a certain amount of home work as well. Every week, however, the Digger calmly handed in an empty exercise book for revision. At last he was ordered to write an essay on the points of resemblance, if any, between the Roman and British Empires, or justify his behaviour before the Governor.

I never saw his literary effort, which he hammered out one night when he was on D Hall duty, but I know that he was never troubled again. This youngster was a most serious pedagogue. His pronunciation of proper names like Zeus and Herodotus showed that he had never enjoyed a classical education. But he had the root of the matter in him, and knew his subject well.

The teacher of World History allowed a wide freedom of discussion, and the class frequently took on the appearance of a debating society. He had a strong tendency to preach the doctrine that one man was as good as another, and that our alleged superiority over coloured peoples was based on an illusion.

The South African, who had been brought up amongst negroes, and despised them as an inferior race, caused some fun one night. The instructor was trying to tell us that given suitable conditions, and the means of absorbing the lessons of science and civilization, native races very quickly rose to the same level as our own.

He had spent the previous week in the company of a West African doctor, a man of wide culture and high intellectual attainments. Would anyone there refuse to trust his wife in the professional hands of such a man simply on the score of colour?

And the South African promptly said that he would. "Why?" asked the teacher. "Because," replied the South African, with all the solemnity and conviction he could command, "it's against all the laws of cohabitation." But nothing could persuade him to disclose what the laws of cohabitation were. Although he claimed to have been an editor at one time, and had more confidence in himself than any man I have ever met before or since, his command of English was never anything but shaky, and he kept on repeating his certainty that the laws of cohabitation would be violated by the employment of a black doctor, until the instructor had to give up his questioning as a bad job.

One evening the Digger and the instructor engaged in a tussle. The latter was speaking of the growth of our Empire, and touched on the question of the loyalty of the Dominions overseas. Did anyone really believe that the Dominions were heart and soul with us in the late war, and was it not possible that in another European conflagration they would stand aloof, and allow the Mother Country to fight it out without striking a blow on her behalf?

"If you have any doubts on that point, I think I can remove them," said the Digger rising from his chair. "New Zealand has a population of approximately one and a half million people. She trained and sent abroad 120,000 men a distance of 11,000 miles. Multiply those figures by four, and you have Australia's contribution— a stupendous effort when you consider that Australia relied entirely upon the voluntary system. Apart from the provision of men, there was the question of money, and both countries burdened themselves with debt to achieve the common goal. They would cheerfully do the same thing again if the safety of the Motherland were menaced, because they realize that their own freedom and security are inextricably bound up with hers."

The teacher mentioned one or two experiences he had had of hostile feeling in South Africa, where he had spent eighteen months on exchange.

"There," said the Digger, "you make the mistake of drawing hasty generalizations from one or two particular incidents in South Africa, a country with internal racial animosities, and problems which are not shared by Canada, Australia, and New Zealand. Those problems will be solved in time. They cannot be expected to disappear in a generation, but that the whites in South Africa are drawing closer together in a common allegiance to the Commonwealth through the nexus of the Crown there is not the slightest doubt."

It says much for this young teacher that he never resented informed criticism from his class. In fact, he seemed thoroughly to enjoy a spirited controversy, and any man who could express himself at all was always assured of a sympathetic hearing.

The class on biology was a large one, and was presided over by a woman, who was said to be an expert of national reputation on her subject. As far as I know, she was the only woman to give her services to Wormwood Scrubs.

I have a faint recollection that at one of her classes two prisoners, one of them a member of the Digger's table, were cased for surreptitiously releasing a live mouse from a cage in which it was imprisoned. The little animal had served as the object lesson for the evening, and as it scuttled across the floor the scientific spirit was ignominiously put to flight, and the good lady made a sudden leap at a table, with her skirts clutched tightly about her legs.

Another large class studied the history of the City of London. The gentleman in charge was an enthusiast, and was also, I understand, a writer of some distinction on his pet hobby. He was so word perfect in exposition, and spoke with such rapidity, that it was often difficult to keep pace with him, but he generated quite a lot of interest in his subject. He also addressed us at Christmas time in a humorous vein on cricket, and some of the better-known characters of Dickens.

The opening of the educational session gave rise to a rather amusing incident in connexion with this lecturer's class. Word came through that all books on the history of the City of London were to be collected and taken to the Governor's office. The Digger was instructed to bring in such as were in use from the cells. He gathered together a very respectable assortment of big and little volumes, and one day the Librarian said to him: "Well, Leader, if you're ready, and can manage it, we'll take those books along to the Governor."

The load was a formidable one, and was arranged like a pyramid, the big tomes forming the base, with the little ones piled on top to the level of the Digger's nose. He marched behind the Librarian, gallantly struggling to keep a proper balance, and behaving much like a juggler on the stage. Within twenty minutes he was back and shaking with laughter.

It was the time-honoured custom of warders in charge of parties to address passing superiors in this fashion: "Twenty men, sir, all correct," or "Eighty men, sir, all correct," as the case might be.

When the pair were half-way to headquarters they ran into the Governor himself, whom the Librarian saluted with the words "*One* man, sir, all correct," and halted to explain his errand, while the Digger cavorted round in circles, performing feats of juggling and balancing that would have done credit to a professional, much to the Governor's astonishment.

The Debating Class also enjoyed a large measure of popularity, until the gentleman in charge introduced the experiment of calling on members haphazard to speak for five minutes on any subject which he might propose, and for which the wretched prisoner had no opportunity to make the slightest preparation.

The night this innovation was made, fifteen men, who could not face the ordeal, absented themselves, but they were all cased, and awarded punishment of some kind. I did not attend this class, but the Skipper took a prominent part in the discussions, and frequently led either in proposing or opposing a motion.

One week he was down to oppose a motion that the submarine should be abolished, and he indicated to us the attitude he intended to adopt.

In his opinion any belligerent with its back to the wall and faced with the prospect of overwhelming disaster was entitled to use every weapon, whether prohibited by international agreement or otherwise. The readiness of our own Government to abandon by agreement the use of submarines was based solely on expediency, because we stood to lose more by unrestricted submarine warfare than any other country.

The great object of war was to seek out the enemy and destroy him. To-day the enemy meant not only your opponent's effectives, but every enemy national of whatever age or sex, and it was sheer madness on the part of a Government confronting the possibility of defeat to refrain from the use of any destructive weapon that science placed at its disposal. In such circumstances the law of self-preservation must obliterate all regard for the sanctity of covenants and the humane treatment of civil populations.

Someone remarked that the Germans in the late war had not scrupled to violate every rule of civilized warfare, but that we had behaved with a chivalry that was almost absurdly quixotic. "I wouldn't go as far as that," interposed the Digger. "Our people always did, and always will play the game when humanly possible, but we were not such fools as to expose ourselves to unnecessary risks for the sake of appearing *le preux chevalier sans peur et sans reproche.*"

He went on to illustrate his point, by telling us the story of his last trip across the Mediterranean. They set out from Port Said, a mighty and imposing armada of forty ships escorted by a dozen destroyers, with aeroplanes wheeling overhead and leading the way. He would not easily forget their passage to the open sea, past the great statue of de Lesseps, with destroyers of every allied nation on either side, fully manned, and cheering them to the echo.

The *Ellenga*, their troopship, was packed with Australian and New Zealand soldiers, and as the most

precious cargo in that argosy, occupied a position immediately behind the Commodore's flagship, and right in
the centre of the fleet.

It was not necessary to describe their daily experiences,
the Digger said. Suffice it to say that they were attacked
by a horde of submarines the moment they left Egyptian
waters, and the troopship trembled to the shock of depth
charges every day.

When the fleet passed Malta two Italian ships slipped
away at dusk one Sunday evening to rendezvous with a
flotilla of Italian destroyers the following day. They
never reached their destination. A couple of submarines
broke off from the pursuing enemy, came to the surface at
dawn, and sank the Italians with gunfire.

Twenty-four hours later, about noon, a torpedo missed
the *Ellenga* by eight or nine feet. A French ship, *L'Atlantique*, carrying civilian passengers from North Africa, was
stationed some fifty or sixty yards away from her, and
she received the torpedo in the bows.

The shock of the explosion threw the Digger to the
deck, but he rose in time to see the gun, which French
boats carried in the bows, and the gun's crew, about a
hundred feet in the air, just turning over to drop headlong
into the sea.

A fairly heavy sea was running, and then, to their
horror, a panic seized the passengers on the stricken
ship. Men and women, some with little children in their
arms, hurled themselves overboard in a sort of mad
ecstasy. They saw them disappear for ever, arms raised
aloft as if appealing to Heaven, and piercing screams of
terror rang in their ears.

It was one of the most harrowing scenes he had ever

witnessed, not only on account of the fate of the poor
victims, but also because of their position as helpless
spectators.

The fleet passed on. *L'Atlantique* was sinking fast by
the head. Two destroyers remained behind, but the
troops never knew what happened, and all they could
do was to hope that she might be towed safely to port.

The next day the sea had moderated. A brilliant sun
shone on the bluest water in the world. White gulls
wheeled overhead, and looking at the wonderful pano-
rama one might have been tempted to believe that
Nature, in any case, was on the side of the angels.

At ten o'clock the Digger was on the top deck with a
friend. "What do you think they will do this morning,
Mac?" he inquired. "The bastards haven't had breakfast yet," replied Mac cheerfully, from the depths of a
French dictionary.

Hardly were the words out of his mouth than a dozen
shells plunged into the sea in front of them, drenching
the *Ellenga* in spray. The peaceful atmosphere of a
moment before was torn and sundered by the thunder
of our destroyers' guns, but it ceased as abruptly as it had
begun.

The gulls swept away in discordant flight, and the
troops dashed to stations. The Digger's job was to call
the roll, detail instructions for the manning of a raft, and
inspect the lifebelts of his platoon.

And so they stood rigidly at attention, waiting for an
explosion that would send them all to Kingdom Come.
The strain was terrific. An eerie stillness brooded over the
whole scene. The phantom fleet moved on.

Not a sound could be heard on the *Ellenga* but the

pounding of the ship's engines and occasional howls from the lascar crew as they were booted back to their posts.

And then the supernatural quiet was broken by a cheer coming from the right horn of the crescent. It grew in volume and intensity, and it was impossible to mistake that note of savage triumph, with which men grew familiar in the day of battle, when the enemy shows signs of yielding, or goes to his doom.

The troops broke ranks and rushed to the side. At the sight that met their eyes a hoarse and blood-curdling yell burst from the crowded ship, above which could be plainly heard the exultant "Hah Hahs" of a group of Maori warriors in the rolling rhythm of the war dance.

There, lying within twenty feet of them, was a German submarine, her crew struggling wildly to get out of the conning tower. The first shells had found their target, and the *Ellenga* passed over the submarine, which then came to the surface, apparently as helpless as a stranded whale.

But our people were taking no risks. As soon as the *Ellenga* had moved out of the danger zone the violent cannonading from the British destroyers reopened, and the enemy were swept off the surface of the water.

"Do you mean to say," asked old Howlett, "that no effort was made to rescue these men?"

"Not the slightest," replied the Digger. "You must remember that we were followed and attacked, not by one submarine, but by a flotilla of the blighters, and any attempt at rescue might have been rewarded by another torpedo. It would have been madness, beset as we were by these under-water assassins to run any risk; and you can take it from one who knows, Howlett, that after spending eight or nine days in the company of enemy submarines, there is no room in one's mind for courtesy and charity, or even common humanity."

The Digger agreed with the Skipper. It was unreasonable to expect belligerents engaged in a life and death struggle to adhere strictly to the use of agreed weapons or methods of warfare. If it were possible, why did we not return at once to the use of bows and arrows?

One evening, when the Digger and I were strolling down D Hall on our way to join the class on Economics, we noticed a wall of men, two or three deep, in one of the washing-places.

The hangdog expression on the faces of one or two of them suggested that some mischief was afoot, and we halted. Then we heard blows and stifled curses, and the noise of stertorous breathing. "Make way, you lads," called the Digger, "and let the ferret see the duck!"

With some reluctance a lane was opened up, and he passed through, presently to emerge dragging Scotch Bob by the ear. "Confound you, Bob," cried the Digger, "you're no sooner back from a stretch in C Hall than you ask for another. Clear out of this, and don't let me see your ugly mug again to-night!"

Bob didn't wait for any more telling, but moved down the Hall as fast as his legs could carry him. We dispersed the men, and then Bob's opponent, a quarrelsome, sullen sort of fellow, came shambling out.

"What are you going to do about this?" inquired the Digger.

"Nothing," replied the man. "It was a fair fight, and I'm not squealing."

"You realize," continued the Digger, "that it is our duty

to report this disturbance, and that you and Bob will be punished.

The man agreed, but pointed out that there were no warders present, and that he would do anything rather than return to C Hall, where he had spent three wearisome sojourns. "As long as you can keep a still tongue in your head," answered the Digger, "we might be able to hold our peace, but I'm promising nothing." And we left.

Two, three days passed. Nothing more was heard of the incident, and I began to breathe more freely again. When all chance of danger had disappeared, I asked the Digger why he had dared to run such risks when there were so many witnesses, any one of whom might have informed a warder, with serious consequences to both of us.

"I had to take a chance," was the reply, "and events have justified the decision. You see, Scotch Bob was due to complete twelve months in prison the following day, a circumstance which entitled him to a small but attractive addition to his rations, and he had faithfully promised me the rind off his cheese, and one pickle a week."

CHAPTER XVIII

ON two occasions only were the Digger and I put down for duty together in D Hall. We appreciated each other's company, and the work was always congenial, but the arrangement meant that one of us had to go without *The Times*, and we both preferred that paper to any other.

Every evening the Leader in charge of the recreation-room brought back the day's newspapers. Those Leaders who were prevented through other duties from attending the recreation-room made their own choice, and could enjoy the inestimable privilege of reading the day's news in their cells between eight and nine o'clock.

The following morning the newspapers were returned as soon as the cells were opened up, and taken to the hospital. Hall duty lasted a week, and the Digger and I took *The Times* and the *Daily Express* alternately. An argument arose in the library as to the merits and demerits of the Press to-day.

Naturally, and for very obvious reasons, *The Times* was not popular with the majority of readers, but the Digger contended that it was the only paper for the man who needed solid food, and not scraps.

The Times, he argued, stood for all that was best in the old order, and never stooped, for the sake of pelf, to tickle the ears of the groundlings. It had dignity, restraint, and a sense of proportion, and faithfully and accurately reported the things that really mattered in the affairs of men and nations.

It was impossible to imagine anything more ridiculous than the methods employed by newspaper rivals to stimulate sales. Look at the baits offered to subscribers: pounds of tea, furniture, books, free insurances, and money prizes, in fact every device that the modern box-office mind could suggest to appeal to the universal human weakness of getting something for nothing. The principles for which the newspaper claimed to stand did not seem to count very much. They did not necessarily have any influence on the new subscriber, who was only anxious about his sideboard or his *Robinson Crusoe*.

And so the mad game went on, with the Advertiser as the milch cow, dazzled and hypnotized by the Chartered Accountants' certificates verifying net increases in the circulations.

Old Howlett referred to the increase in superstition since the war, and the part played by the popular Press in fostering and encouraging it. He thought it was disgraceful that great newspapers with millions of readers should deliberately propagate the idea that there was anything in the pseudo-sciences of astrology and numerology.

The Aussie was an ardent admirer of the *Daily Express*, but there was one contributor with whom he would have nothing to do. People who pretended to see anything funny in Beachcomber's column were not fit to be at large, and the man himself should have been certified as an incurable lunatic years ago.

The Digger replied that the Australian would have to number him amongst the feeble-minded, for he thought that Beachcomber's column was one of the finest things in modern journalism. And behind all Beachcomber's jesting one could easily detect the sincere purpose of a good and humane man. A proper appreciation of his work, though, required a fairly good educational background.

"But for sincerity," remarked the Skipper, "should not the palm be handed to Jimmy Douglas?"

"Yes," assented the Digger. "Jimmy wrings our withers." The Digger often wondered how his soft heart withstood the shocks and bruises of this cruel and callous world. What would happen to him in a Utopian world, of which one could say: "Nothing is here for tears, nothing to wail or knock the breast?" Like Othello, his occupation would be gone. As a weekly cleanser of female tear-ducts, none could stand against Douglas.

The Aussie lamented the dullness of the Sunday papers authorized for prison use.

What a commentary on our vaunted civilization it was, said the Digger, when men could build vast fortunes on the foibles, the weaknesses, and the crimes of mankind and be respected and honoured in the process! But money opened every gate. Put money in your purse, and there was no enemy but death.

So far the men in charge had not abused the immense power they enjoyed. Lord Beaverbrook, for example, by continuous and intensive propaganda in his powerful group of newspapers, forced the pace set by the Government towards the goal of tariffs, and the country was the gainer by his action.

But was it not conceivable that Lord Beaverbrook or Lord Rothermere, or any other newspaper baron, might formulate and propound a policy altogether opposed to the true interests of the people, and as a result of ceaseless propaganda reduce any Government to impotency? Great power and great ambitions formed a dangerous combination.

"But," objected the Skipper, "you must credit their readers with a modicum of common sense. If circulations decline rapidly, these fellows have a habit of changing their tune."

"Yes," assented the Digger, "perhaps the solution of the problem lies in the spread of knowledge, and one of the main objects of our educational system should be the production of people who refuse to accept unreservedly what they see in print."

One night, on Hall duty, I had occasion to reprimand two prisoners for quarrelling, and in order to separate them I called for the Digger's assistance. One of them was a typical Yorkshireman, blunt, bull-necked, rather coarse, and decidedly aggressive. The other man was not one whit behind him in truculence, but his speech was more refined. I first took an interest in their conversation when I heard the latter say: "Yes, I have always understood that they produce very fine cricketers and very excellent pigs in Yorkshire, and I have no doubt when they take the trouble and find the time they will turn out a few gentlemen."

The Yorkshireman was on his feet in a second, his face aflame with anger, but I was in time to prevent a collision, and the traducer of the Rose was packed off to another table at the far end of the Hall.

I remarked to the Digger that the man appeared to hold a very poor opinion of Yorkshiremen. "And yet," replied the Digger, "there was a grain of truth in what he said." He had met Yorkshiremen all over the world, and it was difficult to pick and choose between them. They all seemed alike, physically and mentally, and their main characteristic was an overwhelming faith in their

R

own ability, for which there never appeared to be a sound and adequate reason.

A Leader's duties in Hall were not very onerous, especially after the Third Stage men had settled down comfortably at tables to read, or to play games. The general behaviour was uniformly good, but although a very wide latitude was allowed, there were times when it became necessary to put a stop to filthy conversation. I very soon discovered that most of the really objectionable talk arose through the presence of sexual perverts, of whom there was a fair number in Wormwood Scrubs.

The almost unanimous verdict on these wretched people could be summed up in the words one so frequently heard: "They can't help theirselves!" But there were plenty of bullies of a low and coarse mentality, who loved nothing better than to refer openly, with a wealth of unpleasant detail, to the circumstances of these crimes, and to bait the offenders unmercifully.

Poor old Marshall was one of the worst sufferers in this respect. It is true that his own low and vulgar conversation contributed not a little to these personal attacks. We had to rescue him again and again from little gangs of hooligans, who, unless they were closely watched, pursued him relentlessly with all the fervour of inquisitors, and roared with laughter when he lost his temper under their disgusting cross-examination.

The problem of what the Digger described as the Cohorts of the Damned was one which the authorities never seriously tackled. It is true that nothing in the British Pharmacopœia can ever cure moral degeneracy, but if the claims made for modern psychological treatment have any basis in fact, surely some attempt might have been made to transform these social outcasts into normal citizens.

To my mind it was a disgraceful state of affairs that homosexualists should have been allowed to mix with ordinary prisoners. There was not, indeed, much risk of contamination. The decent man turns from unnatural practices with loathing and contempt, but it was a punishment of the severest and most uncalled-for kind to be compelled to sit at the same table with these creatures, and to breathe the same atmosphere.

The knowledge that they were repulsive to their fellows did not seem to worry the sexual perverts very much. Some of them talked freely, and even boasted of their depravity, and on the slightest provocation would engage in the lewdest and most offensive talk without a trace of self-consciousness.

On one occasion somebody twitted the Digger with being unusually quiet, to which he did not even venture to reply. Pressed by the Skipper as to the cause of his depression, he said that he was mentally ill. Probably nobody would ever have guessed that he was pining for the return of his two by twos, but the sooner they were home again the better he would like it. The Jews happened to be celebrating the feast of the Passover at the time, and lived and ate apart.

In place of one of them the Digger had a prisoner, a man of considerable wealth, who had been convicted for corrupting boys, including his own two sons. "He sits next to me," continued the Digger, "and he tries to be civil, but I would sooner have my meals in the lavatory. Lacordaire's *tout comprendre, c'est tout pardonner*, is probably right in the last analysis, but this is more than ordinary flesh and blood can stand, and if he's not shifted soon I shall go crazy and break things."

Although the general opinion was that homosexualists were pathological cases, who ought to be subjected to expert medical treatment, the Digger's explanation of his depression accurately represented the feelings of the vast majority of prisoners.

The presence of these men poisoned the air and stifled normal social intercourse. I leave it to the reader to judge of the value of any quasi-reformatory penal system which makes no distinction whatever between a man who offends against the laws of property and another who violates the laws of nature.

One of the most prominent members of this fraternity was a man known to everybody as Brown Jack. He was middle-aged, with close-cropped greying hair, and had occupied a lucrative position in commercial life.

Brown Jack was a man of high intellectual attainments and great business talent, yet it was said that he openly boasted that he had destroyed the virtue of seven boys in one family, and made no secret of what he intended to do as soon as he was released.

I never spoke to this debonair gentleman. He was a social pariah, like the less gifted of his tribe. But he must have had influence of a sort, because to everybody's astonishment he was appointed to Leadership a fortnight before his discharge. Men were seldom made Leaders unless their sentence had a few months to run, and it was an unwritten law that sexual perverts were barred from taking office. Fortunately these moral throw-outs were not allowed to serve their time in the library.

A young clergyman was another figure to attract

general attention. Tall, straight as a guardsman, and with clean-cut features like a Greek god, he looked the perfect type of athletic beauty and symmetry, but there was something about his eyes that betrayed the muddy springs of his inner life.

Within this last year the same man has been sentenced to a term of penal servitude for a long series of offences against boys. The Judge described the case as one of the worst that had ever come before him, and despite Counsel's plea that the accused was prepared to enter a home and undergo any form of treatment that medical science might prescribe, he packed him off to gaol for another four years, to live the life of an ordinary prisoner, and to return to the world with his impulses unchecked.

This man was a voracious reader of good literature. Poetry, essays, philosophy, all were grist to his mill, and he was an ardent and unremitting student of the Scriptures.

One afternoon half a dozen of the depraved brotherhood were brought to the Scrubs. They had been arrested in some kind of bawdy-house, taken before a magistrate, and remanded in custody for a week. Some of them were attired in women's clothes, and behaved with all the boldness of common harlots. Eventually all were sentenced to varying terms of imprisonment.

For a time this little group were segregated, and worked alone in the coir shed, but after a few weeks they were dispersed to other prisons, leaving only two to mingle in due course with the rest of the Scrubs community.

And the two who remained were a precious pair of scoundrels, who openly gloried in their nefarious trade.

I had occasion to reprimand one of them very sternly. He was briskly and seriously explaining to a co-worker in the tailors' shop that imprisonment in the summer-time did not inconvenience him in the least. The summer was his off season, when there was very little doing, but when days grew short and nights long and dark and cold, that was the time he expected to make enough money to carry him through the year.

Perhaps the most notorious figure of all this obscene collection was a man who lived in the hospital and worked in the tailors' shop. There was nothing amiss with his general health, but it was deemed advisable to keep him under constant supervision on account of the sexual abnormality with which he was afflicted.

Up to the age of twenty years he passed as a woman, but some extraordinary change took place in his physical organism, which thereafter brought him within the male category. In the meantime he had married a man, continued to live with him as his wife, and as a consequence was thrown into prison.

This *lusus naturae* was beautiful in a womanly way, with luxuriant masses of wavy hair as dark as night, and great liquid brown eyes. I well remember the first day he appeared in the library. The Digger was busy writing at his table when he looked up to see standing before him the Party Leader from the hospital, and the phenomenon about which the whole prison was talking.

The hospital Leader explained that he had brought the man along to make his own selection, and would call for him after he had delivered a message at D Hall.

While this conversation was going on, the man constantly pushed his long hair backwards, shifted his weight from one leg to the other, moving easily from the hips, and gazed curiously about his new surroundings, but with all the aplomb of a reigning beauty accustomed to go abroad under batteries of admiring eyes.

"Well," said the Digger after a pause, "what can we do for you?"

The man replied that he would like to choose at least two books.

"What kind of book have you in mind?" inquired the Digger.

"A book of letters," was the answer.

"Belles-Lettres, perhaps you mean?" suggested the Digger.

"No, no," replied the man, shrugging his shoulders, and speaking in the mincing tones of a young girl in her teens. "You know what I want: the sort of things that people write to one another."

"Come this way," said the Digger, "and we'll probably find something to suit your taste."

The man followed him with the exaggerated mincing steps of a woman in very high-heeled shoes, but as soon as they had disappeared in a recess at the back of the library a loud smacking kiss resounded through the room.

The Digger's head appeared with startling suddenness round the corner, and if looks could have killed, one of us must have dropped dead, but each man seemed to be engrossed in his work, and the silence remained unbroken.

In a few minutes they emerged, the library card was written up, and the hospital Leader arrived to claim his charge. When they had gone not a word was said about the freak, who in other circumstances must have caused a buzz of talk. On two occasions, at least, I noticed the

Digger look up abruptly, in an obvious endeavour to catch the Aussie's eye, but the latter studiously avoided the temptation, if it existed, to gaze in the Digger's direction, and behaved as if he had suddenly discovered a new and enthralling interest in library tasks. And so the incident passed.

In all my experience of prison life this was the only man for whose mental and moral welfare the authorities adopted special and extraordinary measures.

Every week he was taken to a specialist in Harley Street, with the object of curing him of his girlish habits. How far success attended the doctor's efforts I do not know, but it was commonly reported by the patient's colleagues in the tailors' shop that he made no secret of his intentions to return to the man he loved as soon as he was discharged from prison.

A peculiar characteristic of men who had been convicted for sexual offences was their ostensible devotion to religious worship and practice. With very few exceptions they were all communicants.

One man who was on very friendly terms with the Digger and myself comes to my mind. He was intensely interested in religious and philosophic subjects, and he spoke with a clarity which suggested an excellent education and a first-class intellect.

One day he visited the library to collect a book which had been sent in by a friend, a decription and eulogy of the Oxford Group Movement. The Digger scoffed at the Buchmanites as offenders against common decency, and described their methods as an attempt to carry American business efficiency to the very throne of the Most High. It was ludicrous to think of all these fellows sprawling about on their stomachs with notebooks in their hands, and solemnly jotting down messages, the origin of which they fondly ascribed to Deity. And their insistence on a full and detailed confession of sin from their adherents would, if generally followed, make life unbearable.

St. Paul described himself as the chief of sinners, but as far as the Digger's memory went he did no more than generalize, and never descended to revelling in particular sins, or involving other people. Very few men could tell the exact truth about themselves, their inner thoughts, and secret actions without exposing themselves to universal contempt. On one occasion Doctor Johnson advised a friend never to tell a story to his own disadvantage, and Doctor Johnson knew as much about human nature as Doctor Buchman.

"Could you," he said, addressing the man, "publicly expose your basest thoughts and actions to the world in the belief that you were cleansing yourself from sin, and fortifying your soul against the further assaults of the devil? Perhaps," he added as an afterthought, "it might be making a fool of oneself for Christ's sake, but it appeals to me as an indecent show, which can do no good to the performers, and only excites the contempt and derision of the spectators."

The man said he knew too little of the Oxford Group Movement to offer an opinion, but when he had gone the Aussie suggested that the Digger's remarks must have hit him on the raw.

"Why should they?" inquired the New Zealander. "I said nothing which could cause offence."

"But don't you know why he is here?" pursued the Aussie.

"No, I don't," replied the Digger. "All I know is that he is one of the most interesting and intelligent personalities in the prison."

And then the Aussie, who made it his business to ascertain the nature of the criminal record of every prisoner with whom he came in contact, related the man's history.

He had been convicted of one of the grossest and most revolting acts of bestiality I had ever heard of. The Digger cursed the Aussie for a foul and malicious scandalmonger. It seemed inconceivable that this man, with his cultured accent and his impeccable literary taste, could ever be guilty of such a beastly crime against his own nature, but a little inquiry confirmed the Aussie's report.

From that time onwards our friendly intercourse ceased. He guessed the reason, and never made the slightest attempt to return to the old footing, but it was obvious that he felt our defection acutely.

Although the barrier that had suddenly sprung up between us was insurmountable, I felt deeply sorry for this man, who was the strangest blend of intellectuality and moral depravity that I have ever encountered.

The Digger and I finished our tour of duty in D Hall on a Sunday morning. We were standing with the warder in charge at his desk, and the men were waiting for the command to fall in for exercise.

Presently the door at the far end of the Hall was opened, and in trooped the communicants, the majority of whom were men who had been sentenced for sexual offences.

An elderly man hobbling along on two sticks brought up the rear of the procession. He had been convicted for assault on a young girl of fourteen, a brutal act in which he had been assisted by the child's mother, who had pinned her to the bed while the old satyr had his way.

Late breakfast stood ready for them at a special table, and they took their seats at once. But no sooner were they ensconced at the table than a howl of rage and dismay arose.

It appears that the orderly detailed to carry the bucket of porridge from the cookhouse had fallen down and spilt the whole of the contents on the ground, and on this occasion, at least, replacement was impossible.

I have heard a variety of curses in all sorts of places and in all sorts of circumstances, but never in my life have I listened to such a sustained flood of filthy and uncanonical language as on that Sunday morning, and from men who had just returned from taking part in communion.

The officer turned to me in despair. "I have been in this prison five years," he said, "but I will never understand the mentality of these fellows. They are all professing Christians, and have just celebrated the most solemn rite of their religion. And yet look at their behaviour now."

The Digger suggested that most of these men were emotionally unstable. "Furthermore," he said, "I am under the impression that a good number take communion in the hope of influencing the Chaplain as a member of the Discharged Prisoners' Aid Society, and lastly, they are damned hungry, and nothing good ever flourishes on an empty stomach."

"Well, whatever the reason," said the officer, "this din has got to stop!"

He advanced to the table, shouted an order, and the noise ceased as abruptly as it had begun.

CHAPTER XIX

THE hospital accommodation in Wormwood Scrubs was very limited, and with few exceptions the patients were all men suffering from minor complaints. Serious cases were treated in the neighbouring infirmary.*

There were two rather bad outbreaks of influenza while I was in the Scrubs, and the great majority of the victims were confined to cells until they were fit to get about again. In D Hall the sufferers were transferred to the second floor, which resembled a large hospital, and I fancy a similar policy of segregation was followed in C Hall.

Fortunately there was only one fatality. I was one of the first to go down. For two days I could hardly drag my legs about, and early morning drill was a torture. At night delirium had me in its grip, and on the third morning, although the worst of the fever had passed, I decided to report sick.

My temperature was 102°, and the doctor ordered three days in cell. And so I lay there alone. An extra blanket was served out, but there was not the slightest change in the ordinary prison dieting. At meal-times the cell was opened up, and a table companion brought me my rations.

He was the only person I saw for seventy-two hours. At the end of the three days I was still too weak to face the early morning drill, and reported sick again, although it lay with me entirely to decide whether I was fit or unfit.

* Since this time Wormwood Scrubs has been equipped with one of the most up-to-date hospitals of any prison in England.

That was one of the weaknesses of prison medical administration. Many men went out in the early morning cold and performed their ordinary duties when they should have been in bed, rather than put up with the solitary life of the cell.

I was ordered another three days' confinement. The officer who brought me the doctor's decision was one of the most hateful persons in the prison. Broad, low-browed like a gorilla, and inveterately lazy, he always reminded me of some poisonous species of toad as he squatted over his desk. This man never had a pleasant word for anybody, and he spent his life complaining of the stupidity of prisoners and the hardships of a warder's existence.

"You stay here another three days," he announced abruptly as he entered the cell. "Three days?" I gasped. "Yes, three days," he replied, mimicking my voice. "You prisoners are all alike. You can never take your medicine. Nobody asked you to come to the Scrubs. Nobody asked you to get influenza, but you insist on calling in the doctor, and then when he prescribes for you, you don't like it. I've got no sympathy for you whatever. You deserve all you get, and a damn sight more!"

And with this pleasant little homily the fat, greasy fellow banged the door, and I was alone for another seventy-two hours.

The Digger also fell an early victim to the prevailing influenza scourge. He had been complaining for a long time about the temperature of his cell, which he declared was colder than a Jew's heart. He explained to us that every night he had to spend at least half an hour prancing round the cell on his toes in order to stimulate the circulation of the blood: otherwise his feet were so frozen that it was impossible to sleep.

For two days the Digger presented a most woebegone appearance, and then suddenly disappeared for nine days, all of which were spent in the seclusion of his cell.

The day before his retirement he had ordered one of the men at his table to report sick. This prisoner suffered from inherited syphilis. Part of his nose was eaten away— a most unpleasant sight. On admission to Wormwood Scrubs he had been treated in the medical cells in C Hall, which were reserved for v.d. and verminous patients, and after some weeks had been pronounced cured, or at least free from contagion. But the discharge from his nose had started again, and the Digger had insisted on him seeing the doctor. The man was loath to do so. As long as his illness was not too burdensome he preferred the amenities of D Hall to the solitude of a medical cell elsewhere.

To the Digger's disgust this man had been selected to bring up his dinner, but ill as he was he shouted for the officer who had opened up the cell, and the afflicted but very disgruntled prisoner was taken off to C Hall, where he finished the remainder of his sentence.

The official view seemed to be that solitary confinement was an infallible cure for malingering. Probably experience justified this conclusion, but it never seemed to occur to the authorities that dozens of men would go on until they dropped rather than face three or four days in the utter loneliness of a cell, with nothing to gaze at but a few inches of sky.

When the epidemic had passed its worst phase, the Skipper was compelled to take to his bed, but he had the disease in a very mild form, and at the end of two or three days he was with us again.

On his return to the library he questioned Pelling closely as to his reasons for joining the choir. Did Pelling raise up his voice in song for his own gratification or for the glory of God?

The Digger chimed in to say that the Skipper must have been reading that stupid book *The Narrow Way*. This was a religious manual issued to every Protestant. It was the composition of monkish minds, steeped in the presence and power of evil, and if read by prisoners, which it wasn't, must have brought religion and religious practice into contempt. Readers were enjoined, when waking in the middle of the night, to refrain from indulging in lascivious thoughts, and to think rather of that narrow bed in which we must all lie at last.

"Imagine the Aussie," commented the Skipper, who pleaded guilty to studying this precious manual during his illness, "imagine the Aussie struggling valiantly to divert his usual train of thought by contemplating mental pictures of the grave. The thing's too ludicrous for words!"

But the Aussie only remarked that he would be comparatively happy even in Wormwood Scrubs if the other inhabitants would only mind their own business.

Readers were also invited to think of their final passing whenever they heard a clock chime, and to repeat a certain prayer against sudden death. "But Pelling here," continued the Skipper, "stands in danger of hell-fire, because he openly admits that he sings because he likes it, a sin which, according to *The Narrow Way*, is peculiarly offensive to God."

Pelling, however, swore that he would chance his arm and go on singing for the same old reason.

I observed that it seemed to be no worse than *The Garden of the Soul*, which was issued to Roman Catholics. "It is," replied the Digger, "because Rome has always and openly exploited human fear. It is one of the chief weapons in her armoury, but Protestantism boasts of a more humane and enlightened view of man and his salvation. But here all the magic and mummery of priest-craft are employed to scare us into being good."

Another book which the Skipper had read when locked up in his cell was Brigadier-General Crozier's *Reminiscences*. The General had a New Zealander attached to his Staff, and was so enamoured of this gentleman's character and personality that he vowed that if he were not an Englishman he would like to have been born a New Zealander.

Where New Zealand shone, said the Skipper, was in the high general level of education, and in an abundance of strong common sense, which made good business men, good officials, and capable administrators.

It looked as though the Skipper was launched upon a favourite subject, but at that moment a warder strode into the room and announced, in a loud voice, "Visiting magistrate, any complaints?" Behind him stood a short, broad-shouldered man, nervously fingering a bowler hat. We all looked at one another like Cortez' lads at Darien, and like them said nothing. A pause and they had gone. I do not think that visiting magistrates were ever troubled by complaints from prisoners. It is not wise policy to criticize one's gaolers.

CHAPTER XX

ALL things, good or evil, have an end, and a prison sentence is no exception to the general rule. The days, which were long and dreary enough at first, merged slowly into months, and the months into a year. When half of a man's sentence had been served he began to experience a new sense of hopefulness, for he felt then that the worst had been passed, and that every day thereafter brought him within measurable distance of freedom.

Brice was the first to go. A saturnine and bad-tempered man, he was not popular with his fellows, but his *bête noire* was the Digger, who had got under his skin with biting references to the banking system and the monetary policy of the Bank of England.

The Skipper was the next to leave us. He had already been visited by the official representative of the Discharged Prisoners' Aid Society. This gentleman called on every prisoner a month before the latter's release, and inquired if he needed any help in the way of money or clothing. The Society also offered to find work for men, and was, I understand, instrumental in securing jobs for numbers of skilled and unskilled tradesmen, where a clean character was not of the first importance. To men who had occupied positions of trust, the Society was of little use.

Within a week of his discharge the Skipper appeared amongst us in his own shoes. He had discarded the heavier and bigger prison footwear. This concession was made to prisoners to enable them to walk out in their own footwear with some degree of comfort. We were more than sorry to lose his gay companionship, but we swore vows of eternal friendship and made ambitious plans to meet again in happier surroundings, plans which, I am afraid, never materialized.

I well remember the Skipper's last Sunday night in the recreation-room. He elected to tell stories of his life at sea during the war, when he commanded an Australian gunboat in Eastern waters. One of these anecdotes, which dealt with malingering, brought down the house.

The commonest reason given by applicants for discharge from the naval service was deafness caused by gunfire. One day an A.B. by the name of Jones applied for release on these grounds. He was examined by the ship's doctor, who found that although Jones seemed to be as fit as a fiddle physically, he really behaved as if he were as deaf as a post. Nevertheless, the doctor suspected malingering.

Every trick that medical knowledge and experience could suggest was used on Jones, who, however, conducted himself on all occasions as if he were shut up in a stone cage, and completely cut off from the ordinary world about him. Unexpected commands, sudden and startling noises—to all of these Jones was sublimely indifferent. Nothing ruffled his Olympian calm. Either he was stone deaf or he had a nerve of iron. The doctor never wavered from the latter view.

One day the boat was lying in harbour sweltering under the fierce blaze of a tropical sun. The air was motionless, and the heat so intense that the ship itself seemed to be on fire. The doctor mounted to the top deck, where Jones was on duty, with his back towards the companion way, and his eyes riveted on the shore.

The doctor was wearing rubber shoes, and he made up his mind then and there to try the last device in his bag of tricks. Slipping up quietly behind the afflicted mariner he said, in a low, conversational tone of voice: "How would a nice cold glass of beer go now, Jones?" And Jones whirled round to face his questioner as if he had been stung by a serpent. The idea of a cool glass of beer in that torrid atmosphere had broken down his iron self-control at last.

"We won't hear any more of that application, eh, Jones?" continued the silky voice of the triumphant medico, but Jones gazed stonily towards the coast, his mind a welter of raging emotions. To think that the thing he loved most in the world had betrayed him at the moment when success seemed inevitable!

The Skipper's exit made a great gap in our little society, but there was compensation in the knowledge that our own great day was drawing nearer and nearer. Within a week the Aussie had followed him. The two last days of his sentence the Aussie was almost hysterical with excitement. Advice to shun registrar's offices and churches was showered upon him on all sides, and he gleefully assured us that the choicest female in the world could never persuade him to sign away his liberty again.

I fancy the Aussie's emotional disturbance was due more to the knowledge that there would be two claimants for his person on the day of his release than to the prospect of immediate freedom. He had gradually unburdened himself of the information that during his prison sentence he had received confirmation of a belief long harboured that his legal wife had never been in a position to marry:

that she was, in fact, guilty of bigamy, and that he had suffered for a crime he had never committed.

This, coupled with the fact that the last young woman to "marry" him had taken up residence in London left us in little doubt as to the Aussie's ultimate intentions, but he managed to convey the impression that he was torn between two loyalties, and that a final decision would not be made until he had found freedom and a little leisure for reflection.

The Digger's turn came next. A goodly part of his cheerfulness had vanished with the Skipper, to whom he was deeply attached. Besides, as with all of us, the necessity for earning a living in a hostile world loomed large and even menacing, and the ordeal of facing friends as well as foes was not altogether pleasant to contemplate. One is at least sheltered from contempt and pity in prison.

Another circumstance which contributed not a little to his uneasiness was the fact that he had never been photographed in prison, and that the omission might be discovered at the very last moment. Within three weeks of admission every man was supposed to be photographed in two or three positions, and the pictures were sent to Scotland Yard to swell the Rogue's Gallery. The Digger, for some unexplained reason, had been overlooked, and he was afraid that instead of enjoying an early release he might be detained for half a day at least until the authorities had secured a permanent record of his features.

That his fear was not baseless was proved by the experience of a man who had been discharged a month before. Every prisoner was entitled to a bath the day before he left, whether he had already had his regular weekly bath or not.

As he was on the point of leaving, the man was asked the customary question as to whether he had any complaints. He promptly answered, with a show of truculence, that he had. What was the nature of his grievance? He replied that he had not received a hot bath the previous day.

When this information percolated the official mind, the officers present wallowed in sympathy. It was an inexcusable oversight on somebody's part. Such a thing had never happened in Wormwood Scrubs before, but— and here the wretched prisoner began to take alarm—it was an oversight that must be remedied at all costs. In vain the man protested that he was only joking, and never meant the complaint to be taken seriously. He was stripped of his civilian clothing and ordered to don prison garb again. Then he was taken to D Hall, and an hour or two later had a good hot bath; but instead of passing through the prison gates at eight o'clock in the morning, he did not make his exit until four o'clock in the afternoon.

I recollect the case of another man who was due to leave about this time. As he handed over his prison tunic three unauthorized razor blades dropped out of the pocket. To everybody's astonishment he was back in the Shop at the usual hour that morning, to do another three days, one for each blade.

The Digger left on a Monday morning. On the Friday afternoon he had an appointment with the Librarian in the Schoolmaster's office for the purpose of saying good-bye. Saturday morning was taken up with his final interview with the Chaplain, and his last bath in prison.

When he returned to the library he told us that the Librarian had introduced him to a visiting magistrate;

"and would you believe it, Howlett," he continued, "the Librarian described me as the model prisoner, a man who had never made a mistake, or committed an indiscretion, and whom he would trust with anything anywhere?"

Howlett observed dryly that the Librarian's heart sometimes ruled his head.

"And let me tell you another thing," said the Digger, ignoring the old man's sarcasm. "Our parting was really affecting. There was more than a suspicion of tears in his eyes as he wrung my hand, and wished me luck."

The Digger did not exaggerate. On more than one occasion I saw this officer almost overcome with emotion as he bade farewell to a prisoner, and for a long time he and the Digger had been bound together by the strongest ties of mutual regard.

Although his time was so short, the Digger had a narrow squeak before he left. It happened on Sunday morning, after cells had been opened up, and we were standing at our doors waiting for the bell to ring for exercise. The Digger and I lived opposite each other on the same landing.

It was a balmy June morning, and at that hour the sun was just of a strength to induce somnolence. All the men had finished their washing with the exception of one prisoner on the fourth landing, who was still cleaning his bedroom utensil in one of the washing-places, and whistling cheerfully at the same time.

The officer on duty on the ground-floor raised his voice in loud protest, but the whistling did not stop. Again the officer shouted, with the same result. Finding orders useless, he dashed for the stairs, mouthing vengeance against the disturber of prison quiet, but the man was warned in time, and fled to the safety of his cell.

The Digger was standing opposite me, apparently in a brown study, with the sun pouring through his cell window on to the back of his head. Then, to my surprise and consternation, he began to whistle as blithely as the fellow who had just been put to flight.

The warder, now on the top floor, howled an objurgation, but the Digger was far away, and did not hear. Presently the officer came rushing downstairs. On the third landing he roared: "If you don't stop that bloody whistling, you'll whistle before the Governor to-morrow morning!" I gesticulated frantically from the shelter of my own doorway, and the Digger came back to his surroundings with a start, and stopped dead.

I asked him a few minutes later what excuse he would have made to the Governor if he had been caught.

He answered that he would have pleaded that his whistling was "the earliest pipe of half-awakened birds," trusting to the Governor's sense of humour to let him off.

On Monday morning I went to the ground-floor as soon as cells were opened up to see the parade of prisoners about to be discharged. The Digger was amongst them. He was surrounded by friends, all shaking him excitedly by the hand.

His last words to me were an emphatic admonition to read Browning, about whom I then knew very little, and to read Paracelsus first, in which, according to the Digger, were to be found the three greatest lines in the English language. He was referring to those lines where Paracelsus, in speaking of poor, sinning, suffering, struggling human beings, says that they are:

Like plants in mines that never saw the sun,
But dream of him, and guess where he may be,
And do their best to climb and get to him.

Another moment in which we gripped hands and clasped each other by the shoulder and he was gone.

With the Digger and the Skipper out of the library, life became almost unbearable. Other men took their places, the South African and the General were promoted to Leadership, but the savour of existence in the library had vanished.

I had a letter from the Digger before my turn came to pack up. It was couched in cheerful terms. He congratulated himself on the fact that his palate had returned to normal, and that he was able to drink beer and smoke cigarettes with the requisite degree of pleasure. For a fortnight after his return to the world they had been dust and ashes in his mouth.

But, he said, he had been despised and rejected of his own circle, and could see no immediate hope of re-establishing himself in London. As a consequence he had taken a small job with a Gloucestershire contractor, who unfortunately appeared to be verging on bankruptcy. His employer was, however, familiar with the Digger's history, and that was something. The fear of discovery is ever present in an ex-prisoner's mind. I fancy, though, that the quiet loveliness of the English countryside had influenced his decision as much as the necessity for earning a living. There is nothing like it anywhere for the sick or wounded soul.

The two months I had still to serve passed on leaden feet, but at last, after what seemed years of waiting, the great day dawned. The day before my exit I waited on the Chaplain, in a cell in D Hall, at ten o'clock in the morning. He was a little late for the appointment, and the officer on duty handed me a list of men who had reported sick, with instructions to visit their cells and see that they were all right.

I reported that all were well with the exception of one man, the Redband on the Gate, who seemed to be behaving queerly. "Oh," said the officer casually, "he went off his nut during the night, and I've just sent for two of the hospital staff to put him in a padded cell."

I was astounded and distressed. The Redband was a quiet, retiring man, about forty years of age. He had just been promoted to the post of assistant to the Gate Officer, which was one much sought after by prisoners. His predecessor had sat at my table, and judging from the stains on this man's fingers it was obvious that whatever deprivations he suffered in prison smoking was not one of them.

A little later I saw two officers descending the stairs with the Redband between them. The latter's head lolled listlessly from side to side, while all the time he emitted the cry of the typical London milk roundsman. They were removing him to the padded cell.

The next morning I paraded with half a dozen others as soon as cells were opened up. We were marched to Reception, where all prison gear was handed in and checked. It was a queer sensation to put on civilian clothes again. As soon as we had dressed we sat down to our last prison breakfast, a mug of tea, with bread and margarine.

The Governor was due at any moment. On this occasion he did not appear in person, but was represented by the

Chief Officer. As an ex-Leader, I saw this gentleman first. To his first question as to whether I had any complaints, I answered no. All the while he was studying my dossier, and soon discovered that I had entered Wormwood Scrubs without a penny in my pocket. Would I take at least two shillings to cover my train fare home?

I thanked him for the offer, but assured him that my wife would be waiting for me outside the gate. But he pointed out that unforeseen circumstances—sickness, sudden death, or anything—might prevent her from keeping the appointment, to all of which I replied that in such an eventuality I should have great pleasure in walking.

He strongly advised me again to take the two shillings, but I again declined, and reminded him that the Governor had granted me as a Leader an early release. This seemed to be just the opportunity he was angling for. Settling himself down more comfortably in his chair, and with a provocative grin on his huge features, he began to expound at interminable length the law relating to discharges. Prisoners were set free at eight o'clock in the morning solely as a matter of expediency. Despite the fact that I had an early pass, he could, if he liked, and without incurring any censure, detain me until four in the afternoon, and there were occasions when this was done.

I felt my temper rising, but said nothing. Finding me mute, he signalled to a warder and said, "Take this man away." I have seen pictures in newspapers of departing prisoners shaking hands with Governors. It does not happen with Chief Officers. This man did not even say good-morning.

I was not worrying, however, about the Chief's boorishness. The next minute I was in the open air. We passed the quadrangle in which the Fourth Stage men were exercising. They were all waiting to see me go, and waved frantically. The Gate Officer opened a little side door and pushed me through into the outer world. My wife rushed into my arms. I was free.

*   *   *   *   *

Three years have now passed since my release from Wormwood Scrubs, and those three years have served to confirm the opinion which I formed at the time, and which was shared by all thinking prisoners, that our system of punishment is a waste of time and a waste of public money.

It is stupid, and it is meaningless. One could understand, without approving, the infliction of severer and harsher treatment, such as Commander Foster advocated. A policy of this kind could be defended on the grounds that fear is a great deterrent to crime, but I am certain in my own mind that it would prove ineffective. Men to-day are not afraid of authority, and cruelty or unnecessary hardship would only provoke the spirit of revolt, in which offenders would be supported by the general public. The public is not much concerned with what form prison treatment takes, so long as its sense of justice is not offended, but undue severity would raise a universal outcry.

One would think, though, that in this scientific age prison treatment would be based on a process of re-education—that a rational attempt would be made to diagnose the inner causes of a man's fall from grace, and then to build up his will and character, so that he could return to the world with some sort of confidence in his ability to meet and master the strains and stresses of life.

I met very few evil men in Wormwood Scrubs. There were many foolish men, many weak men. There were men who had been exposed to great temptations, and not a few who had been more sinned against than sinning, but by and large there was very little real vice or moral depravity. The fact that such a small percentage of the population of Wormwood Scrubs renews acquaintance with the law is no tribute to Wormwood Scrubs: it is a tribute to the men themselves.

What are we to think of a system which condemns, say, a solicitor to eighteen months at sewing mailbags because under the stress of temptation he has embezzled clients' moneys? That society must take some notice of the man's delinquency is obvious, but if punishment has its reformative side, as the authorities claim that it has, where does the reformative element lie?

Prison treatment is no doubt milder than it was twenty years ago, or even ten years ago. It is irritating and humiliating without being cruel, but it is absolutely unintelligent, and I cannot see that the solicitor, after his long apprenticeship to mailbag sewing, is going to emerge from prison a wiser and a better man. The real problem remains untouched.

To a normal human being the loss of personal liberty must always be an unmitigated evil, but there were some poor devils who regarded Wormwood Scrubs as a sort of paradise. They were assured of bed and board, and the barking of warders was music in their ears. I have seen these men weeping bitterly the day of their discharge.

They had lived all their lives in casual wards and on the roads, and they knew that within a couple of days they would be on the Embankment. And the weather was cold and forbidding.

In a very real sense punishment begins only when a man enters the world again, and joins in the struggle for a living. If he has money, nothing matters very much. The multitude of sins covered by money includes even imprisonment, and somehow or other the most strait-laced people are favourably influenced by a large bank balance.

But to a man who has to seek a position as an employee the experience is terrible. He has a sinister mark on his escutcheon, and that mark has to be concealed. Even if he is lucky enough to secure a post in these days of fierce competition, he lives in a constant state of apprehension that his past will be discovered.

And this fear is not imaginary. The South African, on his discharge, obtained a situation as a traveller for a firm dealing in office requisites. By temperament he was eminently suited for this class of work. And he did well; so well, indeed, that in a few months he was top of the list, and earning as much as £15 a week.

One evening he returned to the office after a satisfactory day's work and was sent for by the Sales Manager. An unknown person had 'phoned through in the afternoon and asked for the South African. The nature of his message was never disclosed. However, the Sales Manager discreetly let him know that the Manager would be obliged if he would put in his resignation, but that in searching for another billet he could use their name as a reference. As far as the South African knew, he had no enemies. He did not owe a penny in the world, and he could only assume that a prisoner, possibly a man whom he had cased as a Leader, had given him away out of revenge. The last I heard of him, he was earning £3 a week.

Of all the men with whom I came in contact after release, none had really prospered. I had another letter from the Digger. His employer had gone bankrupt, and he himself was reduced for the time being to serving in a little inn in a tiny village in Gloucestershire. His letter was full of amusing stories of the farm labourers who frequented the inn, but his main object in writing was to ascertain the address of the Jewish leader with whom he had been on terms of close friendship.

An old dame in the village had died, leaving £100,000 for the conversion of the Jews, and the Digger thought that with his persuasiveness and the Jew's flexibility something might be done with the £100,000. The Jew, by the way, was a man whose name was once one to conjure with in the financial world. The last I heard of him he was running a small social club with a high-sounding name in the East End.

For myself, life became a ceaseless struggle to earn enough to keep my wife and children in food and clothing. Friends were not helpful. Most of them, indeed, behaved as if I had been smitten with some sort of plague, and that I bore in my person the seeds of infection. Before very long it became patent that my company was no longer wanted, and I realized that in the old days I had been admired and flattered, not for what I was, but for what I had. A revelation of this sort always comes as a shock, but it comes to every man who leaves prison without means.

Poor people were the most sympathetic. I had many proofs of this, and the way they expressed their sympathy and regret was really touching. Without exception, not one of my poorer acquaintances ever mentioned the word "prison." With charity and gentle courtesy, they all referred to my "trouble," and sincerely hoped that before very long I would be on my feet again.

One day I passed my old newspaper-seller on the opposite side of the street. I wanted to avoid him, but he dropped his papers, dashed down the street, and brought me to a standstill. I used to speak to the old fellow almost every day on rheumatism, war, or racing—and frequently gave him a shilling for a newspaper.

He was almost overcome with emotion, and wrung my hand until I thought he never intended to let it go. Nobody was sorrier than he to hear of my trouble: nobody would be more pleased to see me make early contact with good fortune, and as we were parting he drew me closer and whispered hoarsely: "And if ever you're in need of a pound, sir, don't forget yours truly."

Commander Foster had declared that few prisoners ever stage a come-back. I agree with him now, and I think that there is much more than a grain of truth in Oscar Wilde's assertion that "all trials are trials for one's life, and all sentences are sentences of death."

For Product Safety Concerns and Information please contact our EU
representative GPSR@taylorandfrancis.com
Taylor & Francis Verlag GmbH, Kaufingerstraße 24, 80331 München, Germany